CORRUPTION
OF THE
AMERICAN HERITAGE

Don Wilbur

Sweelly —
Hope you enjoy,
get your story published
Don Wilbur

Wilbur Press
P O Box 65925
University Place WA 98464

Printed in the United States of America
ISBN: 1491230932
ISBN 13: 9781491230930

Photos by Stan Fouts, of Forks WA and the author
Cover photo by Don Wilbur

DEDICATED TO

Pioneer Missy Barlow, along with many other like-thinking people in the north Olympic Peninsula and elsewhere, who inspired and guided me in my writing.

TABLE OF CONTENTS

INTRODUCTION

My family and I have spent nearly two centuries in the forest communities in the Pacific Northwest. The first of my family began laboring in the Discovery Bay forest in 1859, and the family spent most of their lives into this century being sustained by the wealth of the forests.

Through the evolution of our forest, from wilderness into prosperous forest communities that houses people enthused with their American heritage, it appeared to me that our American heritage was endangered. Also endangered is the forest's wealth, which is rapidly being taken away from local forest communities to be preserved by the intellectual progressives in the cities. The intellectuals' views prevail in the literature and media. I owed my family another point view.

Before writing this story, I spent several years visiting the pioneers' grandchildren on the Peninsula to obtain their views. I found most of them angry at the corruption of their understanding of their heritage and the taking of the forestland from the local communities — communities their families had birthed.

The following story brings forth perhaps an unpopular interpretation of the development of our country. The hardworking people with dirty hands took it away from the British, Spanish, Russians, and indigenous people, mostly by squatting on the wilderness land and developing the land with their families, all the while endangered by a multitude of factors. Modern writers generally credit the greatness of America to the military, explorers, academics, and politicians. The people with dirty hands were the core of our American heritage. They were or became farmers, woodsmen, and entrepreneurs.

This story, to be understood, must be started from near the beginning and moved to the present. The story is not academic with boring footnotes, but a story to entice readers to explore the pioneers' journals, rather than modern writers' interpretation of the journals and events. Hopefully the story will excite the reader with another interpretation of our history.

THE FOREST COMMUNITY LEGACY

Much has been written about the Pacific Northwest forests, but virtually nothing that defines the people and their hopes for their forest communities. Starting in the late 1800s, a great deal has been recorded concerning forest destruction by the greedy timber barons, the mythical loggers, and the quaint settlers. A propaganda campaign was started by the elite progressives and enabled by the National Academy of Science led by Gifford Pinchot and John Muir, who vilified the timber owners (greedy timber barons) and attempted to nationalize the nation's forests. Pinchot used the government through the Forest Service to create a socialized American forest patterned after a European vision of forest management. Muir formed the private Sierra Club to educate the public and to lobby the politicians for preservation of the nation's forests and exclude any commercial activity in them.

The progressives had powerful allies in the government. The foremost were two Presidents, Theodore Roosevelt and Franklin Roosevelt. The Republican Teddy Roosevelt created hundreds of millions of acres of forest reserves by presidential fiat that initially excluded all use of the land. He set up Pinchot as his front man to socialize much of America's land. And, when Americans rejected their leadership in the early 1900s, they formed the Progressive Party to continue the progressive agenda. The American public again rejected their agenda to elect a Democrat for President.

President Franklin Roosevelt continued the progressive's agenda in the 1930s by staffing his cabinet with radical progressives who used the government to viciously attack forest landowners. Again, the American people largely rejected the government's forest policy.

The two Roosevelts were scions of wealthy aristocratic eastern families who purported to represent the common people. As all progressives, these two men supported their positions as being for the "good of "the people", a people they never associated with and largely ignored.

Certainly in the western communities, citizens were treated as if they didn't exist. In 1937, President Franklin Delano Roosevelt met at Lake Crescent on the Olympic Peninsula for a day with only federal bureaucrats before creating the Olympic National Park. Any time a Forest Service bureaucrat gently supported the forest community, he was later removed from his federal position personally by the President, accused of being in sympathy with the greedy timber barons. It never occurred to the President that he was killing the jobs and livelihoods of the local people.

To this day, the productive people in the forest communities have no status with the progressives and are largely ignored in their preservationist agenda, the people who created our heritage. I'm going to tell of my experiences in a forest community in the 1930s through the 1950s and what the forests on the Olympic Peninsula mean to the real people in their communities.

In 1859, my great-grandfather took French leave (deserted) from the British Navy near Victoria and rowed across the Strait of Juan de Fuca to the Olympic Peninsula and America. He was a sixteen-year-old boy named James R. Dickinson, called Jimmie by his acquaintances to his dying day because, one supposes, of his small stature, quick wit, and sense of humor.

Upon arriving on the peninsula, he quickly found his way to S.L. Mastick's Port Discovery Mill for employment in logging. In 1859, logs for the mill were produced on the hills above the mill with timber skidded down the hills to the mill by twenty teams of oxen. Jimmie, an English farm boy, soon became involved with the oxen and, by his own admission, became the best bull whacker (driver of oxen) in the West.

He bragged to his family how he ran down the backs of the oxen to goad them into a faster pace. Log production was all important. (Some literature suggests trotting on the backs of oxen was not the best technique to work the animals.)

Port Discovery was a company town built around the mill. The company (Mastick) built houses for the employees' families, cottages for some single men, and a bunkhouse. There were a hotel and general store among others. In fact, it was the trading, social focus, and economic driver for the area. The Masticks furnished the capital and leadership while California and the world bought the products — mostly lumber. The mill purchased products from the local farmers. Hay for the oxen was always needed, along with food for the mill employees and timber from the settlers' land, which could be sold for a big chunk of cash.

In the 1860s, J.B. Perkins wrote his parents that he worked at the mill. (He had not seen his parents for six years.) He reported there were 50 cabins or houses on the mill site, and every man could have his own cabin if he wanted. There were seven families in houses. He had a cabin to himself, and his cat kept him from being lonely. The food was second quality and largely salted meat. Mr. Perkins fabricated tools for the mill and tallied lumber loaded on ships with Indian labor.

In 1880, Jimmie had acquired enough wealth to buy the Allen Weir

The schoolhouse where my mother attended classes near their Dungeness farm.

homestead (the present Game Farm) in the Dungeness Valley and brought a bride out from England to start a family on a prosperous dairy farm. Prior to the marriage, a typewritten pre-nuptial agreement was negotiated, which is still in the possession of the family. Apparently the bride's father thought Jimmie was an American barbarian who would not ever profit from the marriage. Jimmie had been a bull whacker for about two decades. During

3

this time, his brother came from England to acquire a dairy farm in the Dungeness Valley and to encourage Jimmie to become a farmer also.

Five American children were produced from Jimmie's marriage. However, the family went back to England in 1889 to manage Mrs. Dickinson's English estate following the death of her father. Nevertheless, as the boys became of age, they scurried back to his Dungeness farm. Jimmie also came back to his Dungeness farm upon the death of his wife in the early 1900s. As Jimmie aged, his son, Rueben (Rue) ran the farm. My mother was born on the farm in 1910.

Jimmie died in 1929, while Rueben and his family moved from dairy farm to dairy farm — that is, Dungeness, Agnew, Uncas, Forks, and finally to Freshwater Bay. Rue's wife's (my grandmother) family lived on Lost Mountain, commonly named Texas Valley. Lost Mountain is several miles southeast of Sequim. A small post office on Lost Mountain was named Exa, also, my grandmother's sister's name. My grandmother's maiden name was Morris, and her mother was a McCoy (Hatfield/McCoy fame). Part of the McCoy clan emigrated to Texas in the early 1800s to colonize McCoy Creek, about 60 miles southeast of San Antonio. A family biographer characterized the McCoy men as: "They valued human rights above human lives and treated outlaws harshly." The McCoys lived in lawless cowboy country and enforced their code of justice. In 1886, the Morris family joined a wagon train in Texas for travel to Lost Mountain. My grandmother was among eight siblings; she was seven years old. The Morris family left a harsh and dry Texas to live on a relative quiet and green Olympic Peninsula.

The tales my grandparents verbalized were awesome; unfortunately, their young grandson did not listen closely or ask questions. And, there were little written documents. The few letters mostly discussed the weather.

My grandfather, Rue, was a gentle man who, with the help of a hired man, milked about two dozen Guernsey cows twice a day for most of his life. He was as gentle as the cows he milked; profanity seemed not to be part of his vocabulary. His friends and fellow pioneer families were of similar nature. Liquor was never used, except for grandmother's medicinal sherry. The males respected people as long as they were productive — and even most of those were not productive, if honest. From the women's viewpoint, cleanliness was the top priority. The house and family clothes were scrubbed continually, while slovenly people were held in contempt.

The early and late pioneers transformed the Northwest and the north Olympic Peninsula from a savage wilderness into a vital part of, arguably, the greatest nation the world has ever experienced. Modern writers romanticize the early explorers like Vancouver, Lewis, and Clark. The explorers were generally paid or perhaps ordered by their government to do what they did. They spent a few months in the Northwest and went home to a civilized world to reap honors. After praising the explorers, the modern writers eulogized the Native Americans while generally decrying the pioneers' rape of the wilderness and the subversion of the Native people. The pioneers are largely ignored or portrayed as selfish. The facts are: the settlers employed the land with their toil, capital, and lives to create America.

So, ignoring the modern writers, I will attempt to understand the logic and motivation of the pioneers who lived and died on the north Olympics Peninsula while attempting to fulfill their dreams. To be honest, modern biases cannot be tolerated while reconstructing the thoughts of the pioneers; their thoughts, biases, and accomplishments have to be paramount. What was Jimmie Dickinson's vision? It was probably to have a peaceful dairy herd and productive family while hoping the rest of the inhabitants of the peninsula also enjoyed a good life as all ethnic groups coalesced into Americans.

In the late 1930s, my maternal grandparents purchased a forty-acre dairy farm on Freshwater Bay about ten miles west of Port Angeles. My grandfather was in his late 50s and had worked other people's farms all of his life. A small inheritance enabled him to buy his own dairy farm to live out his working life doing the work he loved. He would improve the property to create a productive enterprise.

The property was a miniature dairy farm of that era. It was about half-timbered with second-growth Douglas fir, and the rest was in pasture and hay fields. The small Douglas fir trees had no value except for firewood that would heat and fuel the cook stove of the family home. Grandfather's "forest" came into existence after Michael Earles' old growth logging in the early 1900s. A small quantity of cedar pieces remained after Earles finished logging. My uncle cut a few red cedar shingle bolts from these pieces and sold them to a small shingle mill on the Freshwater Road. He also sold two white fir trees (Abies grandis) to a pulp wood logger. The two trees were the only white fir trees on the farm.

The logger fell the trees and cut them into four-foot (in length) cordwood. The larger rounds of cordwood were split to enable the logger to load his truck by hand. He had to peel the bark from the cordwood before selling the cordwood to the local pulp mill. The operation was economically viable only because the logger could drive his truck to the trees through the pasture. The Douglas fir was not useable in the pulp mill at that time because of its pitch and wood quality. Grandfather realized only a few dollars from the pulpwood logging operation. The farm pasture would support about six milking cows that produced a very modest farm income while not over-working an aging farmer.

The farmhouse had one bedroom downstairs and one upstairs under the eaves, accommodating two beds. A hand-dug well was equipped with a pump powered by a windmill that lifted water to a wooden tank reservoir fifteen feet above ground under the windmill. Gravity powered the water from the tank into the house and barn. There was no electricity initially; coal oil (kerosene) lamps and lanterns furnished light after dark.

The house was heated with a wood-fueled cook stove in the kitchen and a wood heating stove in the living room. Grandfather went into his forest once a week to cut wood to fuel them. He would fall a Douglas fir tree about twenty inches at the base, buck it into stove-length firewood, and bring the rounds to the woodshed. These would be split into sticks of cook stove wood two to three inches square, with larger pieces split for the heating stove. The wood cutting chore took more than eight hours a week. The cook stove had pipe coils in the fire box that circulated water from the stove to a steel storage tank that stored hot water for use in the kitchen sink and bath. The wastewater was piped out to the nearby pasture.

The barn was big enough to store winter hay for the livestock, stanchions for the cows, and stalls for the horses. Stored in the barn was equipment for processing the hay: a wagon, rake, mowing machine, single furrow plow, and harrow. All of this equipment was powered by his team of horses.

The farm buildings included a small pig sty, chicken coop, garage/wood shed, and a two-hole outhouse. The outhouse was always a challenge for Grandmother to keep "sweet" and clean and free of summer flies. Granddad was kept busy milking the cows twice a day, separating the milk (for the cream), cleaning the barn of manure, slopping the two or three hogs, managing the chickens, and working the fields.

In their spare time, my grandparents cleared more land of brush. Grandmother liked to take a can of coal oil and her grandson to light fires and burn the piled brush after getting permission from the local state fire warden. Every acre of land cleared of brush and burned created grass for additional cows and income for the family. In the summer, a large vegetable garden was planted. The surplus vegetables and fruit from the small orchard were canned for the winter. The garden potatoes were stored for the winter and were a mainstay to the family diet.

The biggest farm operation was haying. In early summer, Grandfather mowed the grass with the team of horses in the two small fields and let the grass cure (dry), a critical decision since wet hay in the barn would burn the hay and barn by spontaneous combustion. The cured hay was raked, a one-horse operation, into rows. Finally, the hay was piled by pitchfork into shocks on approximately a twelve-foot grid. During this process the weather was critical and Grandfather watched his barometer constantly. A soaking rain would demand the hay be spread to dry again and the raking and shocking repeated. It never rained while I was involved in haying.

When the shocking was completed, the transportation of the hay to the barn began. This was a family affair on a weekend. Grandfather's son and son-in-law (my father) would arrive at the farm early in the morning. The men, in their early 30s, were greeted by Grandfather with the hay wagon pulled by his team of horses. Grandfather, on the wagon, drove the horses to each shock of hay while the two men pitchforked it onto the wagon, until the load reached about twelve feet in height. Grandfather arranged the pitched hay on the wagon and drove the horses to another shock of hay. I was about 10 years old and on the wagon cheering the process.

Meanwhile, the family women were cooking huge meals (lunch and supper)) to fuel the haying crew. It was a joyful family holiday of togetherness and productivity.

Soon local laws were created that required "sanitary requirements" for dairy farms. A marginal dairy farmer could not raise the "huge" capital requirements to conform to the regulations. Grandfather sold his livestock and farm machinery for a pittance to fund his family's living expenses until he could obtain work to sustain them. He was about sixty years old and had no skills aside from his dairy farming expertise. He and his father before him had used the dairy products from their now archaic milking process without ill effects. The working people believed the new regulations were senseless.

Grandfather eventually obtained work to feed his family as a gandy dancer on a logging railroad. A gandy dancer was a member of a railroad track maintenance crew that replaced rails and ties along the railroad grade. The job required heavy manual labor. The crew tried to protect him from most of the heavy work because of his age. Nevertheless, Grandfather had a serious heart attack on his last day of work. He was a senior invalid for the rest of his life, living on meager retirement funds plus aid from his daughter, my mother. The family blamed no one, but a cynic would suggest the government shortened my grandfather's life.

My paternal family's move from Europe to the American east coast, and finally to the Olympic Peninsula is classic Americana that developed our heritage. In the 1600s the first Wilbur family left England and Catholic King Charles II prosecution of Protestants. The Wilburs were Protestants who emigrated to Boston. My branch brought property in Rhode Island, which was occupied by Wilburs for eight generations. Each family for those generations produced eight or more children to occupy and civilize the American wilderness, starting on the east coast wilderness in the 1600s.

My first awareness of the Wilbur heritage was my father's revelation of my great-grandfather's Civil War uniforms and memorabilia. Unfortunately, I never met him. My great-grandfather, Egbert Wilbur, joined the Union Army at age sixteen and fought in the Civil War. He was wounded, which left him with a limp for the rest of his life. Upon being discharged from a hospital and the army, he went west to Wisconsin to improve himself. In Wisconsin he worked for a timber company, married and started a family that grew to include ten children.

In 1902 Egbert moved his family to the forests near Sedro Woolley, Washington because his employer (a timber company) ran out of Wisconsin timber. The employer encouraged his workforce to move with the business and file timber claims. The timber claims of about 160 acres would eventually be sold to the timber company. Grandfather preserved his employment and furthered his income from public domain timber. The progressive elements in the country believed these transactions were fraudulent. Nevertheless, the timber company remained a viable business, the employees improved themselves, and forest communities such as Sedro Woolley flourished. In addition, contrary to the progressives' disparagement of these timber transactions, the growing forests in the region continued to serve the people's multiple needs. Great-grandfather Egbert soon was able to purchase a wooded tract of about 100 acres that was cleared to create a farm. Then the family moved into the hotel and livery business. The creation of Egbert's businesses was a family affair, as every child worked the farm, hotel, or livery stable until they were old enough to make their way in the world with families of their own.

My paternal grandfather came to Clallam County in the early 1900s to work in the shingle operation at Ramapo, several miles west of Freshwater Bay. He soon moved to Port Angeles to involve himself in converting the forest into wood products in a small, independent operation. Among other small endeavors, he cut pulpwood for a while. He purchased trees from the local farmers, fell, and bucked the trees into cord wood. He trucked the cord wood to the local pulp mills to receive funds to continue his entrepreneurial enterprise.

This enterprise evolved into a full-blown logging operation, commonly called a gypo operation or logger. He purchased a steam donkey to yard the logs and purchased timber just south of Port Angeles in the Black Diamond area, delivering logs to the Port Angeles mills.

His family (including my father) lived on the logging site for several years. When World War II began, logging supplies and equipment became unavailable to the small entrepreneurs. The larger operators could obtain supplies because logging became a war priority. Grandfather took his donkey and went to work for a logger in Forks. He converted the donkey from steam to gas by scraping the wood-fired boiler and installing a truck engine for power. His oldest son (my uncle), who had mechanical skills, did most of the work. He also rigged the donkey to load logs for his logger employer. The son also built his father a "logger bunkhouse" to house him during the working week in Forks. My grandmother

A facsimile of my grandfather, John Wilbur's, steam donkey.

stayed at home in Port Angeles. We visited my grandfather only on occasional weekends.

The house was patterned after the classical logging camp bunkhouse that lodged between four to six loggers. It was eight feet wide and about thirty feet long, built on skids, runners similar to a sled. The skids were small logs that enabled the building to be dragged across the ground or loaded on a rail car or logging truck, to move as logging activities moved. Grandfather moved his house from logging site to logging site. In the late 1940s, Grandmother moved into this house in Forks. The building burned in the 1950s during the Forks forest fire. As my maternal grandfather loved his dairy farm, my paternal grandfather loved logging and his ability to produce logs for the local industry.

The paternal grandparents raised five children, three boys and two girls. The older boy worked as a master mechanic in the Rayonier mill for his working life; the middle boy (my father) worked at the Crown Zellerbach mill most of his working life, eventually becoming a foreman; the younger boy worked at Fibreboard and in time became a tour boss in the paper machine room.

My maternal grandparents raised my mother and a son. The son initially worked at Crown Zellerbach's lower Elwha Dam and completed his working life operating a tractor constructing logging truck roads.

I was raised in a forest community where everyone produced a product to contribute to America's basic needs. Service people (bureaucrats, lawyers, and clerks) were thought of as inferior people because they weren't producing anything, while people who chose not to work were held in contempt. This contempt for unproductive people did not originate in the early 20th Century. It was expressed early in the 1490's classic, *Tirant lo Blanc*, which chronicles a knight's tales. One tale is of a king who liquidated almost all of his kingdom's counter-productive lawyers.

The Great Depression caused consternation in the family, but they remained employed in their chosen work during this period. However, there was continual fear the logging and the mill work would cease at any time. Wages were minimal and benefits were nearly non-existent. I remember vividly in 1935 (at the age of five) of not being able to sleep on a freezing winter night, as I worried about the family car freezing and the engine block cracking. Father couldn't afford permanent anti-freeze for the family's ancient car and used cheap alcohol in the radiator that could boil away with the heat of the engine. The car was vital to get my father to work.

There was high unemployment in the community, and the Work Projects Administration (WPA) program came to town to furnish jobs for those without employment. The people who worked for the government were looked upon with suspicion. There were many jokes concerning their lack of productivity involved in the program, although they built a ballpark with grandstands and more in the community.

My father's brother graduated from high school in 1938 and couldn't find employment, so joined the Civilian Conservation Corps (CCCs) and was assigned to the Snider Ranger Station near Forks. He left the CCCs and, desperate for work, contemplated joining the navy for a six-year hitch. Thoughts of regimentation, or having to leave "God's Country" were not to his liking; all looked hopeless, until the Fibreboard Company offered him employment.

For my primary schoolmates and me, the Depression was a time of productive fun. The schoolwork was demanding and hard. We believed the teachers were almost God-like, and we hung on their every word. We had organized sports for the boys — touch football and softball. The three local elementary schools were in fierce competition, and we all worked hard to excel. The schoolboy patrol was a prestigious organization that I joined reluctantly late in the fourth grade. I didn't like regimentation. The organization had belts with officers' badges and handheld flags. We marched most of the school body out of school and across Highway 101 adjacent to the school. There were ranks: patrolman, lieutenant, and captain. The ranks were determined by seniority: fourth graders were patrolmen, and only sixth graders could be a captain or leader of the organization. In the sixth grade, I was promoted surprisingly to captain over more senior and popular boys. Shockingly, I learned the hard work of responsibility. It was hard work managing the system with virtually no direction from adults. It was on-the-job training to keep the patrol boys organized. We were rewarded with free movie passes to the local theater's Saturday matinees, all grade-B westerns. The captain was responsible for writing the passes and distributing them without any adult. The trust thrust upon me was flattering and educational.

There was no organized recreation for the children in the community. In that era, we children made up our own activities that continued after school and during non-school days. The boys were particularly active with pick-up football, basketball, baseball, fishing, tree climbing, playing war, and building cabins and dugouts. During inclement weather we shared card and board games at each other's houses. Adults were not involved in our activities, nor were they wanted. Adult lack of imagination would have suppressed our initiative and spontaneity. We rode bikes freely all over town; there was nothing to fear. The boys all had BB guns and most graduated to 22s and larger firearms by the age of eleven.

Dynamite was scattered on construction sites and farms, and we were acquainted with the use of the *powder*, but we stuck to fireworks in and around the Fourth of July, attempting unsuccessfully to blow up the country with firecrackers and cherry bombs. We even shot at each other (carefully) with BB guns. We added slingshots, primitive bows and arrows, and spears to our arsenals. We had a proliferation of cowboy guns to simulate quick draw contests. Our wars were fought against the Nazis and the Japs. Every boy in town knew who our country's enemies were and tried to destroy them with violent imagination. In all this *imagined* violence, there was virtually no real violence or accidents in the town. The biggest danger was hitting a patch of gravel on a bike at high speed and taking a slightly bloody spill.

We had few fights — really scuffles — between boys, but they were soon forgotten. Adults were generally unaware of them. The boys had an ethic of fairness that was inherent in the community. Ethics was not taught or lectured; it was our natural American heritage, perhaps reinforced by the grade-B western movies we viewed on Saturday afternoons. A scuffle usually was preceded by asking an opponent to take off his glasses and put up his dukes. Quite often this request led to peace between two boys. Flagrant bullies were not tolerated; they were ostracized.

In the summer, the main activity was swimming at the local community pool. Sometimes an adult would take a group to the lakes or to one of the two hot springs for a real picnic outing. The kids learned how to swim with little help from adults, nor did we need help. We developed skills by doing. In the winter, snow provided sledding. Roads with hills were covered with groups of youngsters careening down them and trudging back up to the top to do it over and over. The streetlights on the roads carried this activity into the dark of the evening. Speed was all important and competitive. The competitiveness evolved often into *war*, where one group of sledders would try to unhorse (tip over) their opponents.

Adults were not involved, and their requirement was for the kids to be home for meals and bedtime. Girls were involved in all the activities, but avoided the harshest endeavors. The girls preferred skipping rope and hopscotch that most boys avoided. There was no separation of genders. Individual youths participated in the activities they favored.

I thought I had an advantage over my young peers in the late 1930s because of my grandparents' Freshwater farm. My cousin Jim who was two years younger than I, didn't particularly enjoy "farm work". I tried to be at the farm every weekend and during school vacations. As with most grandparents, they wanted their grandchildren with them frequently. A farm can be a lonely place for a couple without young children. In that era, the only recreation was a book, magazine, or radio. The neighbors were not close and besides, the demand of chores kept them close to their farm.

A youth of nine had only the strength to follow his grandfather around while he was doing his chores. It was fascinating to feel that I was contributing to feeding the country through the production of milk (cream) from the cows, eggs from the hens, and meat from the fattened pigs. I watched the butchering of cows, pigs, and chickens, and ate the results. The butchering was not nice and, of course, is never talked about in the politically correct modern world, but this process has been vital to the wellbeing of mankind through the centuries.

Then, the farm endeavor was destroyed by government regulations, to my distress, and Grandfather found unsatisfying outside work. The farm work soon consisted only of cutting wood in the grandparents' small forest to keep the home fires burning. The barn and other outbuildings were vacant, as were the fields.

As I grew older, my interest turned to cutting firewood for the farmhouse. I went into the woods with Grandfather and got on the end of his crosscut saw to fall a tree and buck the wood into stove lengths, then split it with a two-bitted man's ax or maul and wedges. I had not the strength or energy to keep up the effort for long, but learned the simple skills of woodcutting. For Christmas and birthdays I wanted my own wood cutting tools. I started out with a hatchet, but soon needed more tools. Finally, I obtained a five-foot crosscut saw and a boy's ax, a single-bitted light ax. I was eleven years old. I recruited my reluctant cousin Jim to cut wood for our grandfather. It was productive work I thought would relieve my aging grandfather of some arduous work. We had not the strength or stamina to contribute enough to make a significant contribution to the wood supply.

In inclement weather, my cousin Jim and I made up imagined war games in the barn's hay mow and hold off our enemies' assaults on our position with our BB guns. This type of activity is ignored in today's literature or denigrated as counterproductive. Nevertheless, it illustrated the resolve and dedication of the American population to thwart the threat to America from a brutal and evil enemy.

We thought the next step in our maturity should be to graduate from a BB gun to a low caliber 22 rifle. Christmas brought me a 22 rifle and soon afterwards a 16-gauge shotgun for birds. There was no gun training program. Observation of our parents and heritage was enough experience to safely start our adventure with firearms. The youths believed with practice and experience we could supplement the family larder with game animals. In addition, the gun skills would prepare us in case our services were needed to defend our country. But most importantly, firing our weapons was great sport. My cousin and I would walk a couple of miles from the farm to the bluffs above the west shore of Freshwater Bay. We'd walk along the bluffs to the northwest point of the bay and back, firing at random targets in the water. It was a thrill to watch the water splash near the target hundreds of yards from our firing point. We did our shooting from the bluffs many times and never saw a soul on the primitive road or bay, a sharp contrast to today's activity in the area.

December 7, 1941 disrupted the normality on the north Olympic Peninsula. The Japs bombed Pearl Harbor and killed hundreds of Americans. It was a sneak attack that was contrary to American ethics. After all, two American boys scuffling would warn their opponent to take off his glasses. On that fateful Sunday I was on my grandfather's farm when we accidentally turned on the radio (there were no telephones) and got the news of the sneak attack. My grandfather was outraged, angry at the Japs, without fear. He was confident it would take a short war to defeat the barbarians. My grandmother was fearful the Japs would be landing at Freshwater Bay at any moment. I was eleven years old and excited. I got out my 22, polished it, and waited for the Japs to land in front of our farmhouse overlooking the Bay. They never came!

During World War II, the American people universally labeled the Japanese in a derogatory manner — as "Japs". The rape of Nanking and other atrocities are well documented, as well as the later Bataan Death March. Americans directed their hate at the Japanese military, not so much at the civilians. The arrogant Japs also believed the Americans were feeble and a morally corrupt country that could be dominated by aggression. A few million American fighting men taught them otherwise. The Japanese-Americans and the present Japanese people deserve respect, but the Japanese Empire of the 1930s and early 1940s were *Japs*! The politically correct people of today need to recognize the evils of the old empire and applaud the Japanese-Americans and the new Japan.

I traveled home to Port Angeles Sunday evening to prepare for school the next day. My parents seemed nonplussed with the event and continued quietly with their normal routine. However, the town became an exciting beehive of activity for a young boy.

A blackout was required for Father's Crown Zellerbach mill facing the Strait of Juan de Fuca, as were the civilian houses and vehicles. Civilian volunteer wardens were appointed in each neighborhood to enforce the blackout of houses. Rationing of food, gas, and many other essential items was implemented. Fortunately, my father had purchased a new set of tires for our 1935 Chevrolet and, on the advice of the tire salesman, kept his old tires (tires could not be purchased during the war). The meager ration of gas was the biggest hardship, as we needed to visit the grandparents' farm and get our workers to their jobs. There was little or no public transportation in the rural areas. The new regulations were accepted graciously in most cases, and the Japs cursed for causing the need for regulations. In the early days of the war, there was a feeling the Jap fleet could sail down the Strait easily to level the town with a few salvos from their battleships before sailing on to Seattle and beyond. The Port Angeles people knew the closest defense was an antiquated coast artillery fortification at Port Townsend behind their town. The few Coast Guard people stationed on the Port Angles spit were inadequate.

A few weeks after Pearl Harbor, the army moved into Port Angeles. It was a relief for the adults and exciting for the youngsters. My biggest thrill was to watch an army drill where a jeep towing an anti-tank gun roared to a street intersection near our house, unlimbered the gun, and ran through a dry firing exercise.

The fighting army was in Port Angeles and a group of P-38 "pursuit" planes, later called "fighters", was located at the local airport. The P-38 pilots honed their skills and later went to war overseas. They were a wild bunch cheered on by the citizens. The army immediately put checkpoints on the roads coming from the West End into Port Angeles. When my family came from the Freshwater farm back to town, two soldiers with loaded rifles stopped the family car and checked the ID of the driver. Later the checkpoints were moved to the west side of the two bridges crossing the Elwha River, and gun emplacements were constructed on the east side of the bridges that could engulf them with machine gun and cannon fire. The remains of an ant-tank gun emplacement can be viewed at the first through-cut on Highway 101 east of the upper Elwha bridge.

Shortly after the army arrived to establish checkpoints and furnish air support, the construction of fortifications began in earnest. Plans had been made to protect the Pacific Coast with additional coastal fortifications before December 7. The Navy's contribution before the war was five ancient "four stacked" destroyers to protect Washington, Oregon, and Alaska.

Camp Hayden was the only significant fortification built west of Port Angeles, on Salt Creek which flows into the east end of Crescent Bay. My maternal uncle became employed in this project and lost a good friend who was accidentally killed during the construction. Wars are bad, but this war ended the Great Depression and put my uncle and many others back to work. My uncle worked on military installations along the Strait for several years. Camp Hayden was comprised of barracks hidden in the trees along Salt Creek. A six-inch and two sixteen-inch batteries were built and test fired in the spring of 1945 at Camp Hayden. Of course, in the dark days of 1942, the Camp Hayden installation gave little comfort to the Port Angeles folks. The question was asked over and over: Where is our Navy? There was no answer in early 1942. People were angry at the Japs — but also at our apparently inept government.

The local people wanted action, action that only the people could generate by joining the military or producing arms for our fighting forces. In our family, there was initially only one male of military age — Uncle Bob, my father's younger brother and my mentor who helped me polish my fishing skills. He was a young single male who was obligated for military service. He had viewed the movie, "Wake Island" where the Marines fought off the Japs until it was a hopeless fight, as judged by their leaders. The rank and file Marines would have fought to the end. Uncle Bob joined the Marines.

Port Angeles was a navy town and Bob's peers derided him for not taking the "safe" service by joining the Navy. Bob said no, he wanted to kill Japs, not float around on the water safely out of the war. Bob was a Marine on Guadalcanal and several other Pacific Islands before returning to the states for further schooling. His outfit was on the verge of participating in the invasion of Japan when the war ended. Bob believed he would not have survived an invasion. After I finished college in 1954, I joined the Marines for two years, but fortunately there was no shooting conflict at that time.

The older family men in their early thirties would be drafted into the military if they weren't employed in work critical to the war effort. So, my family chose to leave Port Angeles and Father's pulp mill to work in the Navy shipyard at Bremerton. The Wilbur family moved there early in the war where Father plied his painting craft in the shipyard. My mother and I believed he was more useful to the country keeping the fighting ships in the conflict than carrying a rifle. We thought he was too decrepit for strenuous army life. However, I was ready to go to war at age twelve.

In junior high school at Bremerton, I was closer to the war; I was thrilled. The school had an anti-aircraft gun sandbagged on the roof. Unfortunately in my opinion, the cool barrage balloons had been done away with and the anti-aircraft gun was unmanned. My peers and I could walk to the Navy yard fence to peer into the dry docks to watch the ships being repaired. My father reported that when the ships' flooded compartments were opened for repair, dead bodies often floated out.

Our hate for Japs was very real. I would think of my Uncle Bob on the Pacific Islands. At that time my paternal cousin was on a destroyer off the Island of Okinawa, and he wrote to me frequently of the horror of the battle. I imagined his body floating out of one of those ships in dry dock. Today I read reams from the academics suggesting we really didn't understand the Japanese of the 1930s. I suggest the academics are in another world.

With the war over in 1946, the Wilbur family moved back to Port Angeles to resume a normal life. My father went back to his old job at Crown Zellerback, and I entered Port Angeles High School. The forest community was booming with a plentitude of jobs. The logs were moving out of the forest into the mills, and there was full employment. The Depression of the 1930s was a thing of the past. There was no fear of another economic disaster or an invasion by a brutal enemy. When I was about eight years old my parents had told me I was going to college, and took me to the bank to open a savings account. I deposited about $1.50 and started saving money and working where I could — mostly in the berry and pea fields during the summers. A paper route served me for a while, and the state fire crew employed me during my high school summers. The savings were meager, and my family and friends had no expectations of college. The industrial jobs paid well, offering security in the mills and woods.

I was a mediocre student without adequate funds, but I programmed myself to finish college without financial help from any source except my work ethic. My work with state foresters related to the summer fire crew, and my love of the forests set my goal to be a graduate forester educated at the University of Washington.

Because of my father's employment at the CZ pulp mill, it was easy to obtain summer employment there. During the course of my college studies, I experienced every menial job in the mill. I worked each summer and came home from the university to work Sundays in the machine room at time-and-a-half — big money. The job entailed wiping grease off the huge paper machine with a rag soaked in a solvent that was hard on the hands and dirty. All the work was simple, repetitive, and boring. The "money making job" was working in the machine room as a spare hand, wheeling huge rolls of newsprint on a dolly from the machine room to the finishing room. The money was made by working double eight-hour shifts on occasion and working six days a week. It was shift work, and graveyard (midnight to eight in the morning) was nauseating. The smell upset my stomach and I would go to a corner and regurgitate before finishing the shift. I was not going to lose money by letting an upset stomach send me home.

The older workers at the mill had more interesting and meaningful jobs. I had a job where I could observe the grinder room where my father started to labor in about 1930. He worked for eight years before obtaining a skilled position and went on to become a foreman. The men in the grinder room fed cordwood into a furnace-like machine that ground the wood that was the basic ingredient of newsprint. The cordwood was four feet long and weighed over a hundred pounds apiece. The room was filled with steam and, to me, looked much like a hell. After learning this, I sympathized with his terseness with me when he came home from a graveyard shift. He was exhausted.

Of course, I had time to visit with my high school buddies during the summer. My close friends mostly found employment in the local mills. Several years into my college studies, one friend met me for recreational tennis. He drove to the courts in a new Oldsmobile 88, the hottest car of the day. He had been working in the Rayonier mill about three years. My thoughts turned to the good life with new cars relative to my frugal life in college; many times I ate only one meal a day. Many of my friends had married out of high school and started families. But then, I thought of my father in the grinder room struggling to support my mother and a baby, me. I went back to my studies and forgot my selfish greed for an Oldsmobile 88.

The Korean War came to Port Angeles, and the draft started again. Most of my friends enlisted in the military while I had a college deferment. My conscience bothered me as I thought I should join them, but I believed I would never obtain a degree if I interrupted my studies. Only one friend ever saw dangerous combat; the rest were never in harm's way. Most of my friends came back home from the service to attend college paid for by the GI Bill. My peers' military experience matured them, and the GI Bill motivated them financially to better themselves and the country. The high school classes of the 1940s-'50s were an extension of America's greatest generation, that is, devoted to their American heritage, strong in basic education and a belief that productive work was honorable. Not unusual, almost all of my friends returned to Port Angeles, and those that didn't still considered it their home and heritage.

In 2012, the entire country honored the World War II generation as the greatest in the nation's history. What they didn't say is this generation and the generations before them created the highest standard of living the world had ever experienced for all American people through dedication to productive work. In the 1960s, the academic social engineers began to publish myriad publications to improve American education and the standard of living, resulting in a degeneration of the American work ethic and heritage. The academics now suggest the greatest American generation is the last generation to thrive in America, a defeatist and unacceptable suggestion to the real American people.

Port Angeles was a forest community that depended on the productive utilization of the forest and land, allied with a skilled work force. It was much like other communities across the nation. Starting in the 1930s and continuing for decades, there were three pulp mills, a plywood mill, and smaller wood conversion facilities that were supported by a spirited logging and forestry group. The town depended for its existence on the land. By 2012, there was one lone pulp mill and a log export facility. Port Angeles and the surrounding area's forest-working population have been largely replaced by local retirees and an influx of outside retirees — people who are mostly uncaring of the region's past heritage of productive labor. The outside retirees have accumulated their wealth apart from the north Olympic Peninsula and have little interest in continuing the growth of the productive forest, mills, logging and of growing trees. Many of the local priorities are directed in converting the original industrial sites on the Port Angeles waterfront into parks and recreation areas, along with the inland landscape.

The progressives of the late 1800s almost made the Peninsula into the preservationists' Forest Reserve. The reserves on the Peninsula were reduced by the outraged western people, but increased by forest preservationists incrementally through the efforts of the progressives like the two Presidents Roosevelt, along with John Muir's Sierra Club. The preservationists have a host of designations that take the forest away from the forest workers, such as *wilderness, wild lands, wetlands endangered species habitat, scientific areas, archeological and wildlife reserves, scenic rivers, roadless areas...* and the list continues. Almost all of the extensive forest preservation areas can have multiple uses. Clear-cut logging and planting will not permanently disrupt the preservationists' designation. A forest of any structure is wilderness even with limited access roads. These roads serve to protect the forest and make it available to the old and handicapped. The common assertion by the progressives is that the cost of commercial economics in the communities will be replaced by tourists. The so-called environmental damage costs are unacceptable. But, logging has never deterred the tourists from the Peninsula. To the contrary, commercial enterprises have made the Peninsula more accessible to the tourists. The peninsula scenery and environment have never seen permanent human disruption except in the towns that were developed.

Among the many disruptions of the natural environment that soon returned to a normal wilderness were the Tubal Cain Mines and Iron Mountain between the headwaters of the Dungeness and Quilcene Rivers. By 1902 hundreds of claims had been filed on the almost 7,000-foot Iron Mountain located just south of the better known Mt.

Townsend. There were no trails into the rugged area of near-vertical mountain slopes that in the winter were covered with avalanche-prone deep snow. Nevertheless, the miners soon built trails into the mountain and, in many instances, blasted the trails with dynamite into the mountain.

By 1904, the mountain was a beehive of activity with miners in what was thought to contain the largest copper deposit in the world. The Tubal Cain Company consolidated eleven claims and began to build the mining town of Copper City. All the construction material came to the city via horse, mule, and burro pack trains. A sawmill was the first construction project, and a creek was dammed to power the mill. The lumber was used to build a cookhouse and a two-story bunkhouse for 35 men. The miners also built an office building, machine shop, sheds for a blacksmith shop, and storage for dynamite — even a club house for recreation.

The town was built and the mineshaft started. Again the creek waters were harnessed to furnish compressed air to run the rock drills needed to open the mineshaft. A two-inch iron pipeline ran over a mile from the creek to the mineshaft. While the Tubal Cain operation was active, another mine operation was working the other side of Iron Mountain. The Tubal shaft extended 2800 feet into Iron Mountain with side shafts, but by 1913 the operation was abandoned.

Tubal Cain became a local legend that attracted local and outside hikers to the site in the Olympic National Forest, a part of the forest that is pristine, without roads. I hiked into Tubal Cain in 1990 and had difficulty finding the mineshaft. A person unacquainted with the legend could never separate it from the surrounding pristine wilderness. There was no permanent environment impact created by the mining activity.

The early miners simply filed a mining claim and went to work with little or no government interference. In today's world, it would require a miner to spend millions of dollars just for government permits, plus millions for scientific impact studies and restitution agreements. In the midst of the permitting process, public hearings would be required, and the miner would need public relations and lawyers skills costing another million dollars or so. Of course, the progressives would bring a lawsuit against the miner, which might take years to move through the courts, plus another million dollars.

In reviewing the early 1900s Tubal Cain experience, it would appear the progressives had stopped productive enterprises on the Peninsula for a goal of non-existent environmental concerns. The Peninsula's federal land is largely taken from the forest workers, while the remaining private and state land is sharply restricted from use by the progressives' government restrictions; probably up to 20% of the private land is preserved. The trend is clear: started by the Forest Reserves that almost encompassed the Olympic Peninsula in the late 1800s, alive today, and growing out of control.

The efforts of the Port Angeles city fathers in the 20th Century are in jeopardy. The Elwha dams are gone; most of the mills are gone and forest activities have been minimized. The Peninsula's land is largely fallow but awaiting a revitalized greatest generation to get back to work to maintain the highest standard of living the world has ever seen and to help the world emulate the American success.

In 2011, the lumber imports from Canada almost equaled the lumber produced in America. This trend of lumber production is mirrored in many other resources across the country. We are a country that is quickly becoming dependent on other nations for our raw materials because the progressives have dictated land use policy decisions for several decades. Their vision (published many times) is to preserve resources and lower the American standard of living created by our forefathers. In the Port Angeles area, people like G.M. Lauridsen, K.O. Erickson, Thomas Aldwell, Micheal Earles, John Huelsdonk and many others who built a forest community would be shunted aside in favor of Utopian visions fueled by the progressives obscurantism (government) bureaucracy, while the progressives enervate the productive people of past and future great generations.

In a 1993 book, *Federal Land, Western Anger,* R. McGregor Cawley describes the Sagebrush Rebellion that has been renewed in the state legislatures recently in Utah, Nevada, and elsewhere, and how it will continue. This rebellion will eventually prevail to save our forest communities and our American standard of living, sooner rather than later. The following stories will tell of the plain folks who turned the north Olympic Peninsula into civilized American communities for future Americans to expand.

The Beginning

In 1596, Juan de Fuca claimed he entered the Strait of Juan de Fuca. His claim stirred interest in Europe because of their engrossment with the Northwest Passage. However, the exploration and the settlement of the northwest began in earnest with the Russian activities in Alaska, starting in the 1740s. The Russians founded Fort Archangel in 1799.

The Russian activity prompted the Spanish to move into California in the 1760s to counter the Russian threat to colonize the West Coast. The Spanish sent a band of Franciscan monks and a hundred-odd soldiers to establish a string of missions that evolved into huge feudal farms staffed with the natives. The Native population was forced to work and live at the missions in slave-like conditions. The economy in California was largely dependent on the mission farms.

Mexico became independent from Spain in 1821, and the mission farms were eliminated, replaced by large ranches. By 1840, more than a thousand massive ranches in California were owned by California Dons. The new aristocracy dominated California. Meanwhile, small farms were not a significant factor in California.

In 1792 the Spaniard, Fidalgo, established a fort at Neah Bay and proclaimed "An Act Possession" which told the world Spain controlled a large portion of the Olympic Peninsula and beyond. During the same period of time, the Spanish were at Nootka, a port on Vancouver Island almost 100 miles north of Neah Bay. Nootka was nearly an international port visited by Russian, American, British, and Spanish trading and military ships. Spain and Britain vied for control of the port and the Northwest.

Neah Bay was occupied for a very short time and then Spain, for practical purposes, withdrew from the Northwest because of the dominance of Britain's numerous trading vessels, combined with the beginning of trading posts on land, plus the dominant British Navy worldwide, whereas the Spanish had a small military force. A military of a little over 100 men and a band of monks took control of the mostly grasslands of sunny California. It would take much more in the Northwest to compete with the British.

The Spanish had explored the Straits of Juan de Fuca in 1790 and named a vacant harbor "Port Angeles". The Quimper geography near Port Townsend is named for a Spanish explorer. But it took Captain Vancouver to discover the inland sea he named "Puget Sound". Vancouver was charged by the British Navy to explore, and his significant discovery was Puget Sound.

Also in 1792, Vancouver met the American merchant Captain Gray off the coast of the Olympic Peninsula. Both captains compared notes; Vancouver went north to discover Puget Sound, and Gray went south to discover the Columbia River. Because Vancouver was in the military, his findings were published widely (including Gray's discovery), while Gray, a merchant, kept his findings quiet. Both Vancouver and Gray are praised by historians. But with all the military and trading ships sailing around the Northwest during that era, the discoveries were probably overdue.

The Lewis and Clark expedition reached the mouth of the Columbia River in November 1805 and wintered at Fort Clatsop, a fort they built. Lewis and Clark hoped an American ship would enter the Columbia River during their stay at Fort Clatsop to offer them passage to the east coast or furnish them with supplies. However, that never happened, and the expedition made the hazardous trip overland back to the East in 1806.

Lewis and Clark received a huge amount of credit for opening the west to the settlers, and their report did much to publicize the western opportunities. However, others were already in the process of exploring and utilizing the western resources.

The American, John Jacob Astor, planned a trading empire at the mouth of the Columbia River. His ship, the *Toquin*, arrived in the river in 1811 to build a trading post, Fort Astoria. Astor also sent a party overland to Fort Astoria in 1811. After extreme hardships, they arrived there in 1812. Unfortunately, the Northwest Company, soon to be the Hudson Bay Company, in 1812 visited Fort Astoria and informed Astor's people they were in Canada.

In June 1812, a Fort Astoria employee, Robert Stuart, set off with a party to the east to inform Astor. In the course of the trip, Stuart found South Pass. The pass made possible the use of wagons between the east and the northwest that enabled the future migration of Americans to the Northwest.

At the outbreak of the War of 1812 and the threat of British naval action against Fort Astoria, the fort was sold to the Northwest Company. Unfortunately, Astor's business acumen dictated that his business adventures not be publicized. The British and their surrogate, the Northwest Company, took control of the Northwest.

In the meantime, the American mountain men were infiltrating the west. Manuel Lisa, exploring a business venture before the Lewis and Clark expedition, built a fort in 1807 on the Yellowstone River to trap and trade furs. The mountain men were numerous in the northern Rockies and into Idaho by 1810. They were adventurous wild men who were entrepreneurs that acquired and sold furs.

Jedediah Smith was an outstanding example of the numerous small businessmen, called mountain men, who made their livings and sought their fortunes in the west and who in the course of their business, explored the West. Smith rediscovered (Stuart was first) South Pass and communicated his discovery far and wide to enable all to take advantage of the pass. Smith's greatest business travel started in 1827 from Salt Lake to the Sacramento Valley and to the mouth of the Klamath River on his way to the Columbia River then back to the Salt Lake vicinity. He wrote a detailed report concerning wagon travel over South Pass and the fertile Columbia River lands. He was killed by Comanches on the Santa Fe Trail in 1831, but not before he killed at least two of them.

The American government sponsored several military or quasi-military expeditions into the west in the early 1800s, but the American businessmen (mountain men and sailors) had been there first and were prepared to guide and lead further development of the West.

BRITISH OCCUPATION

The War of 1812 forced the Americans to leave Fort Astoria at the mouth of the Columbia River. The North West Company took possession of the fort and the name was changed to Fort George. And the British took control of the Pacific Northwest on land and water. In 1821 the North West Company merged with the Hudson Bay Company (HBC), and shortly thereafter, the reorganized and the more powerful HBC solidified the control of the northwest. The HBC's principal officer brought Dr. John McLoughlin with him to Fort George in 1824 and delegated the responsibility of consolidating the HBC in the northwest. Fort George was inadequate, and McLoughlin established Fort Vancouver in 1825. In 1827 McLoughlin had Fort Langley built on the Frazer River near the present Vancouver, British Columbia. By then the HBC had two forts that bridged the northwest.

With the establishment of the two forts, the communication between them became vital to the company's business. While the sea route was obvious and used initially, it was unreliable or very slow during winter storms, especially with the hazardous Columbia River bar. So a more dependable route was explored and documented. The route was from Fort Vancouver down the Columbia and up the Cowlitz River to Cowlitz Landing (near Toledo) by canoe, then by horseback to the lower Puget Sound and finally by canoe to Fort Langley on the Frazer River. The canoes and horses were usually furnished by the Indians — with or without guides. The route was advantageous to both whites and Indians as the Indians were compensated for their services, and both parties had opportunities to trade.

The HBC traffic proved to be relatively safe as the traffic was non-threatening and of economic benefit to the tribes. Also, the HBC people were well armed with efficient weapons. Nevertheless, in January 1828, Alexander McKenzie, with four HBC employees, was murdered by a group of "Clallams". The experienced HBC knew that if retaliation was not immediate, their overland communication would be lost. Further, HBC personnel would be in great jeopardy whenever they left their forts.

The "Clallam Expedition" was planned and implemented. It included a Fort Vancouver clerk who described the expedition in his journal: A land party would leave Fort Vancouver and travel to the Clallam Indian country on the northeast Olympic Peninsula. The British ship *Cadboro* with its cannon would meet the land party on the upper Puget Sound. The land party on reaching the lower Sound bartered for canoes to continue their journey and, in the process, was approached by a tribe whose members had been murdered by the Clallams. The Clallams had taken one of their women as a prisoner, and the tribe requested the HBC people obtain her release. The tribe then asked to join the expedition.

Eleven canoes traveled to meet the *Cadboro* in Clallam country. Apparently, the news of the avenging expedition had reached the Clallams; the villages were deserted until the expedition reached New Dungeness. The *Cadboro* cannonaded the village as the natives fled to the woods. The land party then went ashore and burned what remained of the village. The Indian woman was exchanged for a captured Clallam warrior. The expedition group was assured the murderers were mostly killed, enabling the HBC people to return victorious to Fort Vancouver.

The expedition demonstrated how vulnerable the Puget Sound tribes were to HBC's armed ships. The tribe's villages were mostly located adjacent to salt water and were easily destroyed by the ship's guns. Also, their canoes were easy prey to sea power. Canoes were essential to the tribe's livelihood. Perhaps the expedition was a strong factor that allowed the HBC to dominate the northwest for years with no army and a small staff. During the Indian War in 1855, the HBC at

Fort Nisqually requested help from the U.S. Army to garrison the fort, since there were only five white men in the fort. The army sent a corporal and six men.

In 1833, Fort Nisqually was established to furnish a presence on Puget Sound and be a half-way house between Fort Vancouver and Fort Langley. But above all, it would make money for the owners in faraway England. As usual, the fort was located on the Nisqually Prairie or Plain, a location that did not require the arduous work of removing the giant Douglas fir and cedars. Eventually, the fort would utilize about ten square miles of the plain. The Native population was not a consideration; the company took what they wanted, albeit with diplomacy and good will. The soil was poor; however, this was compensated by a lack of giant trees on the mostly level ground.

It would seem the HBC forts would dominate the northwest, and they did. They also loosely controlled the tribes, but the HBC only "settled" or controlled the land immediately adjacent to their three major forts plus a few satellite posts or forts in the region. There was an agriculture endeavor of over a thousand acres north of the Cowlitz River near present day Toledo.

The HBC was an English corporation whose sole interest was profits, large profits. The initial thrusts were the fur trade and agriculture to sustain the HBC staff in their outposts. As the fur resource became depleted, exported agriculture products and retail sales to settlers played a bigger role in the corporate profit picture.

The British mentality dictated the English agriculture model be made to fit their profit requirements; that is, tenant farmers or corporate farms were to be managed by HBC gentlemen. In 1841, the HBC sponsored twenty-three families from the Red River (Canada) for tenant farming on HBC land. Thirteen families attempted to farm for a short time, and all left because there was free land in the Willamette Valley which freed them of English type servitude. A tenant farmer did come out from England at his own expense. Generally tenant farmers did not come out from England at their own expense because tenant farming had little appeal to those British subjects who could afford to emigrate from Britain or Canada. And, the HBC was faced with the Americans who were eager to carve farms out of the wilderness. In 1818, a "Joint Occupancy Treaty" was signed between America and Britain that defined a joint tenancy of the northwest. The HBC feared an influx of settlers would disrupt their business monopoly and ultimately drive them from what in realty was their fiefdom.

Doctor John McLoughlin was the chief factor at Fort Vancouver. He administered a vast territory from northern California to the panhandle of present day Alaska, from the Pacific Ocean almost to the Rocky Mountains during the early 1800s to the mid-1800s. He had an administrative staff of probably fewer than 500 people, that is, people loyal to the company. There was no police force, and the British Army was oceans away; however the British navy was present at times. McLoughlin ruled with diplomacy, dignity (the HBC officers always dressed formally), strict discipline, bribery, and on occasion punitive action against individuals and tribes. There were no prisons in the early days, but individuals could be locked up and chained for short periods. Flogging was used occasionally for the employees as well as tribal members. Punitive action was taken against the tribes as a last resort.

The British brought their homeland's village-class society of clearly drawn lines between classes that only the exceptional individual could pass. Emigration was the only way for a British farm laborer to break the class barrier. For example, my great-grandfather, Jimmie, broke the barrier by deserting from the British Navy in Victoria in 1859 to become an American logger, then a farm owner, equal to anyone in the Dungeness community. But, the British Navy furnished transportation to Jimmie, while the average British labor family's subsistence income held them in bondage in Britain.

McLoughlin and his gentlemen ate their meals in a dining room that could seat between 12 and 30 people. The table had probably the only white tablecloth in Oregon. The table radiated with silver, fine glass and wine decanters, and Spode China. The food was bountiful.

Wine was served only on special occasions; liquor was discouraged throughout the HBC country, including the tribes. After the initial HBC trading days, liquor was not an Indian trade item. Important natives might dine at a side table on occasion. The gentlemen were seated by rank; the junior clerks were at the far end of the table and never spoke unless asked a question by their betters. This protocol was observed throughout the day. Females were not welcome at the table except on a few occasions when the factor's wife or a very distinguished female guest joined the gentlemen.

The gentlemen and skilled people lived inside the fort in very Spartan quarters, while the common laborers lived in huts with earthen floors and limited furniture. Cleanliness was impractical as roads, courtyard, and paths were a quagmire of mud during the winter rainy season. My great-grandfather Jimmy would have been housed in a hut and living on a meager sustenance income with no opportunity for improvement. In addition, Jimmie had no skill with firearms that would enable him to escape to his own farm away from the shelter of the HBC.

Contrary to the white tablecloth dining of the gentlemen, the laborers were given a salary of 17 pounds per year, with 8 pounds of potatoes and 8 pounds of salted salmon provided weekly. Of course, on the four annual holidays, their "masters" treated them with a feast of beef, flour, and a quarter of a liter of rum per person.

However, the laborer's lot was moderated slightly by taking a Native woman as a wife, without the protection of any law or formality. The wife might go back to her tribe at any time and the husband could leave for another post at any time, sans the present wife. The children would usually go with the wife to her tribe or be left at Fort Vancouver as orphans to somehow survive. The wives could also bring another asset to the marriage, a slave from her tribe. The slave was invaluable to perform household chores and hunt and fish to supplement the household with fresh fish and game.

The gentlemen often took Native brides since there were no white women within thousands of miles. McLoughlin himself married a Cree woman and formally sanctified the marriage. Nevertheless, the gentlemen usually took Native wives temporarily or permanently, and slaves were utilized by the wives in many instances. Ironically, Britain abolished slavery in 1833, but the HBC found it convenient to ignore the law, rationalizing that slavery was justified because they were dealing with sovereign Native nations. The company's sole purpose was to generate profits for the owners of HBC, not to care for the Native population in any way. The Native's function was only to furnish furs for the business and provide manual labor. The labor force was very diverse and made up of largely imported labor from Hawaii, French Canada, Scotland, England, the Iroquois, and the northwest tribes. It would appear the northwest tribes could furnish all the necessary labor. Nevertheless, most of the labor came from outside the region. The gentlemen were exclusively English and Scots. The workday started at five in the morning when the rising bell was rung, and completed at eight or nine in the evening, with breaks for meals. Generously, Sunday was a leisure day after church services.

In 1830, a catastrophic epidemic (probably malaria) struck the lower Columbia. Because McLoughlin had discharged the fort's resident doctor, he had to add doctoring to his responsibilities. And, he worked with the sick from daylight until late in the evening. Quinine was the medicine of choice, but the supply was soon exhausted. The roots of the local dogwood tree were used as a substitute — a poor substitute. McLoughlin treated employees and Indians alike when they came to the fort. In the Native villages, the historic treatment was to immerse the patient in the icy cold river. The Indians died in droves because of a lack of a European immune system, and to the worse possible patient care, which included shocking icy baths and lack of warmth in their lodges. The HBC employees were stricken with the disease and were incapacitated, but most survived. Up to 90% of the Native population on the lower Columbia died, with survivors flocking to the fort asking for treatment and/or a decent burial. The epidemic peaked in 1830, but continued at a much lower level for several years.

The epidemic brought forth the caring part of McLoughlin's personality that was otherwise reserved or even harsh toward natives and laborers. Of course, the epidemic depopulated the area and resulted in reducing the potential labor force and trading. At one point, even McLoughlin was sick, as well were the HBC employees. There were hardly enough people to keep the fort functional.

Although Fort Vancouver had a resident doctor as well as most of the HBC posts, this small resource could not serve the region.

Related to inadequate medical care, education efforts of any kind were non-existent. School for the employees' children was an off-and-on affair. The gentlemen in the fort sent their children to Canada or England to school.

Fort Vancouver and the other northwest forts' communicated with the interior by canoes or long wooden bateaux paddled by voyageurs. The voyageurs were colorful French Canadians who sang while paddling from daylight until dark. The furs were pressed into bundles of 88 pounds for transportation by water and carried by voyageurs around portages. The HBC gentlemen never paddled and were carried ashore by the voyageurs, if necessary, to keep their feet dry.

Allied with the voyageurs were the brigades of horse-mounted trappers that trapped where the Indians wouldn't. The Snake River Brigade was composed of 65 to 100 people, including women and children who were kept together for safety. On one winter expedition the brigade traveled all the way to the Gulf of California. The Southern Brigade concentrated in the Siskiyou Mountains of southern Oregon and northern California and all the way to California's Central Valley. As the American trappers started to compete with HBC's trappers, the brigades swept the streams clear of beaver to preclude encouragement of American trappers and the inevitable following of American settlers.

There were virtually no farmers or settlers in the northwest until the American Great Migration of 1843 brought several hundred people in 100 wagons, along with about 5,000 head of livestock to the Oregon country — mostly to the Willamette Valley. And, the Americans kept coming.

The Hudson Bay Company's Dr. McLoughlin was undoubtedly amazed at the number of American families that descended upon the HBC's corporate monopoly. The families were common people (few gentlemen) who used their own resources to cross the harsh plains to better their lives on "free" land. The people arrived diseased and, in many cases, nearly starving. Dr. John embraced the Americans with credit for badly needed food, equipment, and congeniality while sending HBC men to bring in stranded Americans when the need was desperate.

Many of the HBC leaders disagreed with McLaughlin's aid to the Americans, especially furnishing credit to people without proper collateral. And, most of the Americans did not pay off their HBC debt. It appears first and foremost, Dr. John was a humane man and could not stand by while his fellow Anglo-Saxons died outside his Fort Vancouver. But he was a practical man. Well-armed and desperate fathers would not allow their wives and children to starve to death when supplies could be taken by force from a puny and undermanned fort. In the past, an accidental fire outside the fort had been fortunately stopped just in front of the fort's stockade, an occurrence that documents how fragile the fort really was.

Perhaps McLoughlin planned to join the Americans all along as he filed a land claim on Oregon City land where he established businesses. He resigned from the HBC in 1845 to become an American. Some call him the "Father of Oregon" because he partly enabled the settlers to succeed. He did make the settlers lives easier, but the Americans would have come to Oregon with or without Dr. John.

A corporation could not claim land in Oregon under American control, so the HBC had its employees file claims on strategic land, especially on the agriculture land, to preclude Americans from squatting or "stealing" HBC's developed land. Many of the HBC people, like Dr. John, took the claims for themselves and became Americans.

By 1840, the fur trade had diminished in the lower Columbia region, and it was apparent the American settlers would turn the Willamette Valley and beyond into vigorous farming communities. There was no room for a HBC monopoly in the area. The HBC established Fort Victoria on Vancouver Island in 1843, and this new fort soon replaced Fort Vancouver as the headquarters of the HBC in the northwest. In the nick of time, the boundary between Canada and the U.S. was agreed to in 1846 making possible the present states of Oregon and Washington.

It was apparent to the HBC and British that to hold their ground north of the 49th parallel that separated Canada from the U.S., the territory would have to be colonized mutually by the HBC and the British Colonial Office. This contrasted with the American settlers who took the initiative with little help and no direction from their government. In 1849, official colonization became a reality on paper. But, there were few in Britain who wanted to settle on Vancouver Island or elsewhere. A settler had to pay a pound (English money) per acre for land he had not seen as well as pay the expense of a long sea voyage from Britain for his family and his farm laborer families. English farming grouped a farm owner with traditional English farm labor. Also, HBC's harsh control in Canada was also well known in Britain, and few wanted to be at the mercy of an autocratic corporation for services and civil law. However, in 1859 the land laws were changed to something similar to those across the border in the U.S. and the British "colony" experienced a serious settlement of people by 1862. However, Vancouver Island and the adjacent mainland did not become part of Canada proper until later.

In 1854, the population was more than 700 people on Vancouver Island; most of these people owed their livelihood to the HBC. In 1858, gold brought thousands of people through Victoria to the gold rush on the lower Fraser River. The miners were mostly Americans or had the spirit of the American miners. The British attempted to control the influx of Americans, but the British officials had little control at the mines of a motley crew of miners who were notorious for making their own laws.

Fortunately for the British, gold played out in a few short years and the miners moved on. If there had been industry to hold the Americans on the Frazer River, the entire Northwest Coast may have become America. However by 1858 all permanent opportunities and jobs were south of the border because HBC autocrats stifled opportunities on Vancouver Island and the vicinity, except for periodic and fleeting gold rushes similar to the lower Frazer River gold rush of 1858. Sensible people made their homes in the U.S.

It is easy to list events and dates, but to get a feeling for the life and thoughts of any era, a journal written by an individual during that time is the only honest way to understand what life was about — a journal written to express feelings without concern for ones superiors, family, or special interest groups. Joseph Heath was one such individual who arrived at Fort Nisqually in 1844 after an adventurous sea voyage from England. He was the wastrel son of an English gentleman. After the son gambled away his resources, his father forced him into agriculture in England. Subsequently, he contracted with the HBC to become a tenant farmer in the northwest. He was touted as an agriculturist by the HBC.

After a long sea voyage on a HBC's ship from England to Fort Vancouver, he writes of his sea voyage and subsequent adventures. (His family paid for his passage presumably to rid themselves of a prodigal family member.) He left Fort Vancouver to travel to Fort Nisqually by canoe to Cowlitz Landing and then by horse to Fort Nisqually.

At Fort Nisqually, Doctor Tolmie, in charge of Fort Nisqually, helped Heath survey the Nisqually Plains for a suitable farm. He also looked at sites near Fort Victoria. Heath chose a site where Western State Hospital is now situated, a site of poor prairie soil on mainly open grasslands, with scattered Oregon oaks. A dilapidated cabin on the site was abandoned by a previous tenant farmer.

Heath's contract stipulated that the HBC would furnish farm tools and supplies in return for half the profits of the farm. Of course, there would be no profit until he converted the prairie into an operating farm. Heath started work on his farm at five in the morning and finished at eight in the evening when weather permitted. Two meals a day were adequate, a boiled gruel of wheat or peas in the morning and salted salmon in the evening. This diet was supplemented with game or domestic meat at times. By the middle of 1846, Heath had 170 acres fenced and 60 planted to wheat. His livestock consisted of a substantial flock of sheep, plus cattle, horses, oxen, chickens, and pigs. His numerous buildings utilized logs, and the fences were poles. He was in debt to HBC who charged 5% interest on articles supplied to him.

Surrounding Heath's farm was the HBC's agriculture endeavor that encompassed the whole Nisqually Plain from the Nisqually River to just south of the Puyallup River. The agriculture centered around sheep, cattle, and horses raised on the open prairie, with some cultivated crops on the better soils. There was only one other tenant farmer on the HBC property besides Heath. The remaining prairie was a corporate farm worked with company contract employees and day laborers.

In the tradition of old England, Heath required farm labor. As his journal suggests, "Indian labor" was the only resource available, so he started hiring semi-permanent employees and day labor from the local Nisqually Indian villages. Soon, he had an Indian village close to his house, as the Indian families moved their lodges to his farm. Heath trained, fed, disciplined, protected, and doctored them.

The Indians had to be watched all the time or they would steal household items, tools, and farm produce that included potatoes, and peas. In fact Heath did not locate on Whidbey Island because prior settlers gave up farming there because the Indian thieves would harvest the settlers' crops in increments before the settlers were ready to harvest. Heath periodically caught his people stealing; he described them as "people he pays and feeds". Yet, he could not survive without the Indian laborers. And the laborers would do little unless Heath was there to observe their efforts. They would intermittently not report to work until Heath learned to stop feeding the village when the work was not done. His Indian shepherd walked away from his flock one day, leaving them unprotected and scattered to the winds. Heath thrashed the shepherd and discharged him. The HBC on occasion caught Indians butchering their livestock, and the culprits were locked-up for short periods and sometimes flogged. Heath believed this treatment was used too infrequently.

The Snoqualmie Indian raids, both real and imagined, were not infrequent. The Snoqualmies hoped to enslave the women and children in Heath's village and murder the adult males. Also, they wanted Heath's head on a pole in their Snoqualmie village. On one occasion, Heath's Indians rushed into his house seeking his protection from their enemy; the enemy didn't come. On several other occasions Heath gave his people ammunition and even loaned them muskets to defend their village. He wrote in his journal that he was not afraid and welcomed the challenge of an attack. On the other hand, Heath reports several of his Indians went out on war parties against other tribes.

Slaves were gambled to be won or lost, used to buy a bride, do the work in the lodges and to work on Heath's farm. One of Heath's Indians beat his slave for giving Heath information about thievery. Heath stopped the beating and struck the Indian master with his fist so hard it split his eyebrow to the bone. Heath's "law": no one will ill-use a slave while under Heath's protection. Heath suggested that his farming success was really an Indian success. One wonders if Heath's farm was worked only by Indian slave labor. The writings of Heath and his peers rarely mention slavery or the slave trade among the northwest tribes. Certainly, modern writers don't touch the subject; only chiefs and warriors are noticed.

Heath believed the Indians' long term passionate and unforgiving vendettas (plus incessant gambling) would interfere with developing a peaceful co-existence with religion or their fellow humans. Murder seemed routine, especially against Indian doctors or medicine men who made bad medicine. On one occasion, two Indians would have killed a medicine man in his lodge fifty yards from Heath's house if Heath and his Indian employee had not intervened. In the scuffle, Heath found the would-be murderer's gun at his chest. He took the gun away from him and the would-be murderer came after Heath with a knife, forcing Heath to club the Indian with his own gun. The two would-be murderers fled for their lives, leaving Heath with a nasty knife slash on his hand. The gun owner sent word to Heath that he had a broken arm and couldn't leave his lodge; nevertheless he wanted his gun back. Heath sent him some provisions and wished him well.

Heath's Indians had many difficulties, but disease threatened their existence. In 1845 Heath had talked to an Indian chief at Fort Vancouver who was the only one of his village of 2,000 who survived small pox and ague. In 1848, word came from Fort Vancouver that many Indians and Sandwich Islanders had died of dysentery that followed measles. Heath's Indians soon contracted the many diseases; most of his village was sick. Many mothers could not nurse their babies, so Heath bought milk and devised a method to feed the babies. Provisions were given to the sick and the well along with the available medicines. He drove the sick Indians away from the icy water they used for medicine and back to their lodges for warmth. The Indian doctors insisted on putting their patients into cold water, a killing cure. Heath brought blankets from the fort; many Indians had no blankets, but only their traditional Indian mats. Almost all of Heath's Indians survived. The results would have been better if the Indian doctors had not tried to practice their medicine with some success. It is hard to imagine sick people in a smoky and drafty lodge with a lack of warm blankets surviving a simple illness. Heath had to sleep two feet from the fire in his then "modern" and insulated house, with adequate blankets to keep warm during cold winter nights.

Heath was a lonely single man who yearned for his family in England. His major thrill was his productive farm, the thriving animals, and crops. He agonized when his wheat was diseased or his potatoes yielded only ten bushels per acre because of drought. The wolves tried to destroy his sheep, and he poisoned them. The eagles came after his lambs, and he shot them. The crows ate his seeded wheat, and he shot them too. But, he had no defense against the mosquitoes that periodically almost crippled him. He suffered through summers (well over 100 degrees in the sun) and the cold winters, the overly wet weather and the occasional summer drought. In addition, there were two huge summer forest fires at some distance that obscured the sun for days, and local fires had to be controlled by him and his Indians before his farm burned.

He did have a social life, with frequent dinners at Fort Nisqually that was only six miles to the south of his farm and social events with the officers of the visiting British ships. When, the Americans came through his farm looking for places to settle, free lodging, and meals, Heath graciously hosted them and directed them to places to settle. As the American government evolved, he even ran for public office — and lost.

Sadly, in 1849 gentleman Heath died at Fort Nisqually. He apparently had heart problems during his tenure on his Nisqually farm. He had periods of swelling of his legs, chest pains and hard breathing, which he mitigated with a blue pill. (A pill was 35% mercury, and contained digitalis, along with other ingredients.)

In the last few weeks of his life he kept his Indian laborers close to his house. If he couldn't see them, they would sleep most of the day. All this time he was in great pain and spitting blood. His journal states: "I am ill, and there is no rest from my cough". Nevertheless, his concern was to keep his farm producing. He could easily have given up in his misery.

Doctor Tolmie stayed with him all one night during his last days on his farm and bled him, blistered him with mustard plaster, and sweated him. The doctor also used colocynth and colonel pills as well as opium pills.

Finally, Doctor Tolmie took Heath to Fort Nisqually for intensive care to no avail. Heath's estate and farm assets were valued at 300 pounds sterling which were forwarded to his family in England.

Heath's Indians had the free choice to become farm laborers or continue their free and "wild" Native ways that most current academics praise. Heath's Indians chose mundane and disciplined farm work, associated with reliable food, health care, arms, tools, blankets, and protection from their enemies.

Towards the end of Heaths' life, American pioneers were moving through Heath's farm to take land and bring American democracy to Puget Sound. Heath sought American public office and to become an American landowner instead of a tenant of a British corporation. The Americans soon brought relative peace to the land. The Nisqually tribe didn't flee from the Snoqualmie Indians, nor did they raid their neighbors. The Indian slaves were freed to take land or be educated in white schools. The American dream was opened to Indian chiefs as well as slaves. All castes of Indians could work or create commerce and purchase necessities such as like blankets to replace their primitive mats. The American pioneers converted a miserable, violent wilderness into an American dream in a few years.

The Great Migration of 1843 was the start of a massive onslaught on the territory bordering the Pacific Ocean by a swarm of American pioneers. In the 1840s through the 1860s, hundreds of thousands of people came over the Oregon Trail to California and the Oregon Country — one estimate was 500,000 people. The migration didn't stop in the 1860s. My maternal grandmother's family came by wagon train from Texas in 1886 to Texas Valley near Sequim, Washington. The Morris family escaped from the dry sagebrush of Texas to the evergreen of Washington Territory.

Historians speculate on the reasons for the migration and generally credit the politicians, explorers, military, and our government. Common people, like my grandmother's family, sought free land in the Oregon Country by squatting on unoccupied land. Unlike all others credited for expanding America, the pioneer migrants risked their families on the Oregon Trail. It is estimated that 10% of the early travelers on the Oregon Trail died. Death generally came from unexpected disease. Of course, Indian danger and massacre was anticipated and faced as the cost of bettering their lives.

The mountain men were their primary source of information and guides. Jedediah Smith's discovery and communication of South Pass and the fertile Willamette Valley is an example of a host of mountain men who were on the ground to guide and advise. One 1843 wagon train asked for military help in crossing the Great Plains. Lieutenant Fremont and forty dragoons joined the train, not to lead, but to follow docilely behind the train, to the disgust of the emigrants. Fremont was named the "Pathfinder" and was given some recognition in opening the West to settlement. The U.S. government had little or no influence on the migration.

Adam Smith wrote in his "Wealth of Nations" in 1776: "Plenty of good land and liberty to manage their own affairs their own way seem to be the two great causes of prosperity of all new colonies." Adam Smith's observation primarily concerned America; the wagon train government exemplified Smith's observation. As soon as the wagon train was assembled, members elected a government to govern the wagon train through to Oregon. The captain was the executive officer, an executive who could be removed immediately if inadequate. The wagon train government quickly handled criminal cases harshly. The wagon trains usually passed by the HBC's Fort Vancouver. The HBC's aristocrats were awed with the organized and democratic wagon trains led by "commoners". The wagon trains' organization was contrary to the European aristocratic culture.

In 1840, less than 200 Americans lived in the Oregon Country, mostly in the Willamette Valley. The few Americans formed a Provisional Government that was discouraged by the HBC and a visiting Lieutenant Charles Wilkes of the U.S. Navy. The Great Migration of 1843 put 700 more Americans into the Willamette Valley, and the wagon train government reinforced the infant Oregon Provisional Government. In May of 1844, the Provisional Government held an election to form an active government that excluded the HBC, which had claimed the land.

There were many laws enacted by the new government, but land ownership was the priority. The settlers squatted on the land in the

Oregon Country and held their infant farms by unwritten community agreement or force. The new government enacted a law that gave each man or widow a claim of 640 acres or a square mile with the only condition being that they occupy the claim for a period. Now the Oregon citizens had title to their claims and could legitimately buy and sell land. The new government promulgated free land, a first in America. American pioneers had unsuccessfully asked for free land after the Revolutionary War, until 1862, when the Homestead Act was implemented. It was years before an individual could obtain land from the government. Finally, preemption laws were implemented that allowed an individual to acquire 160 acres of unoccupied land for $1.25 per acre.

The Provisional Government also was ambitious. In 1844, it set the boundaries of Oregon from the Pacific Ocean to the Rocky Mountains, north to the Russian settlements and south to the Mexican settlements. Then Oregon petitioned Congress to make Oregon an American territory. In 1846 the U.S. and Britain agreed the northern boundary of the Oregon Country would be the present northern Washington State boundary. The Oregon settlers were outraged. They didn't want British neighbors. The settlers planned to take all the British Pacific coastal land as they took the Oregon Territory, that is, by squatting on the land until it became a part of America.

The Oregon settlers were thought to be in need of protection by U.S. military and justice systems. However, the wagon train justice worked very well without federal government justices, and the settlers' military prowess was demonstrated after the Whitman massacre. The Whitman Mission near Walla Walla was overwhelmed by the Cayuse Indians. Dr. Marcus Whitman and his wife Narcissa were killed, along with several others. The Indians took prisoners that included women and children. The HBC ransomed the prisoners and they were returned to the Oregon settlements — and the prudent HBC hoped this would end the tragedy.

The settlers thought otherwise, and in 1850, a hundred volunteers approached the Cayuse villages, well-armed and eager to fight for justice. A modern writer/historian calls the 100 settlers "vigilantes" that only wanted to kill Indians. Today writers universally condemn the settlers' action against the Indians, without understanding the bravery and the risks the settlers took. The hundred farmers went into a hostile Indian "nation" to challenge at least several hundred seasoned warriors, warriors defined by progressives today as noble fighting men. It was not noble to kill defenseless missionaries and be paid for their atrocities by the HBC. The settler/farmers were in the Indian nation to kill Indians or be killed to enforce pioneer justice. The Cayuse Tribe wisely didn't want to be destroyed by a few farmers hundreds of miles away from their families in the Willamette Valley. Without a real fight the Cayuse Tribe surrendered five Indians that were taken to Oregon City. After a perfunctory trial they were hung. Supposedly, the Indians that were hung were the murderers, but logic suggests the Indians that were condemned by their tribe were lower cast Indians, even slaves, who were expendable.

As the Oregon settlements grew, the pioneers transferred their wagon train values to the settlements, and their governments began with the Oregon Provisional government in 1843, which matured to the Oregon Territory in 1848 and finally Oregon State in 1859. The north separated and became the Washington Territory in 1853 and finally Washington State in 1889. Each stage of advancement of the local governments brought a better life to the citizens of what was old Oregon.

Indian War of 1855-56

Shortly after Washington became a territory in 1853, Isaac Stevens asked to be governor of the territory. As a political payback for his work on the campaign of the newly elected President Pierce, he was appointed governor as well as superintendent of Indian Affairs, plus several other appointments relative to the new territory. Luckily for Washington, Stevens was not a run-of-the-mill political incompetent and selfish appointee of that era. Stevens was a thirty-four-year-old army brevet major. His personality, ambition, intelligence, and energy were overpowering and, in some circles, considered arrogant. Significantly different from other appointees, his reward would be to be elected as Washington's representative to Congress, which would further his political ambition. Unfortunately he was killed fighting for the Union in the Civil War.

Stevens grew up on a farm, graduated first in his class at West Point, was wounded in the Mexican War, and decorated for bravery. Stevens was not an aristocrat of the era. He arrived in Washington in November 1853. Upon reaching the capital at Olympia, he jump-started the territory government composed of twenty-five territorial legislators and a nonvoting delegate to Congress.

After a lively election pitting Whigs against Democrats, the elected government was in place. The average age of the legislators was twenty-eight years, mostly farmers. Stevens called the legislature into session in February 1854 in Olympia's Odd Fellows Club. At that time, Stevens' government determined there were 1,602 males eligible to vote. It was estimated there were ten thousand natives split almost equally between those east and west of the Cascade Mountains. The voters were west of the Cascades. Stevens' initial challenge was to settle the Indian situation by negotiating treaties with a multitude of tribes. As governor he was responsible to the American settlers.

American emigrants coming into the Oregon country largely ignored the natives in their quest for land. The settlers had no time for anything but locating land and starting their farms or businesses. They ignored the natives or placated them with simple trade goods and defended their new lands with force when necessary. In the settlers view, the natives were underutilizing the land and/or were transients who could join the settlers in creating a new civilization or get out of the way. In reference to the settlers, Thomas Jefferson in 1776 stated, "They will come in spite of everybody." Before Oregon was brought into the U.S. government as a territory, the provisional government did not recognize Native ownership. But the U.S. government, reflecting international law, recognized Native ownership and proceeded to "buy out" that ownership.

In effect, the leaderless settlers conquered the natives without extensive war, genocide, or slavery, as was a historic norm over past centuries by the Europeans. The white man's disease was transmitted to the Natives by the HBC, a multitude of foreign traders, and the oppressive Spanish and Russian settlements before the settlers arrived. On the contrary, the settlers' civilization quickly brought rudimental medical care, education, elimination of tribal warfare, slavery, as well the rule of law, adequate clothing, and the technology of the day.

The more progressive Natives began to join in the pioneers' civilization quickly. The HBC farmer, Heath, had a Nisqually village at his farm in the 1840s to provide labor in exchange for financial compensation, protection from their enemies, and rudimentary medical care. Nisqually Chief Leschi developed his own "modern" farm before the 1855 Indian war. The Clallam chief, Duke of York (Chetzemoka), had a water transport business. He stated at a treaty negotiation that the white man brought blankets and other needed goods into his people's lives and his people should be thankful. These "luxuries" were purchased through labor alongside the white man in the mills, and logging, and tribal labor on the settlers' farms. Meeker, a hops farmer in Puyallup, paid tens of thousands of dollars to the Natives for picking his hops. Through their labors, the Clallam tribe was able to purchase acreage for a tribal community, thus creating Jamestown on the Straits of Juan de Fuca.

Stevens had the authority from the United States to negotiate treaties with the Native nations subject to the ratification by Congress, which would appropriate the funding of the treaty expenses. The reservation protocol was established during negotiations with the western tribes. The critical item was the location and size of the reservations. Modern historians believe the federal government's negotiations were a function of Stevens following national policy. Historians forget the Washington pioneers benevolently tried to incorporate the natives into their civilization. Even more amazing, about two thousand American voters dominated western Washington to create a rude democracy and modern society in face of an autocratic HBC, supported by arguably the most powerful nation in the world — Great Britain. In addition, the American pioneers had to deal with a subsistence Native population who respected only superior technology and armed power. Energetically, Stevens, after arriving in Washington Territory in November 1853, planned and organized the first of many treaties with the Indians. In December 1854 the Medicine Creek Treaty was consummated with principally the Nisqually and Puyallup Tribes. All the tribes west of the Cascade Mountains had treaties a few months later.

The treaties were uniform in nature, as the natives were awarded a small amount of money and a reservation, plus they could fish in common with the American citizens. Of course trading gifts were distributed during the treaty negotiations.

Most critics of the treaties did not recognize that a major angst of the natives was a provision to free their slaves. All modern writers ignore the natives' treatment of slaves that was more severe than any treatment of African-American slaves at that time. There appears to be no statistics of the slave population, except in a northern tribe (Haida) with an estimated one-third of the tribe composed slaves. Settler McAlister discovered an Indian slave left to die on his master's grave. McAlister saved the young slave and brought him to his home.

For the native slave population, there was no emancipation proclamation by the federal government as President Lincoln gave to free the American slaves. Nor was Governor Stevens given credit by his peers or modern academics for his efforts to eliminate slavery. On the contrary, modern academics condemn Stevens for not preserving the Native culture — which would have preserved slavery.

Since the elites of that era didn't recognize native slaves, the existing slaves were largely held by the tribes in bondage after the treaties. Fortunately, slave raiding between tribes — to murder and enslave — was eliminated by a forceful treaty. The native slave culture probably disappeared in a generation. There is little or no information of the fate of the native slaves or their emancipation. Modern historians and writers martyr the great chiefs and warriors and ignore their brutalization of their people. I would suggest many slaves fled their tribes to the American settlements to be incorporated into American society and the richness it provides, while the higher caste Indians largely lived on their reservations.

With the treaties in place, the settlers' objectives were met. The natives were moved out of the way of the developing country while the federal government had the responsibility of administrating the reservation and educating the Indians so they could share the American dream with the settlers. And, in the view of the radical pioneers, the inconvenience of genocide was not necessary.

Many of the Indians and settlers during the treaty process believed the natives were conned and cheated because of the enormous value of their land and resources. This thinking prevails to the present time. However, these critics never consider that undeveloped` land and resources are worthless. Certainly, the Russians, Spanish and British on the west coast for decades during this era mined the natural resources and the natives, while they took their profits to Europe. The settlers in the 1840s and 1850s started the infrastructure of transportation, education, industry, and commerce that gave value to the land.

Contrary to popular belief, the reservations were neither nation builders nor concentration camps. Thinking people at that time believed it was a concentration of Natives to build people who would blend into the American society. It was hoped the next generation of Natives could speak, write, and be as competent technologically as the white citizens of the territory of the middle 1800s. Therefore the reservations, at enormous expense to the government, were structured to accomplish this vision. The Natives were not herded to the reservations at bayonet point by the military. Many Natives were employed by the settlers and businesses in the territory or were themselves entrepreneurs on and off the reservation. In the case of the Clallam Tribe, the majority never occupied their designated reservation. The common belief today is that current reservation Indians represents a monolithic group from the past to the present. However, a large part of the population has left the reservation over centuries to meld into American society. Perhaps, millions of present day Americans have Indian blood lines and do not associate with any tribe. In this sense, the settler visionaries of the 1850s were somewhat successful.

The optimistic American visionaries held that all people will embrace the American dream that includes high morals, freedom, and a high standard of living. James Swan was one of those people who believed the natives would join American society when exposed to his vision and academics. He left a successful business and loving family in New England in the early 1850s to seek adventure in the west. He came to Shoalwater Bay (Willapa Bay) for a period and described the environment, the natives and their slave trade. He also found time to party with the Duke of York of the Clallam Tribe in San Francisco.

Swan studied and wrote exhaustively of his observations during his life on the "Northwest Coast". Germane to the reservation structure, he wrote about his tenure as a federally funded school teacher on the Makah reservation on the northwest tip of the Olympic Peninsula. For the few years he was on the reservation, he was largely frustrated in his vision of enlightening the Native children. The adult Indians even demanded he pay them for talking to their children. Apparently in frustration, he left his teaching position. In the pioneer area in Washington there have been conflicting writings of the natives' character — from a wonderful good-natured people to barbaric savages to be eliminated.

I prefer to subscribe to my great-grandfather Jimmie's experience as communicated to me through my grandfather. Jimmie worked and played with the Clallams from 1859 to 1880. Both grandfathers used the Clallam spelling instead of the current spelling of the tribe. Jimmie and the Clallams were together at work in the woods logging and in the settlements. The everyday association soon mutually integrated the two races. Eventually Jimmie could speak fluently in both languages. By all reports, Jimmie was a jokester, and so were the Clallams. They worked twelve hours a day when daylight permitted, and the winter was a wet depressing time. Still, they could happily make fun of their misery. The Clallams invited Jimmie to their festivities when the intensive labor would allow Jimmie free time.

In 1880, Jimmie purchased a dairy farm in Dungeness and brought his proper bride from England to the farm. Jimmie and his family visited town occasionally for shopping. While his wife shopped, Jimmie visited with his associate farmers and the Clallams on the street to continue in their past levity, to the enjoyment of both parties. Jimmie's wife disliked his association with the Clallams as they, in her opinion, were "dirty indolent savages". And perhaps she thought Jimmie might have had a Clallam girlfriend. Jimmie's son Rue also was sympathetic to the Clallams, and his wife's thinking paralleled her mother-in-law's.

All the current writing of the white/Native situation ignores the reality of the time and the consuming labor of the pioneers who had no time except for the labor at hand (a concept completely foreign to current thinkers). At the end of the pioneer era, I had the privilege of experiencing this labor.

Modern academics write volumes about the difference between the Indian's and the pioneer's culture. The evidence suggests that the basic difference between the reservation Indians and the Americans is their work ethics. The settlers' work ethic turned a wilderness in the Pacific Northwest into thriving communities that added to a free American economy that created the highest standard of living for all citizens that the world had ever experienced.

Governor Stevens quickly completed the treaties with the canoe Indians west of the Cascades without difficulty, but to the uneasy satisfaction of the settlers and Indians. Upon completion of the Indian treaties west of the Cascades, Stevens started treaty negotiations with the great horse tribes east of the Cascades — the Nez Perce, Yakima, Cayuse, Walla Walla and Umatilla. As opposed to the western tribes, the horse tribes were educated on Stevens' negotiation tactics and prepared a strategy favorable to them. The talks began at Walla Walla in May 1855. In spite of the tribe's strategy, Stevens was able to divide the group and prevail to obtain his objectives. Treaties were signed quickly to all parties' satisfaction. Again, Stevens demonstrated he was a most able and unusually gifted political appointee. Now, all that was needed was ratification of the treaties. The tribes believed their reservation land would not be disturbed until ratification.

Almost before the ink dried on the treaty signatures, gold was discovered around Fort Colville. Gold seekers started across the Cascades to Fort Colville through Yakima's country. Since the treaty was not ratified, the Yakima tribe felt the agreement was breeched and attacked the whites crossing their land. The Yakimas claimed one of the dead white men raped a daughter of a chief. Of course, the responsible Indian agent rushed to the Yakima's chief to investigate. Agent A. J. Bolon was shot in the back, stabbed, and cremated with his dead horse.

When Bolon was killed, the army was dispatched to punish the Yakimas and afford protection to the American citizens traveling to

Fort Colville. The army was composed of Major Granville O. Haller with 102 men and a howitzer. On October 5, 1855, Haller met the Yakimas, who chased Haller's force twenty-five miles. He lost five killed, several wounded men, his howitzer, and cattle. It took three days to be chased the 25 miles by 1,000 Indians who were presumably carefully counted by Haller while he was running to The Dalles. So, the "war" started across the Cascades, away from the settlements to the west. The army's rout by Indians with inferior weapons appalled and disgusted the settlers. A settler "vigilante" group of one hundred had revenged the Whitman massacre without loss.

On October 14 the army requested the governor raise two companies of civilian volunteers. There was an oversupply of volunteers who were mostly unarmed because they left their guns with their families at their Puget Sound homes to defend themselves. Acting Governor Charles H. Mason requisitioned arms from two government ships for the companies. Governor Stevens was in Montana negotiating a treaty with the Blackfeet. Mason immediately asked for four more companies of volunteers. The volunteers would not cross the Cascades and leave their families unprotected west of the Cascade Mountains.

The civilian volunteer companies were targeted to help the army suppress the Yakama Tribe in the East. The settlers west of the Cascades were apprehensive, but not overly concerned with an uprising in the West. Until, James McAllister wrote the governor that Leschi (a Nisqually chief in the West) was working to unite the western tribes against the whites. Since McAllister was Leschi's friend and had recently talked to him, his word was reliable. A volunteer company of which McAllister was an officer went out to restrain him. On October 24, a forewarned Leschi fled to the woods. The company spent three dangerous days on his trail. McAllister and a companion scouted ahead of the company and were shot dead in ambush after the three-day hunt for Leschi. War had come west of the Cascades. Almost immediately a friendly Nisqually had carried the tragic word to McAllister's wife on their Nisqually River farm.

The war was validated the day after McAllister's death with the massacre on the White River near Auburn. It was October 28, 1855. Three families were decimated and their homes sacked and burned. It seemed the war wasn't between warriors and the military, but genocide. The Jones family house was battered in, and the husband and the wife plus a hired man mortally shot. The three living children were taken to Nelson, a White River Indian, who directed the attack. Nelson had often visited the family. Nelson put an Indian in charge of the children who led them to another cabin and disappeared. The seven-year-old boy took charge of his siblings, a four-year-old girl and a two-year-old boy, and led them to a cabin to rest, then back to their deserted burning cabin. There they came upon their prostate mother still alive. The mother, as she was dying, told her children to go to a neighbor's. They objected, but left her to die. On their travel they met a trusted Indian named Tom who hid them until dark, then canoed them to the mouth of the Duwamish River where another Indian took them to a navy ship (Decatur) located at a Seattle wharf.

The Brannan cabin was next for the warriors. The Brannans had heard shots and had barricaded their cabin. The warriors broke in after the husband had killed one before being killed. Mrs. Brannan ran with a ten-month-old baby. She was taken from behind, stabbed in the back and, probably alive, thrown head first down the well after her baby. The warriors went to the Kings where they killed a child with an ax and fatally shot Mr. King. Mrs. King fought with an ax, wounding one warrior before she was shot, and beaten to death with an ax handle. The remaining child was taken prisoner and transported to the Yakima Tribe. Leschi claimed the child was to become a warrior, not a slave, as was the norm for captured children. Ironically, the names of Native chiefs were given to monuments, schools, and boats, but Mrs. King, who fought off the warriors with an ax, is forgotten.

The Indians who helped the children escape slavery or worse are forgotten or even denigrated. Such a Native was Shot-face-Charlie. On the day of the White River massacre, Stephen Judson was walking past the current site of the Tacoma Convention Center towards Commencement Bay when he saw his Puyallup friends and hunting companions dancing with strangers. He joined the dancing and thought it strange his Indian friends ignored him, that is, all but Shot-face-Charlie who whispered to him as he danced by to get to hell out of there. And, he did!

The day after the massacre, virtually all the settlers east of Seattle and Steilacoom packed up their belongings and fled to nearby settlements. The settlers acted with horror and panic. They all knew their isolated farms were easy pickings for small bands of Indians. Worse yet, there were rumors of a total uprising of the tribes to drive the Bostons (white Americans) into the sea as the horse Indians streamed over the Cascades to add to the planned carnage.

The pathway to Fort Steilacoom was choked with settlers seeking shelter at the Fort. The Fort consisted of property rented from the HBC in 1849 on the farm of the deceased British farmer Heath. It consisted of Heath's big house and barns plus barracks the army built. There were few troops at the Fort; no defenses had been constructed, not a place to give the settlers confidence. Nevertheless, many settlers believed a few good white men could take the measure of the Native warriors in a pitched battle.

The settlers evacuated the war zone and, amazingly, planned to evacuate the friendly Indians too. In anticipation of trouble over the treaties, Doctor Maynard visited the acting Governor Mason. Governor Stevens had departed Olympia in May of 1855 for six months to deal with the Indians in the eastern part of the territory. Dr. David S. Maynard went to a reasonable Mason and proposed a plan to form temporary reservations away from the war zone. The territorial government didn't have funds for the operation, so Doc Maynard volunteered to fund the operation if Mason could obtain people with cash to purchase his real estate. The cash would be used to build structures on temporary reservations and feed the resident Indians for the period of the conflict. Doc Maynard by many was credited with being the father of Seattle and had business interests as well as considerable platted land in central

Seattle. There was a possibility a benevolent Congress would compensate Maynard for his expenses much later.

When hostilities started on the east side with the killing of Bolon, the construction on the temporary reservations was started with the anticipation the eastern tribes would invade the west. The doctor was appointed as sub-Indian agent at the Fort Kitsap reservation at Port Madison on Bainbridge Island. A second reservation was located on Fox Island, managed by sub-Indian agent John Swan (not to be mistaken for James Swan of Northwest Coast fame). Swan was respected by both Indians and settlers. Both islands were located in Puget Sound and isolated from the war zone.

On November 9, shortly after the White River massacre, Doc Maynard spent a week with an armed guard traveling east of Seattle telling Indians to come to the temporary reservation and avoid the conflict. At this time the army and volunteers were shooting indiscriminately, and the whites were taking casualties. The man risked his life to save the friendly Indians and perhaps awfully lucky. Word spread through the area: go to a reservation or be subjected to the vengeance of the volunteers many who wanted to kill Indians. The doctor believed he had saved many friendly Indians.

Meanwhile, the army and the volunteers skirmished outside Fort Steilacoom to the east and north. There was no uniting of tribes or much evidence of the eastside horse Indians. It was an ambush and run by the Indians while the army fought to minimize casualties. The settlers and army started building stockades and blockhouses that were impregnable given the natives' arms. Fire perhaps could breach the stockades and blockhouses — but it was a typical soggy northwest winter. Nothing would burn but a dry settler cabin, inside out. For the settlers, arms were short. The Victoria HBC even sent rifles, gun powder and balls, arms the Indians believed the HBC owed them. The HBC in Canada did not want the Canadian Indians to learn from a successful Indian revolt. More importantly, the white men could not enable the killing of whites.

While the skirmishes were going on, the settlers were cooped up in the settlements and upset; emotions ranged from anger, to desperation, to squabbles, impatience, and disgust. Families cooped up in block-houses at night were tolerable only given the fear of facing the massacring savages.

On November 24, the army withdrew from the offense to their garrisons. It was too wet and cold to fight. The natives had no one to fight, as their opposition stayed in their impregnable stockades and blockhouses. Now, the army was idle in relatively comfortable quarters nearby. Then the settlers learned that General Wool, in charge of the army on the west coast, believed the settlers were responsible for the Indian War. He wanted only the professional soldiers to do the fighting, not the settlers. Wool also believed the trouble in Washington Territory was just a brush fire that could be damped down with as little fuss as possible.

The settlers became angry, and their misery increased their displeasure with Wool and their situation. Some left the territory; some continued to build blockhouses and moved away from the do-nothing army. When several farms were centralized, it was practical to build a community blockhouse. The blockhouse contained the families at night, allowing the males to farm their land much of the day.

Hope came when Governor Stevens returned to Olympia on January 19 from eastern Washington. He made the trip home through hundreds of miles of harsh winter weather and through the country dominated by the Indians who wanted his scalp and more without army protection. The army was confined to their barracks due to the harsh weather. The governor arrived to a thirty-eight-cannon salute, the cheers of the citizens, a torchlight parade through the frozen mud of Olympia's streets, and a banquet. He promised the settlers an aggressive war against the hostile Indians.

A few days later, Stevens gave a formal speech to the legislature where he reported on the war and the goal. He said: "The spirit of prosecuting this war should be to accomplish a lasting peace — not to make treaties, but to punish their violation." He promised death to Indians who would war against the people of the territory. Contrary to the insinuations of many modern writers, he was targeting a few Indians who wished to kill whites, not the race as a whole. In a near-historic statement, Stevens said he, the governor, would wage the war independent of the United States Army. The territory officially had its own army composed of the volunteer companies, perhaps the only time in its history. Perhaps, Stevens wished to order the U.S. army out of the citizens' territory as the general and the governor waged war against each other, the general lost.

On January 8, 1856, Leschi landed on Fox Island with other leaders and indicated he was there in peace and would not harm sub-agent John Swan or the Indians in his care. He stayed thirty hours while an inept military failed to rescue Swan. Leschi told Swan he was not responsible for the White River Massacre, and that the captured boy was across the mountains being educated to be a chief, not a slave. The Nisqually Indians were only fighting armed men, but they wanted peace. Swan was invited to visit their camp for peace talks. At this point the settlers didn't leave their stockades, blockhouses or throw away their guns and go to their farms.

Governor Stevens's fiery war speech to the settlers was almost discredited when, five days later, the citizens of Seattle were told the hostiles were gathering to attack Seattle. A Duwamish Indian came with the alarm. The citizens expected a thousand or more warriors to assault their city. Furthermore, they believed it could be another White River massacre, only on a massive scale. Modern estimates suggest that not much more than a hundred warriors attacked Seattle. For all the information available then and now — there could have been only a dozen, because all the warriors accomplished was sniper shots at the city. For defense, the town had less than a hundred men. The defense of the city was delegated to the naval vessel Decatur anchored near Yesler's dock. The Decatur had about a hundred sailors and a few marines, plus their cannon and a howitzer. The male civilians forted up in their blockhouse while women and children were mostly on board the ship.

The skirmish consisted of the warriors sniping and the navy returning fire with the howitzer, interspersed with a few naval musket volleys. The "battle" started in the morning, and by mid-afternoon the defensive sailors ashore were brought back to the ship for refreshments. The battle was over the next morning; the warriors were gone. There were two civilians killed, almost by accident, and the warriors' deaths were unknown. The whites were disgusted with the military establishment that again had let harm come their way, but their fierce anger was directed at the hostile Indians who attempted to kill the men, women, and children of Seattle.

Many modern writers suggest the Seattle attack was the work of the horse Indians from east of the Cascades — but where was Leschi, the chief that wanted peace and wouldn't harm women and children? Nine days after the weak assault on Seattle, Leschi and others approached a former HBC man married to an Indian woman on a claim north of the Nisqually River. He told the man he wanted peace and asked him to contact John Swan for a meeting at the Leschi camp. Current historians never examine Leschi logic concerning his authority to negotiate peace when the warriors attacking Seattle were not under his leadership. Was the war west of the Cascades Leschi war? If so, he was responsible for Seattle and the White River Massacre. Most settlers believed the responsibility was Leschi's.

Swan visited Leschi and spent two nights and a day at his camp, located in a near-impassable swamp near the Green river. Swan estimated there were 160 warriors, mostly from the Sound. Leschi said there were no horse Indians from east of the Cascades in the region. Swan also noted their ammunition and supplies were almost exhausted. Still, Leschi dictated to Swan his terms for surrender.

In spite of the peace talk, a troop building structures in the forest was attacked in early March, three times with a few casualties on both sides. The army and settlers were actively building roads, ferries, and blockhouses to contain the hostiles. After several weeks of futile assaults on the white's military, in March 1856 Leschi led about seventy beaten warriors to a Cascade pass where they struggled through deep snow to the Yakima's country and a temporary refuge. The less dedicated warriors slunk back to their villages. About fifty women and children trudged to the white authorities for compassion and food, which was readily given. The war was essentially over. In the Sound country, the war was limited to the area directly east of Seattle and Steilacoom. The war started October 28 with the White River Massacre and ended when Leschi fled to the Yakima's country in March 1856, about five months of war. In history, this was a short affair, but for the settlers, especially the women, a period of hell. The women and children in Leschi's camp also suffered.

With Leschi's Indians east of the Cascades or back on their reservations, Governor Stevens ordered the Mounted Rifles, a volunteer cavalry group, to search out any remaining hostile Indians in the upper Nisqually River. He was to consider all natives hostile, therefore subject to death if they were not on their designated reservations. Unfortunately, he found seventeen on the Mashel River, mostly women and children, who he killed. He took the governor's policy seriously and executed it. A thinking leader of the Mounted Rifles would have herded the helpless Indians back to the reservation and not blemished the white man's war effort. The only excuse was the anger permeated by the White River Massacre and the subsequent burning of settlers' homes and their displacement to blockhouses and stockades.

In the same operation, the Mounted Rifles captured five settlers who lived on their farms during the hostilities. These men were former HBC employees with Native wives, commonly called "squaw men", a group of people who the settlers believed aided and abetted the enemy. Stevens was committed to punish them, even if he had to circumvent the infant territory's justice system. The charges against the settlers were undocumented and weak. The almost impoverished settlers could never have aided the hostiles in any meaningful way. But, the settlers thought otherwise. Hadn't Leschi met with a squaw man who enabled a meeting between Leschi and Swan? Besides, the white settlers fought for their lives while the squaw men profited from the war; they should be punished. Stevens did everything possible to legally punish the perceived culprits, even declaring martial law. Nevertheless, the judges and lawyers prevailed, and the squaw men were free to return to their farms. The white settlers were not happy, and it was obvious to them there were too many lawyers in the territory.

In late summer of 1856, Governor Stevens went to the temporary reservation on Fox Island to hear the concerns of the peaceful Nisqually and Puyallup Tribes. It is significant he ignored Leschi and his hostile warriors. After listening to the tribes, he increased the size of both reservations. After all the tribal angst and a war, both tribes subsequently sold much of their reservation land piecemeal over the years to whites. For the Puyallups, it was virtually the entire reservation that contributed significantly to the size of Tacoma. Nevertheless, the current citizenry is continually bombarded by the remaining reservation Puyallups with the unfairness of the treaty, who ask the now very valuable land should be returned to the tribe — which has been done on a small scale.

The temporary reservations on the islands and the peaceful movement of the Indians to these reservations suggest a generally good feeling between the whites and Natives that developed over the years. The Indian sub-agents who lived on the reservations had no protection from the hostile natives. The reservation Indians shielded Doc Maynard from any hostility from resident Natives or visiting Indians who were unfriendly.

The fighting Indians are currently given all the current publicity, while the friendly Natives are ignored or even named traitors. There was an Indian named Tom, who risked this life, taking the three Jones' children to safety during the White River Massacre. Shot-face Charley told his white friend to flee to safety from the celebrating Puyallups. The McAllister Indian employees staved off the hostiles around the McAllister home until they could flee to Fort Steilacoom. An Indian warned Seattle of a pending attack. And there were many more Natives who actively helped the settlers.

There were also the peaceful Indians who attacked the warring Indians. The governor's wife and her ladies sewed part uniforms to identify the Indian allies, and the governor put a bounty on the heads of the warring Indians. Several tribes participated in the program. The most significant participant was the chief of the Snoqualmie tribe, Patkanim. He is reported to have shipped a bag of heads of the warring Indians' to Olympia, and was paid a price per head. Patkanim was the most aggressive chief on the Sound. Heath reported his tribe raided the Nisqually Indians on HBC grounds. Patkanim also made a feeble attempt to attack Fort Nisqually before the Washington Territory was established. Arguably, Patkanim had the most powerful force of warriors on the Sound and was not friendly towards the settlers. Still he was intelligent enough not to challenge the white establishment. On the contrary, he beset his hereditary adversaries for profit.

Shortly after fleeing over the mountains to the Yakimas, Leschi and his followers surrendered to the army. The army accepted their surrender on the condition they not fight again unless there were reprisals. The Indians were then released to go back to their reservations. They were on their own as the army had in affect pardoned them. But not Governor Stevens, he would not let the leaders on the reservations until they were tried for murder. Leschi asked the army for help, and the army at Fort Steilacoom agreed to shelter him since he was at war and his warriors legitimately killed, not murdered.

However when Leschi arrived in the Sound country, the army told him to hide in the woods because local prejudice ran against him. The prejudice was probably synonymous with a lynching party. So, Leschi hid in the woods. Fifty blankets were offered as a reward for his capture. A white person in similar circumstances would have fled the territory and blended into society far away, but Leschi didn't have that option. On November 12, 1866, Leschi's nephew captured Leschi and turned him over to the civilian authorities. The nephew was later murdered by Leschi's friends.

Leschi's trial started on November 16. The government's case was based on one witness who claimed he saw Leschi at the ambush site where Colonel Moses was killed. The defense contended his nation was at war; therefore the killing was justified. Plus, Leschi wasn't there. The jury went through numerous ballots with hot words used while an angry crowd surrounded the courtroom demanding a guilty verdict. Two jurors held out against a guilty verdict, so the jury was dismissed and a new trial scheduled. The two jurors who held out were honored and well-liked settlers who had experienced the hardships of crossing the plains.

The day after the trial, Leschi's half-brother Quiemuth surrendered to the authorities. Because the territory had no jail, Leschi was held in the Fort Steilacoom guardhouse. Governor Stevens placed Quiemuth in his office for his first night of captivity until better arrangements could be made. A reliable citizen spent the night with him. In the middle of the night, an intruder or intruders quietly entered the office to stab and shoot Quiemuth. He died quickly. The governor was furious, and the primitive justice system tried unsuccessfully to find the murderers. Most of the settlers were disturbed there was even an effort to find the perpetrators.

Leschi's second trial in Olympia began on March 18, 1857. The only question the jury was charged with was whether Leschi was involved in Moses' death. The jury found him guilty. An execution date was set and then delayed when the sheriff was accused of selling liquor to the Indians. The U.S. marshal jailed him. The complaint was by an Indian, and it was obvious to everyone there was trickery involved. The citizens held mass meetings protesting the delay. The whole territory was outraged with the lawyers and the justice system. Leschi was hung in February 1858, and there was relative peace in the territory.

Current literature declares that Leschi was a hero, while the settlers' community was vengeful and bigoted. The White River Massacre horror was brought on by the settlers' misconduct; therefore, those families were sacrificed for the better good in an attempt to obtain justice for

the Indians. Given the era and lack of resources, the settlers were trying to bring swift justice to the territory with the tools at hand, prior to
the establishment of the territory, justice was administered by retribution: "You kill one of mine and I will kill as many of yours as I can, or
run and hide." The HBC, the natives, and the pioneers all resorted to
this method. It didn't matter if the guilty person suffered as long as
the group was punished with destruction and/or death. The Nisqually
Tribe was split. Part went to war and others went to a temporary reservation on Fox Island for sanctuary. Most of the pioneers considered
Leschi outside the tribe and a renegade outside the rules of war.

Leschi stated many times that he led the war, and he could at any
time have denounced the killing and joined the settlers, but he didn't.
Therefore, in spite of statements that he wasn't involved killing Moses,
the White River Massacre, the attack on Seattle, he was responsible because he was the self-proclaimed leader.

The overriding reason for punishment of Leschi was to eliminate
the threat to the isolated farms and small settlements. The settlers
would soon go back to their isolated farms. In their view, unless the
Indians were punished severely, a White River Massacre would happen
whenever a few natives became disgruntled. The Indians would kill,
then negotiate. The justice system, the lawyers, and the army demonstrated to the settlers during the war their families could not count on
their protection. Therefore, they must administer swift justice. Hence
Quiemuth was killed and Leschi would meet the same fate.

After Leschi was hung, there were no more settlers killed in their
homes, while the natives continued to kill within their own society.
For instance: James Swan had a teaching position in the early 1860s
on the Makah reservation at Neah Bay. One day a group of Makah canoes beached, carrying the heads of two Clallam Indians they obtained
from the unfortunate seal hunters on a reef at Cresent Bay — a revenge
killing. Swan watched helplessly as the Makahs did their traditional
celebration over their trophies. Subsequently Swan appealed to the authorities for justice, but a limited and ineffective government could do

nothing. The Clallams in 1868 massacred seventeen northern natives on the Dungeness Spit.

It took time to bring justice to the tribes, but it did come. However, the settlers had demonstrated their justice to the tribes and kept their heads during the period the tribes eluded the white man's justice.

An addendum to the war: In the summer of 1857, Stevens decided to test his territory policies. He ran for the highest office, the territorial delegate to the U.S. Congress. He won in a landslide, confirming his policies were truly representative of wishes of the pioneer voters.

In true dedication to his country, he shunned an easy political office during the Civil War, and its rewards, to join the Union army. In September 1862 General Stevens, led his regiment in an uphill charge on a fixed Confederate position. He died charging with the regimental flag that, as he fell, covered his body. He was forty-four. Only in America in that era could a farm boy get to utilize his potential. Governor Stevens and his farmer legislators personify our American heritage!

PORT TOWNSEND

In late December 1850 Alfred Plummer was aboard the *George Emery*, captained by Lafayette Balch as the ship sailed past Townshend Bay, later to be *Townsend*, when Balch remarked, the bay is the "finest harbor" on the coast and must become a significant future town. Captain Balch was also the founder of Steilacoom, the first American community on the Sound.

While developing Steilacoom, Balch made money with timber products manufactured with hand labor by hewing products from trees and transporting the products with his ship to a booming San Francisco. Plummer, along with others, felled trees and squared the logs for Balch's ship. It was tedious and dangerous work, but the endeavor generated money that Plummer would use to improve land of his own.

Plummer worked through most of that winter. With a friend he hired an Indian canoe with Indian propulsion to make the voyage from Steilacoom to Townshend Bay that took several days. What was Plummer's drive? On the voyage from San Francisco to the Sound, a friend asked Plummer what was in the packet he carried and treasured as gold. The treasure was seed! Plummer's dream was to create productive land and a community.

Plummer and his companion landed at Townshend Bay and were confronted with hordes of Clallam Indians, maybe five hundred. Plummer and his friend distributed a few trinkets, and the natives welcomed them. The records show that Plummer's claim of April 1851 was the beginning of Port Townsend.

The Clallams lived on the beach just above high tide to be close to their major source of food, that is, the fish and claims. The natives valued the beach, while Plummer saw the value in the uplands that would be home for the seed he carefully treasured.

Unknown to most pioneers and natives, Plummer and the following pioneers brought white men with modern weapons and technology to Townshend Bay. It was of benefit to the natives to be secure from their historic enemies. Then, they had employment opportunities that would furnish funds for basic necessities such as blankets and iron tools. Most modern writers ignore the fact that a few white men with a brace of six shooters and a rifle or shotgun were superior to a tribe of natives with their primitive weapons.

Plummer, upon landing and communicating with the Indians, immediately built a log house with the help of Clallam labor, making employment and wealth a reality to the Native residents. The log cabin was 15' by 30' with a roof of hand split-cedar shakes. A fireplace was built of stone and clay and a floor of hewn planks. The door was never locked. A small clearing was created by slashing and burning the native vegetation, and the ground was tilled for Plummer's precious seeds. This phenomenon was of interest to the indigenous inhabitants — technology to be shared with all. However, in 1852 the natives became restive and forbade the settlers from planting. The whites' negotiating strategy was simple: a United States ship anchored offshore that fired a few canon rounds into the woods above the Indians on the beach. The settlers proceeded with their planting, but they also sat down with the natives in a pow-wow where the settlers told the Indians the government would eventually compensate them for the intrusion of the settlers. An informal treaty was agreed to that was never broken. In the spring of 1852, the white population of Port Townshend was three families and fifteen bachelors with more people coming.

Although the settlers made peace with the Clallams on the beaches of Port Townsend, there were Clallams to the west who were not counseled. In 1857, a host of western Clallams landed on the straits just west of Port Townsend to plan the extermination of the settlement. Chetzemoka (sometimes called the Duke of York), the local chief, met with the hostiles to talk peace and warned the settlers that the hostiles intended to kill the white males and enslave the women and children. The Duke found an ally in the son of the chief who wanted war. The Duke attended the war council for nine days and communicated the council's intentions by sitting on a rock every morning above the settlement with a secret blanket signal. On the tenth morning, the Duke signaled "peace". The Duke and the chief's son's peace talk prevailed, and the hostile Clallams went home.

The Duke appreciated the wealth and civilization the settlers were bringing to the area that benefited both the settlers and the natives, and he worked hard to make it happen.

Modern writers would suggest that the Duke saved the settlers, but in reality the duke saved the hostile Clallams from extermination. The Settlers would have repulsed an attack on their fortified positions and soon taken the conflict to the Indians villages on the straits, with fire and death in retribution. At the Duke's death, most of the pioneers attended the funeral to pay their respects. Many of them affectionately called him "the Duke", a name that cannot be used in today's politically correct environment.

Rightly so, the pioneers honored the Duke and admired him. In 2012, he was furthered honored by the Washington state ferry system with a ferry named Chetzemoka, to honor the chief of the Clallams. In today's world, a chief is thought of as a majestic individual without fault. But like most natives of the area, he had a dual personality as described by Theodore Winthrop in 1853. Winthrop authored a book titled *The Canoe and Saddle* that describes his journey through Washington Territory. His journey started in Port Townsend in the Duke's canoe.

Winthrop went to Chetzemoka's Clallam village at Port Townsend to acquire a canoe and paddlers to transport him to Steilacoom, where he would continue his journey by saddle. He found the Clallam chief, Chetzemoka's brother, prone with drink in his "smoky barn" and in disgust kicked the chief with the toe of his moccasin, just as he would a white drunk. But, outside the barn, he came upon Chetzemoka, commonly called the Duke of York, who was almost sober. The Duke agreed to transport Winthrop with his canoe and paddlers along with his wife Jenny Lind, for a payment of several blankets. Husband and wife started to dress for the trip when the Duke discovered that Jenny Lind needed disciplining, and Jenny slumped to the barn's dirt floor crying to take her routine beating. A shocked Winthrop interrupted the beating, calling it uncivilized. Shortly after starting the canoe voyage, the six Native paddlers started drinking until Winthrop took away their bottle. Then, he had six drunken natives making wild talk compounded with gestures. In turn, Winthrop pulled out his six-shooter and told the drunks his gun contained a bullet for each of them. The Natives calmed down slept for a while, and then the journey proceeded. They camped that night, and Winthrop shared some of his food with the Natives, along with a pot of tea laced with sugar and a little rum. His companions soon became good natured and jovial. Still he slept apart from the natives with his six-shooter at hand. The voyage took place in August. Winthrop was thankful the smoke that forced canoes to the beach quite often in the summer did not interrupt his journey. He also noted the smoke haze obscured the foothills, but the snowy top of Mount Rainer was visible.

At their destination, Winthrop wrote that the Clallams were afraid to land at Steilacoom because they feared their rival Indians. With Winthrop's promise of protection, they landed at Steilacoom and walked on to Fort Nisqually to receive their blankets. The Clallams spent the night at the fort in self-imposed isolation and slipped away early in the morning to their canoe and home. Winthrop brought the Clallams into a peaceful association with those they feared. Without bias, Winthrop documented the pollution and unsanitary living conditions in the pristine wilderness of 1853.

A state of Washington professor recently marginalized Winthrop's book and observations in his introduction to the book. The professor dreams of the Northwest as a pristine wilderness and mourns the start of roads, farms, and the harvest of both timber and fish that Winthrop praised. He was appalled at the ethnic and ecological violence that was taking place in Washington Territory. Finally, he even insinuated Winthrop's valiant death fighting in the Civil War for the Union was a result of his ineptness. If the professor's vision had become reality, there would not be a university in Washington State for the professor to work.

The settlers concentrated their labor on clearing their land to produce agricultural products. Contrary to the settlers in the interior, they lived near tidewater that was a natural transportation avenue for their products. Timber was the product that was readily at hand and marketable in San Francisco — timber that had to be removed before the land could be cultivated. Timber that was close to tide water could be rolled down the slopes, by hand or with the help of oxen, where the timber could be rafted and moved to the ships bound to San Francisco. The products were pilings, ships-knees, square timbers, shakes, and shingles. All the products were hand hewn with an ax or equivalent. A claim could produce cash immediately to those settlers near the water.

Perhaps the most significant early promotion of Port Townsend was the implementation of the hated federal customs service. In the beginning there was no customs house, and the pioneers freely traded with the British to the north. The Customs District of Puget Sound was established in February 1851, headquartered in Olympia. In 1859, the Hudson Bay's boat, the *Beaver*, was seized by customs inspectors. From that time forward, responsible shippers carefully adhered to the customs regulations. Olympia was too far away from the shipping traffic, and the headquarters was moved to Port Townsend in 1854. Every ship entering Puget Sound had to stop at Port Townsend. Also, the ships paid off their crews at this port and most of the crews' money was spent in Port Townsend, mostly in the saloons and brothels. Port Townsend became the leading shipping point north of San Francisco, and perhaps the most rowdy and sinful city that was magnified because of its small population of proper people relative to the transient sailors.

To add to the turmoil in this early time, the port was home to a host of smugglers. Both the people on the Sound and the British were in sympathy with the smugglers, as the excise taxes were thought to be unfair. The smugglers were almost never interfered with by the customs people, whose vessels were too slow.

Even though the rowdy city gets the publicity, the backbone of the community was the settlers who continued to civilize the countryside. In 1854, a group of pioneers met to discuss their children's education. Where could they find a school teacher? A pioneer was authorized to seek a teacher in Portland at a salary of no more than thirty dollars per month. A teacher came from Portland, and a vacant log cabin was made available for a schoolroom. Textbooks were also purchased in Portland, one being the famous *McGuffey's Reader*. There were no tablets or pencils. The students numbered twelve. Of course, the teacher was allowed to cut cordwood to supplement his income.

As time went on, the school system was enlarged and the facilities improved. The Indian children were welcome to attend. The more progressive Indian children did, although initially they were rowdy until the Duke instructed them on proper behavior.

Religion came to Port Townsend by canoe. That is, church people traveled from afar to communicate their message for a short time and then retreat to their home bases. They would hold their religious gatherings at private residences, lodge halls, hotel lobbies, log cabins, and any place they could bring people together. The rowdies on the waterfront were a challenge that brought them to the community. In 1865, a chapel was constructed that was 42' by 20' near Point Hudson. The captain of a revenue cutter presented the church with a bell with a request that it should be rung on foggy days since there were no foghorns nearby. The ringing church bell undoubtedly guided many ships safely into the harbor.

The first settlers had no professional medical help, except when an occasional doctor from the south Sound dropped by for a day or two.

The local men could set bones and tend to wounds in addition to the women who assisted mothers giving birth. Typhoid fever was endemic, and diphtheria was common among the young, often fatal. Sailors brought small pox occasionally from overseas. For contagious diseases, there was a "pest house" located away from the town and attended by an elderly volunteer nurse. Pest House survival rates were not good.

In 1855, Port Townsend obtained a resident physician. He acquired a lot and built the first frame building in the town. He also founded the Marine Hospital that was subsidized by the government for sailors. At that time, marine hospitals were a private enterprise that eventually was taken over by the government. The pioneer doctors had little to work with and rudimentary facilities. Most doctors carried forceps to remove teeth. Some even filled teeth with an amalgam of silver and mercury. If a doctor was not available, a blacksmith and his pincers were utilized.

The pioneer doctors' dedication to the community was astounding. In the 1880s, Doctor Seavey in Port Townsend got a call for help from Quilcene. The doctor started out for Quilcene at four a.m. on horseback with a guide and reached the bedside of his patient at five that afternoon. He treated his patient and had to find his way back to Port Townsend without a guide. His fee for his effort was not recorded, perhaps a box of apples! Serious operations were often performed in the patient's home. There were no special operation tables or electric lights, and cleanliness was largely ignored, thus blood poisoning was not uncommon.

The justice system paralleled the doctors in primitive professional practice. The early lawyers and judges convened courts, often in tents or shacks without law books or briefs. The judge might be armed with a gun or knife. And yet, justice usually prevailed swiftly, contrary to the modern justice system. The lawyers in many cases were as rough as their clients. For instance, in 1867, Lawyer Tripp represented a group of seamen over a wage dispute. The lawyer was able through threat of court action to obtain the seamen's wages, but the seamen thought he cheated them out of their full wages. The seamen accosted Tripp on the street and, in the ensuing fight; Tripp killed three seamen and ran off the remainder. Tripp was unhurt, but was arrested and then released, claiming he acted in self-defense. Nevertheless, he determined it was prudent to leave town as the seamen were sure to have their revenge!

The primitive civilized social structure slowly evolved in Port Townsend. However, there was a war to fight. For Port Townsend and vicinity, it was a two-prong war; first with the local hostile natives centered just east of Seattle and Steilacoom, and second, the northern transient Indians from Canada. In the fall of 1855, about a thousand local Indians held a war conference at Port Madison with the objective of forming a unified war effort against the whites. The Duke and Chief Seattle pleaded for peace, and the conference ended with an agreement to not consolidate the tribes to fight the whites. But, in October 1855, the White River Massacre happened, and although the war seemed confined to a few tribes east of Seattle and Steilacoom, all the settlements were apprehensive. In Port Townsend a military organization named the Port Townsend Guards was formed. Plummer was made captain. In December 1855, a large building was converted into a blockhouse. Here the men slept at night and performed their military duties during the day. Mrs. Plummer chose to stay at home and, on two occasions' sighted Northern Indians' canoes approaching and fled to the blockhouse for shelter.

In early February 1856 Captain Plummer with four men went to Whidbey Island on hearing of potential Indian hostilities, and found a number of settlers fortified in a cabin. He left about fifty rounds of ammunition and returned to Port Townsend. In addition to the Port Townsend Guards, a company of volunteers was formed in March 1856 from Port Townsend that consisted of fifty-five men. This company joined other companies from the northern Sound to form the Northern Battalion that was stationed near Snoqualmie Pass for several months, then disbanded when hostilities ceased.

The trouble with the local natives was largely solved by mid-1856, but the Northern Indians remained troublesome. Historically, the

Northern Indians canoed past Port Townsend to access the Sound every summer. They dominated the local Indians probably for centuries. The early settlers soon found the Northern Indians took what they wanted and murdered when it was opportune. The first action against the Northern Indians came in November 1856. The U.S. Steamship *Massachusetts* was instructed to control the Northern Indians at a logging camp on Henderson Bay near Steilacoom where a fight had occurred between the Northern and Southern Indians. Two Indians were killed. The *Massachusetts* located the Northern Indians and followed them to Port Gamble, where they were united with their brethren.

The Port Gamble whites had requested help to disperse the Northern Indians prior to the Henderson Bay incident. The Indians for several years had worked in the Port Gamble sawmill and had always been arrogant while pilfering and stealing. The mill owners were fearful they would burn the mill for perceived insults to their pride.

There were 117 Northern Indian men, women, and children camped near Port Gamble. Under a flag of truce, the Northern Indians were offered amnesty if they would agree to be escorted to Victoria by the Massachusetts. The Indians were defiant and refused to leave. During the night, the Massachusetts and companion ship the Traveler, sent a party ashore with again an offer of peace. The Indians armed themselves and the ships opened fire all day. The next day a landing party went ashore to destroy their last canoe. Without food or canoes, the Indians surrendered and the Massachusetts took the surviving Indians to Victoria. They were told never to come back. Of course, they did and vowed revenge.

The Massachusetts was stationed on the Sound in 1850 as a show of power and continued to prowl the Sound for many years.

The Northern Indians had their retribution the next summer. They landed on Whidbey Island and made inquiries of the friendly settlers, to identify a chief among them. Unconsciously, a settler identified Colonel Isaac Ebey. Early that night, ten Indians left their canoes to hike to his house where they made a disturbance to get Ebey outside. When

Ebey came out, they shot at him. He charged them with an ax handle then retreated and was shot dead on his porch while attempting to talk to his wife. His wife, three of his children, and a visiting woman ran out the back door into the woods. The visitor fled to a neighbor's house to rouse the men, who armed themselves and ran towards the beached Indian canoes, only to be minutes late. To further infuriate the settlers and satisfy their egos, the Indians decapitated Ebey and took his head to their northern village. The neighbor, Engle, stated after Ebey's death: "A Northern Indian never set foot again on the soil of Whidbey Island without biting the dust." Apparently the settlers in turn got their retribution and protected their families.

Early in 1859, the Northern Indians murdered the crews of two small trading vessels on the Sound and burned them. In May 1859, a Vigilance Committee was formed in Port Townsend to deal with the Northern Indians. The committee passed resolutions that would deport all Northern Indians and not allow them to return. The murder of the seamen and the Committee's resolution created a storm of protest, and the Northern Indians were successfully kept from U.S. waters.

The pioneers fought their own local wars to gain a relative peace in the territory, just in time to be plummeted into the Civil War. The first concern was the young and not so young leaving the territory to fight for the Union, leaving the territory undefended to marauding Indians and Confederate sympathizers, Certainly, the Union military would have little or no resources to protect the territory. Their first governor, Stevens, left to join the Union army, but few of the other white pioneers did because of their responsibilities at home and the long journey and expense of traveling to the east where they were needed.

Like the rest of the country, the territory was devastated economically. The cost of all necessities for living increased dramatically, while the market for farm produce and timber shrank, and prices declined. San Francisco, the major market for the Sound, purchases were significantly reduced. Greenbacks depreciated to 35 cents on the dollar. Ships were laid up because of lack of cargo. The federal census reported 264 people lived in Port Townsend in 1860.

The citizens of Port Townsend avidly followed the course of the war, but it took a month for the news to reach town from the East. When critical events were eminent in the East, the wait for news was almost unendurable. Patriotism was intense. A Confederate sympathizer at the Discovery Bay mill was told to leave the area in threatening tones, as happened in other localities. The only threat to the territory would come from the sea. The Confederate steamer, the Shenandoah, was ravaging Union shipping in the north Pacific. James Swan was teaching on the Makah Indian Reservation at Neah Bay when smoke from a steamer (there were few steamers in those days) was seen nearing Neah Bay. An attack from the Shenandoah was anticipated, and Swan was asked what should be done. He replied, "Climb the flagstaff and nail the Stars and Stripes at the peak. And there it shall remain for I will never haul it down to a rebel." Swan's remark could have come from almost every pioneer in the territory. Finally the Civil War ended, and Port Townsend soon recovered its economic vigor.

The Civil War was over and Americans looked to further expansion via a railroad system connecting all points of the country. In 1869, the first transcontinental railroad was completed, connecting Omaha to Sacramento. Immediately, farms and businesses sprang up along the line, giving people the means to transport the efforts of their labors to market.

California was joined to the eastern markets, so the Northwest demanded their country be made accessible to the East. The start of the effort began with the appointment of Governor Stevens, the territory's first governor, who was charged with an additional responsibility of finding a route through the Cascade Mountains of the new territory to tidewater. The first settlers were well aware of the value of land located at the potential town sites, which combined seaport potential with railroad possibilities. Plummer located in Port Townsend with the hope that his claim would eventually become a part of a thriving city that would create added value to his initial farming and timbering endeavors. Plummer's vision was multiplied exponentially as it was in other locations, especially in Seattle, Tacoma, and Portland. Today's critics would label Plummer and like-minded Settlers aspirations as greedy; perhaps, but in most instances, these people risked their lives and meager fortunes to better themselves and their families while contributing to a better society. Plus, the competition between potential town sites was invigorating. The proven results' suggest they were superior to the modern so-called urban planners, corrupted by politically correct politics.

It appeared Port Townsend should be the priority for a terminal of a transcontinental railroad. In 1884-1885 more foreign trade steamers cleared through Port Townsend than anywhere in the U.S. Offshore sailing vessels continually used Port Townsend as a port. The citizens of Portland were interested in promoting a railroad from Portland to Port Townsend. The Columbia River bar precluded extensive shipping up the Columbia River to Portland, and Portland's envisioned the goods from offshore would be marketed through their city. A transcontinental railroad traversing the Cascade Mountains to the Sound would exclude Portland from the rich trade offshore.

The Port Townsend/Portland railroad vision took meaning in 1871 when James G. Swan of Port Townsend was made an agent of the Northern Pacific Railroad and charged with seeking land for a railroad right-of-way from Port Townsend south to the Columbia River. Swan arrived in Port Townsend in 1859 to live out his life in the city. He was well known as an anthropologist, naturalist, author, business promoter, teacher, and an advocate for the Indians.

The Northern Pacific rail plans called for a line to be completed within a year to the Columbia River. Real estate in Port Townsend boomed. When railroad plans collapsed in 1873 because of financial difficulties, real estate values plummeted. And, Seattle and Tacoma became the centers for railroad construction activity.

The city fathers decided to build their own railroad because of the lack of interest by the outside railroad entities. In the summer of 1887, the Port Townsend Southern Railroad was incorporated with local financing, with the optimistic goal of a railroad constructed from Port Townsend to the Columbia River. Lack of funds created little progress until general optimism swept through the country in 1889. Now funding was available. In March 1889, ground was broken for a line headed south from the city. Only a mile of track was built before construction ceased. But, this catalysis brought people to Port Townsend. The town population exploded to 7,000 people. There were six banks, three streetcar lines, and a host of other amenities. The organizers of the railroad were also in the real estate business, and the profits from their sales were more than generous.

It soon became obvious that local resources could not fund a railroad to Portland. Luckily the general prosperity in the country motivated the Union Pacific to absorb the Port Townsend Southern, if the local railroad's assets were given to them, plus $100,000 added to the contract by the local residences. In turn, the Union Pacific's subsidy, the Oregon Improvement Company, would lay tracks to Portland and have 25 miles laid from Port Townsend south completed by September first. The contract was consummated in March. The railroad was constructed to Quilcene in June 1891. By then the Oregon Improvement Company was in receivership, and the country was in a depression that destroyed the dream of a railroad to the Columbia River forever. With this dream shattered, Port Townsend's population shrank to 2,000 of mostly miserable people to match the misery in the rest of the country.

The financial panic of 1893 devastated the country, but probably more so with the Port Townsend folks who had dreams of grandeur based on an elusive railroad. The dreams and financial funding were promoted mostly by the early pioneers whose land claims were the basis of land sales that created their wealth. That wealth was largely reinvested in the community's commercial buildings, sawmills, foundries, canneries, dry dock, and many other enterprises that generally were unsuccessful because of the 1893 panic and depression, along with the unfavorable location of Port Townsend relative to Seattle and Tacoma who now had the terminals of transcontinental railroads. Plummer and his associates risked their lives and modest wealth on Port Townsend's potential grandeur, yet the competition of like-minded pioneers in Seattle and Tacoma prevailed. The competition between pioneer individuals, enabled by a weak government, bought their children and children's children the brightest standard of living in the world.

The Port Townsend promoters got twenty-six miles of railroad built from Port Townsend south to Quilcene. The town of Quilcene was nowhere near the Columbia River. The rail traffic along this rail line could not sustain the railroad, and the section between Quilcene and Discovery Bay was abandoned. The Port Townsend Southern section from Port Townsend to Discovery Bay was used by the Chicago, Milwaukie and St. Paul Railroad for decades, that is, from Port Angeles to Port Townsend.

The pioneers' activities that civilized Port Townsend and the surrounding countryside have been subverted with a continual publication of debauchery in the town. In the formative years, there were unsavory activities taking place largely confined to a small segment of the city, activities that were normal to all port cities on the west coast of that era.

The publicity started with a writer in 1856 who credited Port Townsend's success as: "How whiskey built the city." This moniker has been unfairly repeated to this day to sell the town.

In the early days, there was a saloon with gambling for every seventy-five inhabitants. There was a particular rowdy area near Point Hudson where Port Townsend was rocked with loud reveille every night. "Houses of ill fame" crowded the town, a term used on town plats to designate brothels. Single men, largely transient sailors, loggers, mill men, soldiers from Fort Townsend, Indians and generally outcasts of all nationalities, created a market for the merchants of the saloons and worse. And, this market flourished into the 1900s in spite of the reformers efforts to create change.

Obviously, the largely unregulated saloon culture created numerous destructive incidents and crimes. Perhaps the most heinous was the smuggling that matured from the 1850's harmless evasion of excise taxes to the destructive smuggling of Chinese workers and opium. A multitude of Chinese in Victoria B.C. were willing to pay good money to be smuggled to the U.S., and there were men in Port Townsend who were happy to provide that service.

Port Townsend was the center of the smuggling, from 1880 to 1887, because of the lack of government inspectors. The smugglers would pick up their Chinese near Victoria and transport them to Discovery Bay or West Beach, where the newcomers would usually work in a Chinese garden near their place of landing several weeks then mingle with the Chinese in the local area or move on. The smugglers were seldom caught because of their swift boats and knowledge of the government's activities. If they were approached by a government boat, their chained Chinese would be put overboard into the Straits watery depths, and the evidence was gone.

There was a Chinese community in Port Townsend and scattered through the countryside. Commonly, they operated a laundry or raised and sold vegetables. They were respected by the Port Townsend community, and the citizens were hardy concerned with the smuggling. Smuggling was thought to be a problem for the unpopular government customs service. Few smugglers were prosecuted although the smugglers methods seemed to be common knowledge. The lives of the Chinese smuggled across the Strait seemed to be of little concern to the general public perhaps similar to today's lack of concern for the welfare of people crossing our borders illegally.

Opium was smuggled into the country with or without the Chinese. There were smugglers' boats and professional smugglers, and ordinary people who used commercial boats, to bring opium into the country illegally. The use of opium was legal in the U.S., but it was profitable to avoid paying the custom's duty. The government's confiscated opium was sold at public auction. The highest bidders were usually Chinese firms!

Probably the most violence associated with Port Townsend involved so-called shanghaiing, that is, putting sailors aboard ships by force or trickery. Most readers think of shanghaiing as a sailor being laid unconscious and carried aboard a ship, and that certainly happened in Port Townsend. But less violent means were preferred.

"The Sailors' Boarding Houses", an enterprise in every west coast port, came into being about 1890. The ship captains needed a source of sailors, and the sailors needed a place to stay until the next ship was available. The boarding houses fit a need. Unfortunately, it was a sailor's habit to come to port with money and an uncontrollable urge to have a roaring celebration in the saloons of Port Townsend. The town welcomed this quick revenue, but the sailor was broke in a few days and his only haven was in a boarding house. The house gave him room, board plus a little spending money. Then the boarding house operator would be the sailor's agent to sign him onto another ship.

When a ship was available, the boarding house operator was paid by the ship's captain — a head count for each sailor, plus his board bill. The sailor's board bill would be deducted from his earnings during the forthcoming voyage.

However, the sailors might not want to ship out in a" hard" or "hell" ship. The operator usually prevailed by using various degrees of coercion, including shanghaiing. The operator might have the problem of not having enough sailors to man a ship, therefore, he searched the town for potential sailors, willing or unwilling. He avoided the local families' young men and Indians who were protected by the federal government. To add to the turmoil, the Seamen's Union was being organized to replace the boarding houses to serve the seamen and eliminate the boarding house evils.

After years of violence in Port Townsend and other port cities, the union prevailed. In the 1890s, it was common to see ten to fifteen sailing ships at anchor at Port Townsend, sometimes with only a watchman on board, waiting for a charter. The charters took the ships all over the world on long voyages. The seamen's life aboard these ships was brutal, just from the nature of the work. One can only imagine the near-horror of working the sails far above the deck in a gale or worse. The hard nature of the work was often combined with the brutality of the mate who might drive the men to work under the urgency of the task. All too often, brutality became ingrained in their nature.

The tales of mistreatment abound. On one occasion, the crew refused orders by the captain in an emergency and the captain shot one of the crew members, perhaps saving the ship from destruction. On another occasion, an 18-year-old Coupeville youth signed on to a ship in Port Townsend to experience the romance of the sea; then experienced the realities of life at sea while the ship was in port. He chose to jump ship with two life rings off Whidbey Island. His body was found on the island's beach.

The large sailing ships were used well into the 1900s off shore, but the watercraft in the Sound that plied between British Columbia and Olympia were another breed of cat. The evolution of craft was unique to the Sound. First there were the canoes, then the small sailing boats, and the powered boats, the stern-wheelers and side-wheelers, and finally the propeller boats. The Beaver was the first powered boat on the Sound and was active before the American settlers arrived. In the 1850s and for decades there was a mixture of craft plying the Sound, but the large sailing ships were offshore vessels. The seamen on the Sound were not subjected to the harsh offshore sailing ships' long voyages and could escape mistreatment, while the seamen on offshore ships were by the nature of the long voyages prisoners for months. However, when modern propeller driven ships replaced the offshore sailing ships, life became much easier for the sailors.

The early tales of the horror at Port Townsend concentrating on the marginal society are overwhelming! But, what were the ordinary people doing? My grandfather moved from his father's dairy farm near Dungeness to a dairy farm in Uncas at the head of Discovery Bay about 1914. Port Townsend was the center for doing business for the area surrounding the town, including the people from Uncas who made infrequent trips there for their necessities while ignoring the more unsavory parts of town. The cows needed milking twice a day and there was little time to be concerned with the saloon culture. There was mostly hard work and tranquility in their life. Then granddad's younger brother Jack disappeared. Inquiries and search through Port Townsend and vicinity over weeks was futile. So, the family suffered with concern and fear for months. Finally, Jack wrote a letter from Australia telling the family he had gone to sea and was in good health — but little else. Jack was never heard from again. My grandfather would only tell his family that Jack just had gone to sea.

Port Townsend quietly lost their offshore ships to Seattle and other ports in the south Sound. A natural evolution of the shipping was to the ports having transcontinental railroad terminals. Also where ships docked, the businesses followed and so did the saloon culture in Port Townsend.

The town's future looked dismal until 1927 when Crown Zellerbach, a large paper corporation, located a paper mill in the town. Initially, the mill employed 500 men. In addition the corporation, in conjunction with the town, brought water from the Quilcene River to the mill and the town. The town desperately needed water. Water was always in short supply because of a lack of funds for a modern water system. The system required a costly piping of water from a considerable distance from the town.

Port Townsend was finally made viable by a simple formula — the utilization of our natural resources, water and timber, plus an infusion of capital and technology by private business. A formula that seems lost to society today.

PIONEER SAWMILLS

The pioneers in Puget Sound displaced the Indians, British, Spanish, and Russians to create our present culture. Perhaps an equal force contributed to today's society, that is, the often-defamed sawmill entrepreneurs who created steam sawmills/villages on Hood Canal and Discovery Bay. In 1853, four California-owned sawmills were built. Port Gamble and Port Ludlow were first, while Port Discovery and Seabeck started several years later. All of these pioneer industries were almost structurally and philosophically identical.

In 1850, 29-year-old Andrew Pope and 31-year-old Frederic Talbot came together in California to establish Pope and Talbot to sell consigned lumber products mostly in California. They were the younger sons of Maine families who came to California to make their fortunes. They had little money, but more importantly they had the family business background in lumber and trading.

In 1849, Bangor in Maine sent thirty-nine ships with five million board feet of lumber around the Horn to California. This lumber was very expensive in California, and the tiny water-powered mills of the west were inadequate to supply the market. Lafayette Balch, of Steilacoom fame, was a relative of the Talbot family and described the opportunities on the Sound. It was obvious to the two Yankees, Pope and Talbot, there was a real business opportunity for a modern steam sawmill on the Sound. The Yankees formed The Puget Mill Company with two minor partners.

Talbot took a ship to the Sound to locate a mill site and the minor partner took a ship to Maine to load the machinery for a mill and recruit experienced sawmill workers. In June 1853, Talbot cruised the upper Sound and Hood Canal, awed at the size and quality of the Douglas fir timber extending to the water's edge on both sides of the relatively narrow Canal waterway. Accessible timber seemed unlimited. Logging technology at the time dictated accessible timber must be within a mile of navigable water. Port Ludlow and other potential mill sites were already taken. The Puget Mill Company's minor partner had a claim on Teekalet Bay, soon to be Port Gamble. So, a mill site was acquired with no cost to the business, allowing more funds to go into the mill and village structures.

The Talbot ship's party began work on the Teekalet Bay mill site immediately. By the time the mill machinery arrived, the site preparation was well underway. Their shipment included a steam-powered sawmill, supplies, and store merchandise. The new resident manager, Captain William Talbot, settled in with his wife, daughter and a young son in a crude sawmill/village that included a cookhouse, a general store, and a 45'-by-70' sawmill building. There were twenty-four men, women, and children in the Teekalet village.

It took about six months to get a sawmill up and running. In their first year, 1854, the mill produced 15,000 board feet a day in the eleven months of production. In today's measurements, that is equivalent to about four truckloads of logs. But of course the facilities at Port Gamble were rapidly expanding. By 1870, Port Gamble had two private hotels, a Masonic lodge, a school, church, library, theater, brass band, and other amenities. The population was 246 people, with a third of the residents from Maine.

In the 1850s, companies could not purchase land or timber in the government's public domain, which included most of the land on the Sound. Companies had to purchase land or timber from an individual. A Pope and Talbot minor partner filed a 320-acre Oregon Donation Act claim later to be deeded to the company; the company obtained a mill site and 320 acres of timber at no cost. Because this Act was implemented for the emigrant pioneer farmers, The Puget Mill Company people referred to their mill as "the farm". However, tradition opened up another option.

Settlers considered frontier land free for everybody to use. The settlers treated the so-called *public domain* as common ground unless someone was occupying the ground. Why shouldn't the mills? It wasn't until the passage of the Timber and Stone Act of 1878 that timber acres could be purchased from the public domain at $2.50 per acre, limited to 160 acres per person. The federal government considered cutting trees on public domain as thievery, but in the 1850s the government was too small to define the problem or administer a timber sale program. More importantly, the pioneers and San Francisco market could not wait for the government. Perhaps it was thievery, but the mills could have just raised the price of lumber to compensate for the price of the stumpage (trees), and the people in San Francisco and other parts of the world would, in effect, have paid the government.

The first people to get the products from the trees to the market were the settlers who logged on their claims and public domain. These products were handcrafted for loading on ships in the Sound. The construction of the numerous sawmills in the 1850s created a need for professional loggers.

The loggers were of two classes. The one-or-two-man operators working on water's edge had a saw, ax, peavey and a hand windlass. They usually worked on the public domain and paid for only a few tools. They fell the trees towards the water and then muscled them into the water, a low cost operation.

The big loggers of six to ten men utilized four or five yokes of oxen to power the logs down a skid road at a snail's pace. The crew was composed of a cook and six to ten other men who lived in a primitive camp on the logging site. The hand equipment included saws, peaveys, axes, chains, and heavy blocks. The skid roads were located carefully on a gentle downgrade to the beach, only wide enough for access of the oxen, with short poles spaced at two to three feet across. The cross poles were lubricated with dogfish oil or other grease to provide a slippery surface to slip the logs down the skid road. The oxen logged about 28,000 board feet a day; in today's world, that is about seven truckloads of logs a day.

A writer in this era stated that the loggers, settlers, and mill workers were not drones, and people who would not work were not tolerated. For example, a logging boss was knocked unconscious during logging; the crew picked him up to carry him to camp. Within a quarter of a mile from camp, the boss came to his senses, angry at his crew for leaving their work. The crew placed him under a tree and went back to work. The boss then crawled the last quarter of a mile to camp, suffering a permanently damaged eye.

The skid roads were rarely located more than a mile from Hood Canal because of the cost, and as loggers from 1850 to the present day know, the shorter the skid road the greater the profit. My grandfather was a bull whacker (oxen driver) in a camp like this for twenty years.

After the logs were skidded to the beach, they were rafted. That is, boom sticks (poles) were chained together to encircle the logs. When sufficient logs were rafted, a tug from one of the mills towed the rafts to the mill. The mill scaler measured the length and diameter of the logs to determine the board foot volume, paying the logger by a previously negotiated price, in dollars-per-thousand-board feet. The scale was usually made to favor the mill, and a smart logger would understand this when negotiating a contract and adjust his bid accordingly. The logger's crew got paid only when the contract logger was paid by the mill people.

Surprisingly, there were drastic improvements in falling trees since the settlers began cutting on the Sound. Before 1870, it took two men using single-bladed axes at least an hour to fall a medium size fir tree. Western ax choppers switched to double-bladed axes that saved time. Then a thin-bladed ax evolved for falling with a broader-bladed ax for utility purposes. By the 1880s, crosscut saws, many over six feet in length, came into vogue.

The two-man saws were used for the undercut, which helped to direct the tree's fall. The fallers sawed a third of the way into the tree, chopping out a wedge above the saw cut. Then they started on the backside of the undercut. Iron wedges were sometimes used to facilitate the fall of the tree. The faller's placement of the undercut and the wedges directed the fall. A good team of fallers could direct a straight tree in any direction and hit a stake driven in front of the tree before falling. The saw and the improved ax were labor savers. The next improvement came with the chainsaw that was generally adopted in the 1950s.

Milling and timbering created jobs and wealth on Hood Canal for the residents and the three sawmills. The mills that used most of the timber were at Port Gamble, Port Ludlow, and Seabeck. About twenty loggers and fifty farmers along the canal depended on the health of the mills for their livelihood.

The pioneer sawmill era extended into the 1880s when logging railroads displaced the oxen in the woods, and the transcontinental and other railroads opened up lands away from the water to utilize further timber resources. In the meantime, the Puget Mill Company and other mills aggressively created the predominate industry in the area. The Maine sawmill technology and machinery were utilized to create the state-of-the-art sawmills while a railroad system was developed to deliver logs to the mills.

The log supply was generated from many sources. Companies structured their own logging camps, but, there were other sources over that period that could be more efficient. The independent loggers, big and small, existed because the mills required logs. People had a ready market for the trees they cleared from their claims to facilitate their agriculture endeavors.

The mills bought logs delivered by both loggers and land owners. But, most people with logs got their logs rafted near the logging site, where the mills' tugs towed them to the mill. However, logs from people independent of the mills were inadequate to the mills' needs. So the mills loaned money to enable the loggers to get into the business or to stay in business. In addition, the loggers obtained most of their supplies from the company's store on credit because there were no other sources to fill their needs. The competition between loggers and mills was usually uneasy. The prices at the company store were considered to be exorbitant. However, no one has reported the multitude of bad debts written off by the companies. A logger could move out of an area without paying off his debt, and log for someone else.

In brief, the mills obtained logs on the open market or logs from the company's loggers, plus independent loggers. In addition, the company bought stumpage from landowners and arranged the logging.

The source of logs was not easily defined with the multitude of groups delivering them to the mills. Nonetheless, the federal government continually tried to stop the trespassing on public domain. The mills were readily identifiable, but not private individuals logging on the public domain. Finally in 1861, the federal government indicted the mill owners for criminal theft. But, the federal prosecutor had a problem knowing that no jury in the logging communities would convict anyone of timber theft; after all, the jurors were mostly timber thieves too.

Edward Clayson, a writer in that era who lived at Seabeck, writes that Kitsap County was the richest county in the United States in proportion to population. The five large sawmill towns of Port Gamble, Port Madison, Port Orchard, Port Blakely, and Seabeck were running night and day loading fleets of ships with lumber to California and ports as far away as Australia and South Africa. And probably, to the amazement of today's society, there were only a few professional people in the county — three doctors and six gamblers. A lawyer and newspapers were not needed.

The federal prosecutor had to save face, so he negotiated a timber domain trespass settlement with the mill operators and offered a token punishment for a guilty plea. The punishment: the criminals were locked in a jail cell in Port Townsend for the time it took to smoke a cigar with the judge and sheriff, who joined them in the cell. The mills also paid a small fee to the government based on the mills' estimate of timber removed from federal land.

The timber theft problem was never solved by the government; on the contrary, private sector thievery diminished when the Northern Pacific Railroad charged a fee for timber removed from their land and put their agents on the ground to administer the program. The other landowners soon adopted the railroad's program. The Northern Pacific Railroad obtained their forest land through a grant from the government. The grant was a subsidy that made it economical for the railroad to build a transcontinental rail line.

The mill owners/managers were tough-minded competitors who needed several superior skills to remain in a risky business. Their motivations appeared to be the fun of the game of lumbering and establishing estates for their children. Most worked long hours both physically and mentally under stressful conditions. Those with less ability believed greed drove their entrepreneurial efforts. But, entrepreneurs with money need not work, and those with little wealth wanted a better life.

The risks were great. The sawmill was a tinder box set to burn, literally. The Seabeck mills burned to the ground in 1886 in an accidental fire; the Port Discovery mill lost its ship at dockside to fire; its lumber ships or cargos sometimes were lost at sea. In the 1850s, the local and northern Indians were a threat to both assets and life. The lumber markets were erratic as was the financial health of the nation. Perhaps most of all was the risk of losing capital invested in the mills if the government stopped the logging on public land. A largely hostile federal government was continually trying to jail mill operators for thievery. As usual, the government was inept, counterproductive and, in that era, sometimes corrupt. The mill owners desired a dependable timber supply and were willing to pay for it.

Competition in the lumber industry was brutal, with many sawmills in the Sound competing for logs. Landowners and loggers could sell their logs at any number of mills unless they were under contract with a particular mill. At various times the mills tried to cooperate on setting log prices. In turn, the loggers countered with price-fixing programs. Consequently, no agreement lasted long and the free market prevailed.

On the other end of the timber pipeline were the lumber marketing and sales in San Francisco and elsewhere that was all-important to a mill. Those that had a marketing group active in San Francisco had a distinct advantage over their competitors. The mills were sending shiploads of lumber all over the world and selling locally. It is hard to visualize how the Port Gamble mill could send a ship to Australia with a cargo of lumber and find a Seabeck mill's ship there to usurp the Port Gamble-Australian sale. Communication between buyer and seller took months, as letters were carried by slow-sailing vessels. Thus, delayed communication demanded selling skills beyond the understanding of today's world. It is obvious that the lumber sales strategy and execution were critical for the mills' success.

The lumber sales competition was vigorous between the Sound mills as well as the mills in both Oregon and northern California. Several efforts were made to form a consortium of mills to manage competition by standardizing profitable lumber prices. Attempts were made regionally to form a west coast consortium. All efforts were short-lived because of the independent spirit of the entrepreneurs. (Some would suggest greed and dishonesty were the driving factors.) In today's world, business collaborations on pricing products is illegal. In the pioneer mill era, the natural competition between businesses made government intervention irrelevant.

Unique to the 1850s was the startup of numerous sawmills by like-minded men on uninhabited and wilderness sites. There was no time to wait for a settlement and infrastructure to evolve through a government bureaucracy. Besides, the owners demanded an attractive environment for their family-oriented villages that would attract excellence in their workforce.

Life and facilities were surprisingly similar at the mills. There was a dormitory for single men and assigned housing for families, small cottages for the laborers, and better houses for the skilled labor and managers. A mess hall and a company store for the employees were shared with the surrounding countryside.

Many of the owners /managers joined the work force during the day doing menial work to further production or to work off nervous energy. Nevertheless, there was a hierarchy. The managers and the office force ate together; the skilled people ate together, other employees ate in assigned seating in the mess hall. A shocking concept for today's progressive thinkers. But not unlike today's real world where there executive dining rooms and military dining are segregated by rank.

In the business world there is a strong reason for segregation: business is discussed over meals — in most cases almost exclusively. The mill managers were absorbed in lumber production, markets, shipping, timber supply, taxes, and long-term planning. The skilled workers discussed the allocation of the work crews, improvements to be made, and personnel problems. Management and skilled workers had no time for idle talk. In that era, personal problems were quickly solved by replacing the worker — and replacement was easy. In the late 1800s, a gold rush created a shortage of labor that was overcome with creativity.

Life revolved around the sawmill routine. Usually a whistle woke the village at five a.m. A later whistle opened the mess hall, and the six a.m. whistle signaled the mill to begin an eleven-and-a-half-hour day. A whistle announced lunch, and another stopped the mill in the evening when the day was done, unless the mill ran a second shift.

In the start-up period, the urgency of the moment dictated the village be very rudimentary because the initial effort centered around the lumber production facilities. One manager suggested the long workday would keep people occupied and out of trouble. Nevertheless, the mill leaders wanted to attract responsible and hard-working families to their sawmill communities. Many amenities were slowly added: a barbershop, bowling alley, dance hall, community hall, library, theater, and church. The company store carried books, newspapers, and ladies fashions. The village was improved aesthetically with shade trees, flowers, and picket fences. And, the amenities were at company expense, while the value of the property rose to the pleasure of the county's tax assessor.

The mills also were expanding and improved. Most complexes began building ships for sale, as well as adding to the company's lumber-carrying sailing vessels. A network of transportation was developed between villages, towns, and logging camps with a fleet of schooners, both private and company-owned. A schooner sometimes carried the company baseball team to play other teams throughout the Sound. It is amazing that people who worked eleven-and-a-half hours a day, six days a week, found time to play.

The mill owners and managers believed a moral and disciplined community contributed to their business endeavors and were of mutual benefit to the individual. A benevolent paternalism was practiced. This was certainly different from the workshops in Europe and elsewhere in America of that era, where the labor force was expendable. Mill owners of the 1800s were forward thinking. An injured or crippled worker was generally provided with a job he could handle, and money was collected to help the family. The competitive lumber business limited the aid given the labor force, since bankruptcy was always a threat.

The mill owners/managers were almost desperate in their attempts to keep their communities wholesome, both for an effective work environment and their moral responsibly to strengthen their employees' family structure. The mill management worked hard to maintain a family friendly environment in the mill/villages. The rough and tumble single men's lifestyle did not produce a responsible workforce. The activities in the dives of the port cities, like Port Townsend, were destructive to the individual and the American community.

The mill owners/managers sought to eliminate misbehavior. First, was to keep out the scoundrels by requiring the ships entering their ports for lumber to hire and pay off their crews in Port Townsend, thus eliminating the disreputable sailor boarding houses with their associated Barbary Coast environment. Adulterers and prostitutes were not welcome. Hotels with liquor and gambling were considered undesirable, but impossible to eliminate because of public demands. Also, this undesirable activity could and should be located off the mill property to minimize the bad influences on the mill families. Mill culture was leveraged by the owners simply by not employing *undesirable* people and furnishing family-oriented activities, such as dances on Saturday night, competitive baseball games between communities on Sunday, celebration of the Christmas, Thanksgiving, and the Fourth of July holidays. These activities were encouraged, to keep people away from the saloons.

The part owner of the Seabeck mill, Marshal Blinn, went further than most owners in attempting to eliminate liquor in the mill community. He purchased a hotel that sold liquor in Seabeck and reopened it without liquor thus, making the hotel an economic failure. Further, he entered politics to institute prohibition in the area, and was defeated easily by his opponent, a saloon operator. Blinn then sold his interest in the Seabeck mill and retired, apparently in disgust, to enjoy his wealth in a community more to his liking. The new mill manager put his effort into managing the mill and largely ignored the hotel/saloon activities.

And, activity there was. As an example, a woman and her daughters came to Seabeck during the usual big Fourth of July celebration. She obtained a room in the hotel located on the second floor above the bar. The family retired about the time the loggers came to town to celebrate The Fourth, breaking the monotony of months in the nearby logging camps. The celebration went on late into the night until toward morning, when there was the roaring of gunfire. The terrified lady and her daughters spent most of the night under the bed.

The next morning when the family walked past six loggers who lay out on the street, she thought they were dead. The saloon keeper explained they were only sleeping off their drunken stupor of the night before. This was behavior not conducive to family living. Nevertheless, these were single men blowing off steam as single men do today after periods away from a civilized community. Loggers were fortunate not to be in Port Townsend, where they might have awakened on a ship headed to China.

The mill/villages were relatively peaceful and provided quality places to live. Critics suggest they were oppressive and undemocratic. Not so. People voted, and mill owner Blinn discovered, to his discomfort, that people chose liquor over prohibition. The mill hierarchy had few votes, while the people held the vast majority of the votes and could change the direction of the Washington Territory at their will. When the federal government tried to convict the mill owners of thievery for logging on the public domain, the people's jury turned the government away. While some of the evils, like prostitution, could have been changed, the reformers obviously didn't have the votes.

It must be remembered the territory was largely populated by single young men, and women did not have a vote. Restrict today's population to mostly young single men and this would be a different country. As for being oppressive, my great-grandfather didn't think so. Unlike many single men, he saved enough money to buy a prosperous dairy farm, a farm that enabled him to offer a proper English lady of moderate wealth a life, which she had to think was in a wilderness populated with wild loggers and Indians.

For several decades, the pioneer sawmills, utilizing the wealth of the forest, turned a wilderness into thriving forest communities. Commerce, trade, and local governments were funded largely by the activity of these mills. The mill owners, allied with the settlers' families, arguably fought to bring moral American fiber to the forefront in the region.

CHINESE ANGER

The first Seabeck sawmill had been in operation since the late 1850s and was one of the economic mainstays of the Hood Canal community. In 1883, the Seabeck operation built a modern sawmill to complement it, expecting it to be staffed with traditional sawmill workers.

The community was looking forward to expanding the traditional workforce and adding to the village population, increasing the economic value of the entire region. So it was with shock and anger when the new mill was staffed exclusively with cheap Chinese contract labor. Furthering the community's angst was the fear that the white men's jobs in the old mill were in jeopardy. It was thought other mills would be forced to use the cheap labor to remain competitive with the Seabeck operation. Many Americans believed the thirty years of building American families in the region was under attack by the wealthy and the Chinese.

Traditionally, the Chinese were housed and fed in dormitories on the mill site and chose not to circulate in the community. Their meager earnings mostly went back to China for their families or to defray their debt to the labor contractor. They were unlikely to form families in the Seabeck community.

The rest of the community seemed to have no alternative to the intrusion of the Chinese. The government and politicians had passed innumerable laws and regulations concerning Chinese emigrants, laws and regulations the progressives at that time thought were unfair and discriminatory. Nevertheless, the community faced losing its livelihood. The people were not passive, since they were of pioneer stock that had fought its way as individuals to the promised land. They didn't decry their situation or wait for very long. They just let it be known they would burn the new mill to the ground, preferably with the new mill workers in it. The wooden mill was literally a matchbox; one spark and the box would explode. The spark could be one man throwing a lantern into the box.

A few weeks passed and the Chinese were deported from the mill and replaced with traditional mill people, people who were mostly white, but not exclusively. Many ethnic groups filled the workforce — the American way.

Few people, past and present, understand how the Chinese got to America, and that understanding is important before judging the Chinese/American relationships. The California gold rush of 1849 mesmerized Chinese peasants. Many wanted the free American gold to improve their lives in China. Chinese peasants — "coolies" — were subjected to periodic starvation and debilitating wars. The coolies had no money to get to America. Chinese labor contractors were eager to control the coolies in China and in America after funding their ocean voyage to profit from coolie labor. In 1852 the contractors brought 18,000 coolies to America and they continued the flow of Chinese to America.

The Chinese labor contractors or merchants (they had other businesses too) numbered six in the U.S. The six companies controlled the Chinese emigrants who numbered about 151,000 in 1876. There was a potential to bring unlimited Chinese into the U.S. if there was a market for contract Chinese labor. The contract companies sent Chinese immediately into the gold fields of the 1849 California gold Rush, as well as smaller labor opportunities. The companies acted as the emigrants' agents. Before the government of China had offices in America, the companies spoke for the Chinese government, keeping their people in touch with their homeland and furnishing common meeting grounds for them, along with helping organize Chinese societies.

But the companies could go much further than communication by offering educational, recreation, and medical services that included hospitalization. In the event of death, members were given burial, care for their tombs, or shipment of their bones to China. The companies settled internal disputes and offered money to help in lawsuits. In short, the companies controlled the lives of the Chinese laborers in America. If the Chinese were able to vote in America, the Chinese companies would control their voting.

The Chinese companies had agents wherever there were Chinese. Eventually, that meant throughout the west. The agents provided direction to employment and, when necessary, arranged supplies and housing, and even provided advice and guidance. The list of the companies' services seemed only helpful. But the so-called agents were the organizers and directors of the companies' labor force. The companies' income and profits depended on the coolies working and returning money to the company that invested in them.

The Chinese coolies went into the California gold fields as a funded and organized group by a well-directed Chinese corporate identity, in competition with the individual American miners for the free gold in California. The American miners and the American public believed there was only a jumble of poor Chinese working the gold fields; instead they had health insurance and other benefits. By instinct and observation, the American miners knew they were being displaced by foreign competition and reacted with harsh treatment directed at the Chinese while they implemented laws to level the playing field. The progressives of that time, as well as those of the present day, condemn the white miners as bigots or worse. In 1859, a Chinese company sent 2,000 Chinese to Fort Victoria to mine the Fraser River bonanza. There wasn't another country in the world that transported organized miners to the gold fields. On the contrary, the Fraser River Gold Rush was composed of free individuals from many countries that made their own arrangements.

In 1864, the Chinese miners moved into eastern Washington by the hundreds. The majority of them were "contracted" by the Chinese companies, shipped directly to Portland from California and China, and dispersed throughout the region. The larger Chinese mining camps were well organized and supervised by a Chinese boss responsible to the company.

Although there was some friendly interaction between the whites and Chinese, there was also harassment meted out to the Chinese by the whites. The California-type laws were implemented, taxing the Chinese. Sadly, the Indians also massacred a group of Chinese miners in 1875 near the Methow River. The Chinese must have been an easy target for the Indians, since the white miners suffered no such indignity. The white establishment didn't see fit to seek retribution for the barbarism. In a few years, the gold was played out in eastern Washington, and the Chinese moved on.

The transcontinental railroad was completed in 1869 and the Chinese companies furnished 10,000 coolies to do the labor; most came directly from China. Then railroad construction continued on a smaller scale. The Northern Pacific line from Kalama to Tacoma began in 1871, and 2,000 Chinese were employed to build it. Shortly afterwards, the demand for Chinese railroad labor became minimal. Mining and railroad employment become incidental; but contrary to ideology, the Chinese didn't all go back to China. They made little effort to integrate into American society. American ministers were frustrated in their efforts to educate them. For a population of 700 or 800 Chinese in Tacoma, there were three Joss Houses (Chinese temples), but nearly none approached the community's churches. Their opium seemed popular, but not the saloons of the Sound or other American amenities.

By 1885, the people in the Sound were about to become violent. The wealthy families used Chinese in their homes, a dramatic change from earlier years when all Americans worked together for a standard of living expected in the American dream. Consciously or subconsciously, the non-wealthy visualized wealthy aristocrats served by Chinese coolies.

Many people rejected the white women domestics in their households in favor of Chinese servants. This destroyed a single woman's best avenue for work. Single women who left their families for various reasons had generally two avenues of employment: first was domestic service; the second was the too-easy brothel. Older women with shelter could take in washing, but the Chinese washer houses soon put them out of business. My maternal grandmother left her family to serve as a domestic worker in a respectable Dungeness family in the 1890s, until she met and married my grandfather. Thankfully the Chinese were not a factor in the 1890s.

The progressives, then and now, attribute the anger at the Chinese as intolerance to an ethnic group. The progressive can't relate to Seabeck's community, who faced pain and financial distress because of the intrusion of Chinese labor, who appeared to be mechanical robots that produced lumber. Or, to the Indians and whites excluded from the Puget Sound hop fields by the Chinese. Finally, several Puget Sound coal miners lost their jobs. The Chinese work force had intruded into industry, farms and domestic service. and the verbal outrage turned to violence.

On September 5, 1885, a group of armed white men and Indians approached a hop farmer near Issaquah and asked him to dispense with his Chinese labor force. The farmer turned them away. Several nights later, the group attacked the Chinese in their camp on the ranch. The Chinese were asleep in their tents when the group fired into their tents, killing three and wounding three. The Chinese fled the valley, and presumably, the white/Indian group then harvested the farmers' hops.

A few days later in the same area, about a dozen masked men drove the Chinese out of their quarters at the Coal Creek mine at midnight, burning their quarters and possessions. The Chinese were not hurt, but frightened, outraged. They fled. Again, presumably the masked men and their friends applied for work in the mine the next day.

Given the urgency of the violence that had the potential to flame out of control, citizens called for a statewide conference to address the anger. The conference soon came to be called the "Workingman's Movement". It provided a new thrust and empowerment to the labor groups, such as the Knights of Labor. Furthermore, the Chinese were driving a wedge between the American classes. The upper class was displacing the American lower class with cheap Chinese labor, which gave birth and education to the embryonic anti-American Marxist's world labor movement in the Northwest. The Northwest movement climaxed in Russia after World War I.

The conference concluded that the "Chinese must go". A Committee of Fifteen was appointed to craft and implement a plan to accomplish the goal in both Tacoma and Seattle. The committees were composed of professional people and leaders in the territory. They decided that all the Chinese should be notified that they must leave by November 1, 1885, and that all employers dismiss their Chinese immediately.

There was a proliferation of volunteers to notify employers of the committees' edict and to confirm compliance. Most employers discharged their Chinese employees, with few exceptions. One exception was an owner of a barrel factory when he faced the volunteers (called "a mob" by the progressives) with loaded six guns and drove them away. Shortly thereafter, a bomb exploded under his building, after which he immediately discharged his Chinese. A pro-Chinese minister preached his convictions in Sunday services, and his congregation got up and walked away from the church. The minister, threatened, carried two Colt revolvers when on the street; he was never harmed.

The Chinese residents sought succor from their patrons, the six Chinese companies, who immediately contacted the Chinese consul. The progressives would suggest that the companies wanted to save their improvised countrymen, but logic suggests they wanted to preserve their economic vitality. The leaders of the six Chinese companies were filthy rich by this time, and their cash cow was about to be destroyed by the rank and file citizens of America. The Chinese rich were about to be emasculated by American "laboring peasants". The Chinese consul wired the Washington Territorial Governor to ask for protection for the Chinese, amazed that the Chinese might be expelled from the territory. He shouldn't have been surprised, since the

U.S. Congress had passed "The Chinese Exclusion Act of 1882", which banned Chinese laborers from emigrating to America. In passing the bill, Congress stated the Chinese must go. The citizens felt the act was ineffective, as the Chinese kept coming and staying in the country. The progressives thought the act was an uncalled for attack against the mistreated Chinese, and those in disagreement were agitators to be held in contempt. That thought prevails to this day. In 1885, almost all in the territory were agitators.

As November 1 approached, most Chinese were unemployed and moving out of the territory. However, a significant number remained, either through ignorance, lack of resources, or defiance of the deadline. Unfortunately the progressives told the Chinese to stay because the edict to leave was all bluff. The agitators, now called "the mob" by the progressives, started to forcibly move the Chinese out of the territory. In Tacoma on November 3, a foundry whistle was sounded in the morning, and hundreds of armed men gathered in the streets and marched through the town. At each Chinese business or residence, a couple of men dropped off to inform the Chinese that they had until 1:30 p.m. to leave. The march was mostly orderly, and the mob moved silently like grim reapers.

After the deadline, the mill whistle sounded again and the mob rounded up the remaining Chinese (a few were forcibly removed from their residences) and marched them eight miles to the Lake View railroad station, where they were put on a train to Portland. To complete the deportation, their "shacks" were scheduled to be condemned and burned legally. However, the shacks "accidentally" caught fire and burned in spite of the efforts of the fire department. There were some reports that the fire hoses were cut.

Judge James Wickersham, a Tacoma member of the Committee of Fifteen, knew nothing of the plans to expel the Chinese. When the people gathered in the streets to execute their evacuation, he sat with a fellow committeeman sweating out the event. The judge desired to remove the Chinese from Tacoma, but wanted it done in such a way that the Committee of Fifteen didn't go to jail. He sat with his friend hoping that a Chinese would not be killed or wounded. With this vision in mind, he did everything he could to protect the Chinese from violence.

The judge was perhaps the most forward thinking and unselfish agitator in the territory. He wrote a friend in 1916: "There are millions of Chinese who would flood the Pacific Coast if the bars were once lowered and if they were given an equal chance with our people. The Chinese would out-do Americans in the struggle for life and gain possession of the Pacific Coast. We cannot compete with them. Further, I fear the Chinese good qualities much more than I fear their bad ones."

It seems the judge could have been a prophet given the unique example today in Singapore. The ever benevolent British took Singapore from the indigenous people and developed it into a world-class metropolis. After decades of British rule and culture, the British turned the area over to the indigenous people. But, the emigrant Chinese in the area prevailed, and Singapore remains Chinese. Apparently Judge Wickersham could foresee the Pacific coast becoming another Singapore.

The other major Chinese community in the territory, in Seattle, couldn't meet the November 1 deadline for the Chinese expulsion. On October 15, 1885, the Committee of Fifteen volunteers visited the Chinese quarters and the private homes of whites who had Chinese domestics, to communicate that the Chinese needed to leave. A wit wrote that the upper class households of Seattle didn't like the idea that laborers in heavy boots and cloth caps would pull their door bells to inform them that their Chinese servants had to leave. And, some of these laborers even used the front door. The upper class wrote the description of those organizing to remove the Chinese from the territory: *they were mobs, rioters, rabble, agitators, and generally rowdies without rights to express themselves.* They knew best. In contrast, the laborers at the door of upper class homes, probably with cap in hand, wondered why the householders wouldn't pay American wages for their help and respect their fellow citizens.

The upper class wired the governor for help against the mob. The local sheriff requested troops. Ten companies of troops were sent from the Vancouver Barracks, and martial law was proclaimed. Troops on the train to Seattle were diverted at Tacoma by activists and had to take a steamer to Seattle. In addition, the sheriff called out the home guard and had a revenue cutter brought to a Seattle dock. The cutter pointed its cannon at the city. Nevertheless, the troops — with the governor looking on — were met at the dock with about 300 armed protesters. All was quiet in Seattle for several months.

The Committee of Fifteen was indicted by the grand jury, but were soon free of the indictment. The people had spoken! The verdict for the Seattle Committee of Fifteen paralleled the verdict of the whites and Indians who attacked the hop harvesters who were in their tents asleep. However, a serious murder charge was leveled against the men. Apparently, the anger against the Chinese was so great that there was no jury in the territory that would find the men guilty of protecting their livelihoods; for right or wrong, the people spoke again!

Finally, on September 7, 1886, the so-called Seattle "riot" began. The elected riot leaders led their followers (rabble) and brought the Chinese from their quarters to a steamer that was to take them away from the city. The militia and armed deputies were there to protect the Chinese. However, the steamer captain was served with a writ of habeas corpus. The Chinese were marched back to their quarters.

Ninety-seven Chinese in Seattle appeared in court, and the judge assured them they could stay. But he told the Chinese that the majority of the people in Seattle were hostile to them. The steamer sailed away in the afternoon, loaded to capacity with 196 Chinese aboard, while 150 Chinese remained in Seattle. Meanwhile, the sheriff informed the railroad that they would be charged for kidnapping if they took the Chinese aboard a train.

The 150 Chinese who were turned away from the steamer were marched toward their quarters to await the next steamer that would sail the following week. The marching Chinese were protected by the sheriff and the Home Guards. The protesters interrupted the march and wanted to know why the Chinese were not leaving Seattle. Then someone started shooting. Five people were wounded, one fatally. The casualties were white men, not Chinese. The steamer arrived on February 14, and the Chinese were gone.

Apparently the Territorial Governor Watson Squire and his wife were in a Seattle hotel observing the turmoil. Mrs. Squire described a street filled with angry citizens with words of contempt for the "mob", while the governor issued mild proclamations. Shortly before the citizens' demonstrations, his proclamation was met with emotional contempt by the crowd.

The historians decry the event and describe the citizens' demonstration as "a mob acting with bad behavior" — behavior that represented the will of the majority of the people in Seattle. The progressives could have avoided the casualties and angst easily. The sheriff could have marched the Chinese to the railroad and saved a white man's life along with the anger of everyone. The governor could have issued a proclamation that supported the citizens of the territory. Or, if he had guts and supported his people, he could have faced the angry people in the town square, as could Seattle's mayor, Henry Yesler. But no, the only language the 1880s progressives understood was the use of force against the people of the territory.

The battle between the progressives and the people of the territory was not over. The progressives needed to punish and jail the rioters in Tacoma. Immediately after the people in Tacoma had transported the Chinese out of the city, indictments were returned against twenty-five anti-Chinese residents of the city, including Judge Wickersham. On November 9, 1885, four companies of federal troops and the U.S. Marshall came to Tacoma and took the men into custody. Of course, there was no resistance, a fact that suggests the authorities were completely out of touch with the people they were supposed to serve. A cheering and happy crowd gathered around the criminals, and $5,000 was quickly gathered for the men's defense. The U.S. Attorney later wrote: "the evidence warrants me saying that, short of firing upon the flag of our country, no greater outrage was ever committed against the laws and government of these United States." The U.S. Attorney didn't believe that the people make the laws. Several days later when the indicted men returned to Tacoma, a large crowd gathered again in celebration with a welcome home meeting and a dinner. It took several years of legal nonsense before a grand jury released the men.

The saga of the Chinese riots in the Washington Territory went into the history books, recorded by the progressives. The aristocrats in the country and the world decried the moral tragedy of the riots. It is ironic the Chinese government who held their people in near-slavery berated America and demanded reparations, which they got.

What is carefully obscured in recording the Chinese expulsion, is the result of the election following the riots. The people overwhelming elected anti-Chinese candidates for every office, over their opposition, who were pro-Chinese candidates. The election was one of the few examples in the world where the people prevailed over the tyranny of the aristocratic minority. Further, the people without help from their government; deported a multitude of Chinese without bloodshed. The Chinese were asked to leave, politely, and most did. Certainly they were frightened Chinese taken from their homes and marched to transportation out of the city. However, they chose to be evicted by not heeding requests from the town's citizens. While several Chinese were killed before the riots, the riots prevented further bloodshed. Americans are proud to be ruled by the people. The riots were an example of rule by the people, not a territorial governor and staff appointed by a distant federal capital. The governor was completely out of touch with the people he was supposed to lead.

Today riots are still considered a tragedy. The American people lost something when many of the Chinese were forced to leave the territory. The reality is the territory evolved very well without that Chinese faction and became the envy of the world, while the country of China is still ruled by despots.

The progressives still have their way by labeling the Chinese deportations as a riot, which suggests little rational leadership or controlled behavior. But, Judge Wickersham was an intellectual and proven leader in the community, as were many of his associates who risked their careers and jail time in what they believed was right. Wickersham's dedication to what he thought was his duty to America rivals our founding fathers.

Wickersham's definition of the Chinese situation was even-handed and well thought out, not the emotional tirades of many of the pro-Chinese or the anti-Chinese. He stated emphatically he thought the Chinese were industrious and hardworking, not base and immoral. His concern was that the Chinese emigration in both numbers and organization would overwhelm our American heritage, given what he observed in the 1880s.

Wickersham and his associates certainly stopped the flood of Chinese into the country by taking most of the Chinese out of the work place. There was little market for Chinese labor in the territory for a while. The rough and ready pioneers demanded that the people rule themselves and prevailed over elite progressives with the force of government for support.

Americans have always welcomed people in their midst who wished to melt into their traditions and further American justice. However, the Chinese of the 1800s were funded and controlled by Chinese businessmen whose slave-like work force largely owed their loyalty to China. Where else could China extract free gold from a country and return the resource to their homeland? Progressives of the 1800s and the present are either ignorant or conceal the facts in their effort to control the American masses. And, this control was a struggle between the rich and poor, a struggle that partially inspired the communist revolution that created the Soviet Union after the First World War, a revolution that could have swamped the U.S. except for our pioneer heritage.

The contracted foreign labor didn't end with the Chinese expulsion. Foreign labor was contracted sporadically in American commerce later.

In the 1920s, my uncle in Port Angeles observed imported Japanese stevedores housed in warehouse quarters on the waterfront, where they replaced striking American stevedores. My uncle, at about age eight, joined older youths to throw rocks onto the tin roof of the sleeping Japanese quarters. Awakened angry Japanese rushed out of their bunks to chase the fleeing youths, almost catching my young uncle. The Japanese soon left Port Angeles and left stevedoring to local Americans.

PORT ANGELES, THE BEGINNING

The Puget Sound villages were growing into towns and even cities by 1860, but Port Angeles was nearly an unknown name when its founder came to the Northwest from the east. Victor Smith was unlike the founders of the earlier towns who had crossed the plains in covered wagons or came by ship to build a business or farm. Smith, to be polite, was a promoter whose interest was singularly aimed at promoting himself through use of government connections and influence.

Port Angeles came to the attention of the politicians in Washington City (Washington DC) when the first governor of the territory, now the Washington Territory's Congressional delegate, proposed a significant naval station be constructed at Port Angeles. Governor Stevens believed the Sound's security was in jeopardy with the status quo. He compared the Port Angeles location to the famous French naval fortress at Cherberg in France. In Stevens' opinion, Port Angeles should be the American "Cherberg of the Pacific". Of course, his dream remained a dream.

However, Smith saw an investment opportunity and bought out a homesteader's claim while buying into the Cherbourg Land Company who claimed to control three and a half miles of beach in Port Angeles. The envious citizens of Port Townsend were infuriated at Stevens' Cherbourg proposal and hung him in effigy in protest, an honorable American tradition that has been ignored by today's community leaders.

Smith had invested in Port Angeles and needed a government position to take him to the Sound. Fortunately for Smith, he was an old friend of Salmon Portland Chase, President Lincoln's secretary of the treasury. Both men were abolitionists, anti-Lincoln, and had business deals between them. Chase needed a promoter in the territory to support his vision to run for president.

Chase appointed Smith as collector for the Puget Sound Customs District and a special agent of the treasury. Smith's office was in Port Townsend, a location that a clique in Washington City had already secretly decided should be in Port Angeles. Smith took the wearisome sea voyage from New York to Portland, which included an ox cart crossing of the Isthmus of Panama, then canoe and wagon up the Cowlitz Corridor and finally by steamer from Olympia to Port Townsend. He arrived in Port Townsend at 2 a.m. with his wife and three children. Four men came with him for promised jobs, jobs that would presumably vacate local people from positions so as to assure loyalty to him.

Smith immediately started to alienate Port Townsend's citizens. He took over the local paper for a few months through trickery and treated the citizens with attacks on President Lincoln's policies, along with a multitude of séances and messages from the other world. Then, he moved the Marine Hospital out of Port Townsend to Fort Townsend and replaced the managing doctor with his own doctor. The new doctor was forced to pay $1000 out of his salary to one of Smith's organizations. He also charged the government $40 per month for the hospital's use of the fort's vacant building that serviced as the hospital.

In 1862, Smith left for Washington City on business. He couldn't trust anyone to look after his customs business — so he had a reluctant Lt. James H. Merryman from the local customs cutter assigned to the job. But, Merryman was honest and inquisitive and soon discovered Smith was not bonded; therefore his government appointment was invalid. He also discovered the illegal paybacks from the Marine Hospital. Even more serious, Smith had sold a surplus cutter without permission and apparently pocketed the proceeds. Also, two financial entities were holding government money for Smith. Merryman sent his findings to President Lincoln and others.

However before action was taken on Merryman's report, Smith returned from Washington City aboard the cutter *Shubrick,* When it docked at Port Townsend, Smith rushed ashore to the Customs House to find Merryman had locked himself inside and refused entry to Smith, telling him he had no authority. Smith returned to the *Shubrick* and ordered armed sailors to take control of the Customs House. Merryman turned the sailors away. Smith then ordered the *Shubrick's* captain to shell the Customs House and the town. The captain removed solid shells from the *Shubrick's* cannons and re-loaded them with grapeshot and shrapnel, shells that would have leveled the Customs House and killed innumerable town citizens.

Merryman gave up the Customs House. Apparently he felt Smith was not bluffing. The shelling of an American town by an American vessel would have sent shock waves throughout the country, resulting in Smith and the captain labeled as American pariahs in the history books. Since murder was avoided and communications in that era moved at a snail's pace, the people in Port Townsend were the only folks aware of the near-tragedy. Politics moved on as usual.

Nevertheless, ten days later on August 11, 1862, the governor of the territory arrived in Port Townsend with an examining board. The board swore out an arrest warrant for Smith, charging him with assault with intent to kill. Almost the whole town swore to Smith's intent. Smith was on the *Shubrick* anchored in the harbor at Port Townsend. The U.S. marshal took a small boat to the *Shubrick* to serve the warrant on Smith. The captain forced the marshal off the *Shubrick* into his small boat before he sailed off into Canadian waters. The frustrated authorities went back to Olympia to study the situation.

The *Shubrick* returned to Port Townsend early the next morning and moved the Marine Hospital from Fort Townsend to Port Angeles, sans its doctor-manager who by this time was a Smith enemy. Smith had successfully moved his establishment to Port Angeles and thwarted the territory's authorities. Smith's entourage increased the population several fold to the benefit of the twenty Port Angeles citizens, while the Port Townsend folks seethed with anger.

The town began to grow. People were employed to build the Customs House and the Marine Hospital, and to staff both facilities. In two years, the town numbered 200 citizens — but the boom was not forthcoming. Ships clearing at the Customs House didn't tarry long since there were no supplies to replenish the ships needs or social amenities or adequate saloons for the crews. The ships hurried to Port Townsend and other Sound ports for their needs and cargos. There was no industry and little farming at that time near Port Angeles. The village stagnated.

Meanwhile, Smith's vision became a reality. An act of Congress officially transferred the Custom House from Port Townsend to Port Angeles, and the Port Townsend people again hung Smith in effigy. President Lincoln signed an executive order making a federal reserve out of Port Angeles. The secretary of the treasury, Chase, sold the reserve on the basis that federal land should be sold to help finance the Civil War. Almost immediately lots were auctioned off, and $4,500 was received from the sale — not an amount that would contribute to the Civil War needs.

The self-serving manipulators of the Port Townsend/Port Angeles affair met with disaster shortly after the Customs House was moved. President Lincoln accepted Chase's resignation as secretary of the treasurer, and Smith drowned off the coast of Oregon when returning to Port Angeles from Washington City. However, earlier in Smith's voyage home, he was involved in another shady adventure. As a treasury agent, he was required to transport a fortune of government money from Washington to San Francisco. His ship was wrecked north of the Isthmus in the Caribbean Islands; the money disappeared, and Smith accused the ship's captain of theft. The captain was exonerated. The money was never found.

Perhaps the most ironic event, although tragic, of the Customs House move occurred on December 16, 1863. The Customs House was built near the mouth of Valley Creek, a small innocuous stream flowing through Port Angeles. On that December day, a flood of water burst from the headwaters of the creek to sweep the Custom House into the Port Angeles harbor. Two customs men were killed, while one escaped. The records were recovered, but the ink was washed away leaving blank paper. The empty strong box was washed into the harbor and recovered by an Indian. It was speculated the creek was dammed with a landslide, which collapsed to form a torrent of water, a natural event that never occurred again, perhaps because human activities stabilized the creek. Port Townsend lost the Customs House to Port Angeles amid turmoil and angst to ironically have it returned to Port Townsend in 1866, events that had little to do with the development of the North Olympic Peninsula.

The Customs House activity created a flurry of activity at Port Angeles, and then it was quiet until the Puget Sound Cooperative Colony was formed in October 1885. The Colony chose Port Angeles as home for their vision of Utopia. In the summer of 1887 there were 250 Colonists in Port Angeles. By fall, the number totaled 400. The Colony bought property on the east boundary of the town at the mouth of Ennis Creek, while the locals were settled on the west side, creating the east-siders versus the west-siders. The west-siders were fearful of what appeared to them to be radical progressives.

Judge Peter Good was the Colony's inspiration. The judge, believing Utopia could be established in Puget Sound, visited Mexico and France to observe reform, enabled by cooperative and communal living. It was easy to sell his associate in Seattle, George Venable Smith, his vision of Utopia. Smith was a prominent California lawyer who became the Seattle Attorney in 1885. He and Good became involved in the Seattle anti-Chinese movement and had the audacity to meet with the so-called "radical labor agitators". Like Wickersham, both men went to jail until the "people's jury" freed them. Good died shortly after being released from jail. Some people attributed stress from the humiliation of being put in jail as the cause of his death.

The Colonists visualized cooperative living, cooperative hotels, and cooperative industries, plus free medical care, no taxes and lifelong security, and no unemployment, along with housing in a beautiful model city. Certainly, Port Angeles was the setting for this beautiful city. Smith and Good were looking to get away from the economic turmoil in Seattle and Tacoma, along with the Chinese culture.

Modern writers applaud the Colonists' vision to better themselves. The Colonists believed in an eight-hour, five-day work schedule, equal pay for men and women, and other concepts adopted in today's America. Today's observers believe the Colonists, on the average, were intellectually superior to any other community of that era in the nation; still they were denigrated for their bigotry.

The Port Angeles west-siders immediately resented the Colonists because of their intellect, arrogance, and radical ideas. Above all, they were not *normal* pioneers. The colony published a newspaper, *The Model Common Wealth* that expressed its radical views vividly. An eight-hour day and women rights were disturbing to the west-siders. When the *Commonwealth* published its opinion on the Haymarket Square Riot executions, the west-siders knew they had a problem. On May 4, 1886 a mob of anarchists rioted in Chicago's Haymarket, killing eleven people, including seven policemen. *Four* anarchists were hanged for the murders. The *Commonwealth* denigrated the American justice system; the west-siders applauded the justice system, perhaps creating the most divided community in the nation. There was hope though; both communities agreed on the Chinese problem.

The Colonists had the talent and motivation to start the Colony working immediately with vigor when the 400-plus people arrived in Port Angeles in 1887. First they cleared a roadway from the commercial boat landing to the colony to eliminate the arduous beach pathway. Some land was soon cleared, crops planted, timber felled, and buildings constructed. More important to many, the newspaper immediately blasted out its motto: "Let the many combine in cooperation as the few have done in corporations". Sadly, they had not learned from the history of Port Gamble, Seabeck, and other pioneer towns.

The Colony went on to influence the total Port Angeles community in many ways. Even though their detractors accused them of being atheists, they founded five churches in the community. They built the first sawmill, the first schoolhouse, and the first office building in town. And of course, they brought a newspaper to the community, even though it represented only the Colonists' views at first. In their waning days, the Colonists put in place an eight-hour work day and the first old age and health insurance. They even designed and constructed several ships. In addition, they contributed leadership in developing a modern school system for the community.

The lasting contribution to the community was the design and building of the Opera House in the center of the west end of town on Front Street between Laurel and Lincoln. It was a shared responsibility between the two groups, east and west. The Colonists' energy made it a symbol of reverence and unity for three decades in Port Angeles. Unfortunately by the mid-1888s the Colony was near bankruptcy, and by 1889, the operating Colony was gone.

What Happened? After the initial euphoria of the Colonists' reach for nirvana, reality came to the forefront. First, the Colony was formed by dreamers and lawyers with no experience in leadership or finances. They didn't like money or taxes, so they eliminated a method to raise money. However, their activities demanded a form of money to reward work within the Colony, so they printed script, which was useless outside the Colony. This system failed, and the script was soon devalued. The lawsuits soon followed between the individual Colonists and their organization. The Colonists wanted what they thought was full value for their efforts.

The concept of communal living demanded complete cooperation and unselfishness among people, which is foreign to human nature. The leaders soon became arbitrary for what they thought was better for the Colony to the exclusion of the rank and file. In addition, the people were exposed to activities of the ordinary western town whose people independently made commercial deals to better themselves as individuals. Communal living afforded little privacy.

Finally, many of the Colonists were productive, while many were not. Their organization could not efficiently rid themselves of non-productive people. The goal was to work an eight-hour day, with a shortened work week, while the rest of society worked from dawn until dark and then by candlelight to obtain the finer things for their individual families. This was especially true of homesteaders who quite often worked the farms and held outside jobs.

The Colonists couldn't or wouldn't work hard enough to improve themselves enough to compete with the pioneer society. Hence the Colony was bankrupt.

With the liquidation of the Colony, many left Port Angeles, but many stayed to join the folks on the west side. Marriages between the two groups became routine. The Colonists' leader, George Venable Smith, was elected judge and became a town leader, while a Colonist woman ran for the U.S. House of Representatives — the first woman in the state to do so. The merger of the east side Colonists with the ordinary westsiders made for a solid community, a community of diverse talents that other communities weren't favored with.

In 1890, Port Angeles had a vigorous population on the move, but no place to go. The town sat mostly on the beach hemmed in by the federal government's reserve of about 3,000 acres. The reserve precluded them from moving off the beach; some say it was because of the reserve and the impenetrable Douglas fir forest. The impenetrable forest was only impenetrable to city-bred folks, not to Americans who wanted land for farms, homes, and industry.

Fortunately, an Irish lawyer who loved a raucous town arrived in Port Angeles from Olympia in 1890 and was made aware of the reserve problem by the frustrated citizens. John C. Murphy quickly determined the government reserve was for *the people*, and *the people* lived in Port

Angeles. There were numerous requests by the people to open the reserve — to no avail. Murphy reasoned the only alternative was for the people to occupy the reserve. He and the citizens had numerous rallies, meetings, and probably lots of saloon talk, and it was determined that on the Fourth of July 1890 the citizens would become squatters and occupy the reserve.

The morning of the Fourth, a multitude of squatters moved into the reserve with surveying equipment, land clearing tools, and tents, in homesteader fashion. It was not like the Oklahoma land rush, but orderly, without government leadership. These were American individuals who fairly cut the reserve pie into lots of equal size, with no more than two for one family. The forest (reserve) was lighted with lanterns at night, somewhat like a city. The original squatters were joined by others. They waited for two and half years before Congress acted in their favor. In that long interim, the squatters wrote bundles of letters to the authorities while they sweated out a trespass summons or titles to their new home.

In January 1, 1894, government officials gathered to pass out deeds to the squatters on their proof of compliance, confirmed with witnesses and, of course, payment fees. Some new owners became emotional, while others celebrated at the saloons. Following the squatters obtaining title, the rest of the reservation was put up for an auction that lasted twenty days. The whole affair was done orderly because a united community neutralized any disruptive individual who might want to manipulate the system to their advantage. For example, one of the squatters was a widow who was out of town, and all she had was her lot. When her lot number came up, no one bid against her. The force of public fairness silently prevailed.

By the beginning of 1894, Port Angeles was a whole town of 3,000, united physically and socially. The rush for land into the reserve defined the American passion for land ownership. Families, widows, and single men were willing to live in tents and shanties for more than two and a half years before obtaining a lot in the reserve free. The squatters' sacrifice of amenities for free land is beyond the understanding of modern society. However, there is a downside to this emotion. In 1896, 17,000 parcels of land were confiscated by the county for delinquent taxes and put on the market for resale. Apparently numerous landowners did not have the cash to pay their taxes to an unforgiving county government. The county carried a large inventory of property acquired through tax delinquency.

In the 1940s, my grandfather bought about ten acres of tax delinquent property adjacent to his Freshwater farm and deeded it to me for my college education. I was thrilled to be a landowner, until I got the modest tax bill. The acreage contained 50-year-old second growth Douglas fir that had no market value. Hence no revenue could be obtained from the property, and it couldn't graze my grandfather's cows. Fortunately in 1952, I found a buyer for the property, which paid several quarters of college tuition for a near-starving college student.

There is a lesson to be learned: A property owner must have a cash income from the property or income independent of the property to keep the government from claiming it. In pioneer days, the only income from rural property came from agriculture or timber, and both products had to be accessible to a market to generate cash income to pay taxes. Most of the timber was inaccessible until a private company funded and built a railroad to an area. Property taxes were onerous to the property owner and no less to the counties. The counties needed the tax revenues to fund the almost non-existent infrastructure, like roads, bridges, and schools. In the mid-to-late 1800s, the majority of the county's land was in the public domain and not taxable. Many county improvements were funded by subscription, that is, donation of funds by citizens with discretionary money.

THE RAPE OF THE OLYMPIC PENINSULA

The pioneers on the north Olympic Peninsula and the entire West were well on the way to converting the wilderness into American communities. The basis for the success was their American heritage and the use of the transfer of the public domain to the private sector as fast as the Americans could utilize it. The land was transferred to the public by the Homestead Act, Preemption Act, grants, and land sales.

The Olympic Peninsula was almost taken away from its residents with the implementation of Forest Reserves in 1891. The Forest Reserve action was the dream of mostly academics and the start of the progressive, environmental or green movement in the United States to control land use in America and the people. The progressive aristocrats were mostly people of inherited wealth and academics. They conversely and inadvertently created peasants — that is, the settler pioneers and laborers. The peasants who created excessive wealth for themselves and their communities were labeled by the aristocrats as selfish or even criminal because they raped the wilderness land to create communities. The aristocrats' agenda was to create or maintain the wilderness. In fulfilling their agenda, in effect, they raped the people on the Olympic Peninsula and the West, starting in the 1890s and continuing to the present. Following is the history of the progressive creation and implementation of their agenda.

In 1891, Congress voted to authorize the President by executive order to withdraw land from the public domain for forest reserves. This law reversed more than a hundred years of total land transfer to the citizens. The Forest Reserve legislation did not earn its own legislation;

it was enacted on a rider of an appropriation bill without discussion or even a clear-cut vote. Again, a law was put into place by the East without any communication with the needs of the West. President Benjamin Harrison signed the Forest Reserve Order in 1892, which created the Yellowstone National Park. During his administration, thirteen million acres were pulled out of the public domain to become forest reserves. It was unconscionable that Congress set aside thirteen million acres without provisions to administer or protect this massive area of land.

The American Forestry Association was the driving force pushing the Forest Reserve legislation through Congress. The Association was formed by a physician and horticulturist, Dr. John Aston Warder, who convened people who were interested in the forest in Chicago in 1875. They formed the Association, which soon expanded into similar groups throughout the country. Dr. Bernhard Fernow was hired to lead the organization as its general secretary. He was a strong-willed German forester who was given the position because there were few American foresters available at that time. The Association became a powerful education and political force whose goal was the creation of forest reserves. The effort helped create state legislation resulting in forest fire laws. However, catastrophic fires in the country were the real driving incentive for state fire law.

A diverse group of association members held little expertise in land use. One was a German emigrant employed by the Department of the Interior, who wrote official reports debunking the "inexhaustible timber" theory embraced by the lumbering interests, settlers, and woods workers. His official reports supported the Association's major thought to preserve the timber in the reserves.

A second German emigrant member was in sharp contrast to the rank and file members. He was Fredrick Weyerhaeuser, "timber baron", from a class of people the Association generally believed selfish, corrupt, and desperately in need of government supervision. Weyerhaeuser repeatedly spoke of being in business for the long term and was interested in learning more on how that might be accomplished technically and economically. His immediate concern was wild fires in the forest, and hoped the Association would advance public and political education to address the wrath of fire. Weyerhaeuser and his peers knew forest management was impossible given the fire devastation in the late 1800s and early 1900s. A self-made man, contrary to most members of the American Forestry Association, he started his career as a roustabout in a lumber yard.

The Association, Congress, and the President quietly took millions of acres out of the public domain without informing the public, particularly the western public. Finally, the western people became aware of the progressives' intentions to dominate the West and actively fought against forest reserves to defeat any effort by the Association in Congress to further their forest reserves strategy. In desperation, the Association turned to the federal bureaucracy in the form of the Secretary of the Interior; the Secretary was requested to ask the National Academy of Sciences for a status report on the nation's forests.

In turn, the Academy formed a Commission. In 1896, the Commission was formed of eastern intellectuals that included Professor Charles Sargent, an eminent arbor culturist who chaired the group. In the group were an engineer, a hydrographer, a Yale botanist and agriculturists, and prominent geologists. Gifford Pinchot, a neophyte American forester, served as secretary. John Muir, an American naturalist, was asked to join the group, but declined because he thought he would be more effective in selling his forest preservation agenda as an observer during the Commission's activities.

The Commission started on a three-months tour of the West on July 2, 1896. They spent most of their time at scenic areas like Yellowstone and Crater Lake instead of surveying the operating forests of the West. There was virtually no news coverage to inform those vitally interested in their agenda. Muir and Pinchot spent some of their time fishing and sleeping under the stars, while the rest of the Commission utilized the better hotels in the areas they visited.

Almost immediately after returning to the East the Commission sent a summary report to the Secretary of the Interior that presumptuously recommended thirteen new forest reserves be created immediately by President Grover Cleveland. The President created 21,000,000 acres of addition forest reserves on February 22, 1897. It took the Commission about eight short months from the time it started a secret study for them to transfer millions of acres of public domain land to forest reserves — without public input. The West was outraged.

Four days after the President created the new forest reserves, 30,000 people in Deadwood, South Dakota, held a mass meeting to protest the President's action. The people *stated* it would "affect disastrously all the mining and dependent industries of the region and largely compel its depopulation". A Wyoming senator called Cleveland's action "an outrageous act of arbitrary power as a czar or sultan ever conceived." Another senator from Wyoming called it "an order without the authority of law." *The Seattle Post-Intelligencer* said in part: "At best, the only title which the federal government ever had to the land was based upon concessions which the new states were compelled to make as the price of their admission into the Union."

John L. Wilson from Washington State represented the West's anger best: "It would seem that it was impossible for the people west of the Missouri River to develop their own domain and their own country in their own way.... The people who first settled in New England came and took thousands of acres of land and developed them as they saw fit, and the people who passed from New England across the Alleghany Mountains and settled in the Mississippi Valley took up their lands at $1.25 an acre without those restrictions required under the Homestead Act of 1860.... Our people have had to go forward and develop their country by law, and they have observed the law insofar as it has been possible for any to do so. They do not complain of this. It is right and proper and just. What they do complain of is that their material interests — those very things that affect their prosperity and advancement, nay their very existence as Commonwealths — shall be disposed of by the stroke of the pen, as though we were mere provinces and not sovereign states of this great Union."

Wilson concluded his remarks with a bitter denunciation of the "eastern friends who are so extremely solicitous for our happiness and our prosperity and our growth and our development, who control our incomings and our outgoings with such liberality upon their part." And, "Why should we be everlastingly and eternally harassed and annoyed and bedeviled by these scientific gentlemen from Harvard College?"

The western firestorm over President Cleveland's reserves led to further Congressional action to invalidate the reserves, and the West hoped that the eastern politicians would desire to quiet the westerners. The East had the votes and prevailed. In 1897, the Administration of the Reserves was enacted. The only significant concession was a declaration stating the reserves were established "for the purpose of securing favorable conditions of water flows and to furnish a continuous supply of timber for the use and necessities of the citizens of the United States."

To further the perceived western view of the eastern tyranny of the eastern intellectuals, Gifford Pinchot was appointed as special forest agent for the Department of the Interior to finalize the reserve boundaries. Pinchot, secretary for the Commission and a strong advocate of massive reserves, saw an opportunity to increase the current reserves by a million acres. Looking for advice, Pinchot wrote to his associate, John Muir, the preservation/naturalist. Muir replied, "when running the new boundaries of the new reservations, no doubt small changes should be made. But for every acre you cut off, fail not, I charge you to add a hundred or thousand." These were the men who questioned the ethics of the timber barons and their like.

The Commission brought about change. However, the members soon disappeared from influence. Pinchot and Muir had an almost dominant influence on the Commission's recommendations to Congress and the President. They would dominate the conservation movement, later to be called the progressive/conservation movement, for decades.

Gifford Pinchot was born in 1865 and died in 1946. He was born into a family of great wealth and political influence in the Republican Party. His father made his fortune in lumber and land speculation, an activity that apparently troubled his conscience, as he encouraged his son to study forestry to enable him to reform what he thought was a disordered land system. The father and mother carefully guided and funded his education to further his career as a forester first and a politician second.

Pinchot graduated from the exclusive Phillips Exeter Academy and went on to Yale to graduate in 1889 where he was active in many outside activities, including the notorious Skull and Bones. He excelled in debate, allied with communication skills. The family endowed the Yale School of Forestry in 1900, making it arguably, the most prestigious forestry school in the United States. Further, Pinchot was closely associated with friends and scholars at Yale, and for the rest of his life he utilized the forestry graduates, who went to work for the government, to further his own political career.

The family's wealth and influence opened many doors for Pinchot that were closed for others. In 1889 a young Pinchot, fresh from graduating from Yale, and a friend casually visited the governor of New York — Teddy Roosevelt.

Immediately after Yale, Pinchot studied as a post-graduate at the French National Forestry School for a year and was encouraged to go on for a PhD; but he was anxious to return to the U.S. to use his talents in selling his view of forestry to his own country. Besides his formal training, his family opened doors to the leading forestry experts in the Old World. Two Old World foresters became confidants and advisors for the rest of his life. The two foresters were academics with little experience outside of the aristocratic Old World.

In 1898, Pinchot was made Chief of the Division of Forestry, in the Department of Agriculture, when the forest reserves were the responsibility of the Department of the Interior. Much to his frustration, he had little influence over the government's forestland. He could only educate and advise the private and government landowners. However, that didn't cool his crusade to bring his form of forestry to America. When Pinchot became chief, the staff numbered only 60; he quickly increased it to 500. The Pinchot forest crusade became sponsored by the government. An aggressive education program was implemented that included public and private, and almost more importantly, the American public.

In addition, the forest reserve boundaries were examined by his foresters to prepare for future expansion. His goal was to control America's forests.

Pinchot was probably the first in the country to discard what he considered a corrupt system of political patronage. He believed the government should employ only those who merited their position, based on education, experience, and passing a civil service examination. His government group demanded professionalism built around certified foresters, and they rejected political patronage. This philosophy, along with a dedication to principals of forest management, brought together people devoted to each other and the forests of America.

However, there were numerous differences in the group on the meaning of forest management. To complement his demand for professionalism and certification, Pinchot established the Society of American Foresters (SAF) that was independent of employment, but dedicated to the forests and the growing of trees. The SAF brought credibility to the profession of forestry and its ideals, which led to a professional movement in the United States in other sciences. The SAF went on to certify forestry colleges and universities and to publish a prestigious professional magazine. Pinchot is commonly referred to as the Father of American Professional Foresters.

Pinchot's vision for the American forests became achievable when Teddy Roosevelt became President in 1901. Roosevelt quickly moved the nation's public forests from the Department of Interior to Agriculture with the approval of Congress in 1905, creating a meaningful Forest Service with Pinchot as its chief. Pinchot became the real power behind the conservation progressive movement with a like-minded President as an expeditor. The President probably consulted with Pinchot more than any other person. By the end of Roosevelt's administration

Pinchot's Forest Service had grown to an organization of 1,500 men in charge of 150 million acres of timber, valued at about $1 billion. He had a powerful organization that seemed able to overpower any other private or public interest.

However, the conservative battle was invigorated by the Act of 1907 which repealed the Forest Reserve Act of 1891. The President could not by executive order create forest reserves in six timbered states without the approval of Congress. Ten percent of the forest revenue would go to the counties in which the reserve was located for schools and roads. The Act of 1907 was a major victory for the people of the West. Some would say dirty politics still prevailed. Roosevelt/Pinchot proclaimed twenty-one new forest reserves in six northwest states on the day before his executive order privilege to create forest reserves was abolished. So, Roosevelt and Pinchot increased the National Forest three-fold during Roosevelt's tenure as President.

Alaska revolted against Roosevelt's order of 1908 that withdrew coal deposits on public land in Alaska from lease or sale. Most Alaskans believed Pinchot was responsible for the order. The Alaskans' view of Pinchot was said to be: "No patents for coal, all timber to the forest reserves, bottle up Alaska, and save Alaska for all time to come." They burned an effigy of Pinchot as their own "King George III" and dumped imported coal into Cordova's harbor as their "tea party" protest. They labeled him as the man who "thinks more of trees than people."

In March 1909, William Howard Taft replaced Roosevelt as President, and Pinchot had to work with a President who was not fully aligned with his conservative principles. Richard Ballinger, the Secretary of the Department of the Interior, validated coal claims near Katalla, Alaska — claims that were sold to a corporate mining firm that was about to develop the coal resource.

Pinchot, with conservative zeal, contested the transaction as fraudulent and should be invalidated. President Taft thought otherwise, and Pinchot took his position to the public via the media. Ballinger did likewise. The internal fight in the President's administration was intolerable, and Taft terminated Pinchot's services in 1910. He had served from 1905 to 1910 as chief forester and was the highest forest authority in America, a very short period for a man of his prestige and ability.

The Alaskan protest illustrated his glaring weakness. He fought Ballinger because he believed the proposed coal mine would only serve to enrich a greedy corporation, who without his supervision would endanger the environment. The corporation did not revolt. The people in Alaska revolted. They wanted the jobs and wealth that an operating mine would produce. Pinchot ignored the local people, destroyed his honorable adversary Ballinger and, arguably President Taft. He always contended he was doing his work for the people — but they were only like-minded people. Pinchot had spent millions of his and the government's funds in educating the public to his vision. The views of the local people whose livelihood was a stake were ignored.

The Ballinger/Pinchot fight was resolved, but the effects carried over to the 1912 presidential election. Taft represented the historic Republicans that the Roosevelt/Pinchot Republican progressives (conservatives) abhorred. It was critical to the progressives that the Roosevelt/Pinchot principles be protected and expanded. So, a progressive third party was formed, with Teddy Roosevelt as their candidate for President. It was commonly called the Bull Moose Party, a name that symbolized Teddy Roosevelt. Pinchot served as the principal strategist, speechwriter, and fundraiser for the progressive party that was wholly dominated by Roosevelt's personality. Apparently the American people rejected the progressive movement; the Democrat, Woodrow Wilson, won handily.

The progressive vision was to implement federal control of land use as defined by Gifford Pinchot. His influence was greatest when he was Chief of the Forest Service and had the resources of a federal bureaucracy and a like-minded President to further his agenda. After leaving the Forest Service, Pinchot's influence continued to be substantial because of his talent, dedication, political, and academic friends, plus his personal wealth.

Pinchot was a crusader. He started his crusade in school and began to implement his vision in 1898 when he became Chief of the Division of Forestry, a Division whose sole responsibility was to educate; and educate he did. But, he soon formed an opinion that the government and the major private timber people could not be educated and were perhaps even corrupt. In his opinion, the big timber men, ranchers, and miners were greedy without any social or environmental conscience. So, he concentrated his education talent on the academics and the people, that is, mostly the eastern people.

Timber supply was Pinchot's primary concern. He predicted the nation would run out of timber in a few short decades, which drove his efforts to build massive Forest Reserves, 150 million acres, before Congress stopped the expansion. However, expansion of government ownership continues to the present day. Ironically, there was no timber famine, and most of the country's wood products were sourced from private timberlands.

Pinchot was certain that vast areas would be devastated where timber was being harvested. His major concern was that the forest was being converted to a wasteland. He envisioned a North Africa, along with other historic areas, where permanent deforestation had occurred. In the early 1900s, his protégé, William Greeley, said the Forest Service had no feeling or information on regeneration. Pinchot claimed he was basing his conclusions on science, but science is built on facts, of which he had few.

Simple observations of the primeval Douglas fir forests tells us that these forests were created by devastating fires over vast watersheds that resulted in even-aged fir forests that regenerated naturally following fires. The extensive Douglas fir forests of western Washington and Oregon were a mosaic of primeval even-age trees as old as about eight hundred years. Pinchot decried the devastation left by loggers, but largely ignored the devastating wildfires during this time that were burning millions of acres a year — and sometimes burning the same areas over and over again. If he was a scientific observer, he would have concluded that the fir forests were created by fires and could, in turn, be duplicated by clear-cut logging that were actually regenerating harvests that perpetuated the forests.

The waste wood left after logging dismayed Pinchot and others. A scientist would have been aware of the massive biomass in a Douglas fir forest and lack of markets for the total tree. Over the decades, landowners have searched for markets for the total biomass — such as tree limbs. It has been a slow process to market the whole tree. Landowners would never waste something of value. Even today, they seek a market for biofuel that would eliminate the last increment of waste in the woods, that is, limbs, broken pieces, and brush. Progressives today are being obstructionists by fighting biofuel for electric generating facilities.

Foresters probably defined the concept of sustainability. In the late 1800s, Pinchot believed all forests should be sustainable, and a sustained yield of forest wood was sacred. All forest landowners thought in these terms. One simple definition of *sustainability* is: "harvest (logging) equals growth". In the Douglas fir region, the growth should be about 1,000 board feet per acre per year on good, well-managed land (or one quarter of a truck load of logs). So, a landowner who owned 40 acres could harvest 40,000 board feet a year or ten truck loads of logs. The goal of sustained yield was to stabilize the forest communities, forest landowners, and the nation's timber supply. But the application is complicated and is best not left to a central federal bureaucracy.

Pinchot feared the forest land would be monopolized by a few aristocratic landowners to the detriment of the forest communities. His solution was to form the biggest monopoly of all, the government ownership of hundreds of millions of acres controlled by a fickle government of aristocrats (like him) and academics hundreds or thousands of miles away from the people making a livelihood in the forest communities. The people in Alaska between 1908 and 1910 reflected how they felt about Pinchot when they called him "King George III".

Pinchot couldn't acquire all of the forest land for the government and believed he couldn't educate the private landowners, so he turned to a third solution. He sought federal regulation of all private land to dictate his vision of forestry across all forest lands. But, private landowners had enough political influence to defeat this proposal. Therefore, later in his life he proposed a government takeover of all forest lands as the ultimate solution, one similar to Mao Tse Tung's in China and Josef Stalin's in Russia — where millions starved.

In 1896, Pinchot started his education of private timber interests and was frustrated with their skepticism. His condemnation of clear-cutting universally across the American landscape must have confounded the private timber owners in western Washington and Oregon Douglas fir forests. Pinchot demanded partial harvest of the trees by continual cutting stages, which could create an uneven age forest, that is, small trees intermingled with large trees.

From the mid-1800s to the 1950s, most of the timber harvest utilized old-big trees in the Douglas fir forests, because they composed most of the existing forests. The few younger forests of small trees had scant market value. These forests were mostly even-aged, that is, big trees were not intermingled with small trees. The young or small trees (mostly under 100 years old) produced lumber the public market shunned. The large Douglas fir tree forest contained about 50 trees per acre, trees that varied between 190 to 310 feet tall and four to six feet in diameter at the base.

The fir forest could have an understory of smaller hemlock or other species, which had little value. Of course, there is variation in all the forests. The big trees were spaced randomly about 40 feet apart and mostly obscured the sun from the forest floor, which prohibited or inhibited growth of understory trees.

When felled, a giant fir hits the ground and makes a sound similar to a large charge of dynamite. With the span of its limbs, which could be more than ten inches in diameter, the falling tree would destroy everything in its path for about 200 hundred feet distance and 20 feet wide. When the trees were on the ground, they were bucked (cut) into logs and dragged hundreds of feet by cable to a railroad or truck road. Again, the huge logs destroyed everything in their path.

Pinchot was asking the private timber owners to do this destructive process two or three times. The second and third logging of the same area would be almost as destructive as the first. And, the residual trees from the first logging would have been damaged. Regeneration (if any) after the first logging would be mostly destroyed in the second logging.

The stage logging of the even-age big tree Douglas fir forest disturbs the synergistic protection against the wind incorporated in the forests. The removal of some trees leaves the remaining trees exposed to the full force of the wind that usually results in part or whole destruction of the residual trees.

I observed forty acres of residual trees blown over during a mild windstorm. The Douglas fir forest was composed of about thirty trees that were 400 years old, and averaged 250 feet in height and five feet in diameter at the base. Half of the trees had been logged and removed from the site six months prior to the windstorm. Almost all of the trees crashed to the ground, with many of them splintered as they hit the stumps created by the first logging or by falling across uneven ground. If the residual trees had been cut by loggers, they would have been directionally felled away from stumps and broken ground, and saved. A similar forest of big trees located adjacent to the stage logging suffered little windfall.

The biomass in the Douglas fir forest exceeded that of any forest in America with the exception of the redwood forest. Until the mid-1900s, only a small portion was marketable. That is, no one would buy decayed and knotty lumber, and the mills that utilized small defective wood were in their infancy. Therefore, the biomass (wood) residual was heaped on the landscape, undulating from several feet deep to much deeper, with barely any exposure of mineral soil that is critical for seedling survival. Seed cast from adjacent trees had trouble reaching mineral soil, making tree planting difficult if not impossible.

Pinchot and his Forest Service decried waste of the forest destruction with criticism, but no solution. Private forest owners wanted to sell all the biomass, but needed a market. They finally came up with a solution that was adopted by the Forest Service after Pinchot left. They broadcast-burned the logged areas to moderate the fire threat. Woody debris (slash), deep and tinder dry on the landscape, would burst into fire given an innocuous spark, while green timber needed extreme conditions for fire to occur. In addition, the elimination of the slash created an ideal seedbed to culture the seed cast from trees outside the logged and burned area.

This process mimicked nature that created sequential forests over the centuries by means of destructive fires. This phenomenon was validated by the even-aged fir forest throughout the range of the species. The several hundred thousand acres of fir forest west of Coos Bay, OR was 200 years old, and west of Eugene, OR was 350 years old. These primeval forests of various ages were repeated across the region. The Douglas fir forest region is unique, but there are similarities in all other regions. The tree or plant needs a seedbed (generally mineral soil), full sunlight, and little or no competition for optimum growth.

Historians can write volumes about Pinchot's legacy in praise or condemnation, but his legacy should be defined with case histories. His legacy can be related to one of his namesakes, The Gifford Pinchot National Forest in southwest Washington State. The city of Longview, WA is the largest town tributary to the forest. Longview was planned and built by Long Bell Timber Company. Long Bell built a huge sawmill there in the 1920s and bought thousands of acres from another timber company that had obtained most of its timberland from a railroad. The railroad in turn obtained the land from the government, who subsidized the construction of a railroad with land in lieu of cash.

Long Bell obtained rail rights and built a rail line north of Longview to its timber, where they built a village, Ryderwood, for its logging headquarters and facilities for its work force. It is a retirement town today. Logging railroads were built into timber without delay, and logs soon flowed to the Longview mill. But unusual in that era (by the government or the private sector), Long Bell established a tree nursery and planted most of its logged areas with a variety of species. Douglas fir did well while the other species struggled. Then, most of the tree plantations were destroyed by wildfire. Long Bell and other landowners learned that they had to reduce wildfires before they could successfully plant another forest.

Meanwhile, Pinchot was doing his utmost to denigrate and regulate the timber owners. In 1940, Harold Ickes, Secretary of the Interior in Franklin Roosevelt's administration, published a photograph of a "devastated" clear-cut on private ownership to sell his progressive agenda. Ickes was a political ally of Pinchot and would make statements to the public not based on facts to further their agenda. The photo was taken at Wolf Point between Longview and Mt. St. Helens. Subsequently, the owner took periodic pictures of the site to show a growing forest. The second forest there was logged a few years ago and the logs processed in the area. Now, the third forest is growing and will be harvested again in several decades to once more be processed in the community. Many of us have tramped miles through forests that were harvested (logged) and, without exception, regenerated on private, state, and federal lands in western Washington. Where necessary, newly harvested sites are regenerated shortly after logging. These harvested lands are now supporting a healthy second and third forest because of the commitment of the landowners.

In 1980, the Gifford Pinchot National Forest and the adjacent forest landowners suffered the greatest catastrophe to American forest known to date. Aside from the human deaths and annihilation of all wildlife in the core area, the trees disappeared, were broken up, or killed by the heat when Mt. St. Helens erupted in 1980. Private timberland owners immediately started salvaging the timber that remained after obtaining the necessary permits from the state bureaucracy. More than 600 truckloads of logs a day were taken out of the blast area by the private sector.

Then, the private foresters researched how to eliminate the blast debris (they burned it), and they penetrated at times a foot of ash to plant trees. A few trees were planted within a month following the blast. Then, planting stock had to be obtained. It takes two years or more to grow a nursery seedling. Seed source was carefully chosen by area and elevation. One private owner planted 45,000 acres in several years to create a new forest. Some of the new forest was commercially thinned about two decades after the blast and the logs trucked to Longview where 2x4 lumber was sawed from the planted trees.

What did Pinchot's boys do on the Gifford Pinchot National Forest? Unfortunately, they waited for Pinchot's progressives to give them directions. The progressives demanded them to do nothing. Much of the blast area was designated a national monument to study a natural forest recovery. The monument is Pinchot's barren "North Africa" (for decades) while the privately owned forests will be ready for harvest in about 2020 to sustain Longview's forest economy and to preserve the community's jobs.

A small segment of Pinchot's forest is put aside for study; the rest of the forest should be a multiple-use forest as Pinchot visualized. Pinchot's forest is not managed under a sustained yield (forest harvest) concept where the timber harvest approximates the growth of the forest or any facsimile of the sustained yield concept. The forest's young trees grow and, as an old forester remarked, "the old timber is left to rot on the stump." Pinchot's vision was that the timber harvest would create revenue for the government, and the products coming from the forest (logs) would sustain the local communities and the people's jobs. Contrary to Pinchot's vision, his forest is a drain on the government's treasury.

Ironically, the Wolf Point forest and the vast private forests in the Northwest are operated on a sustained yield concept that feeds the industries in the local communities. The private sector has enhanced the tree growth through research and operations on the ground to increase forest growth, hence furnish more jobs in the local communities. The deer, elk and other wildlife seem just as happy on Pinchot's forest as the private forests, while the streams run clear on both.

The progressive movement was fathered by Pinchot and Muir, who began their journey as friends and like-minded crusaders. They were both brought together by the American Forestry Association in 1896 to further the effort to convert the remaining public domain to forest reserves. However, their newly found congeniality soon turned to anger over the use of the reserves. Muir wished to preserve the them in their near-wilderness state while Pinchot wanted to utilize the reserves to produce timber, grazing, and minerals. Pinchot planned that the private sector would use the government's resources and be controlled by careful permitting and leasing. The congeniality was destroyed when Pinchot publicly stated he would allow restricted sheep grazing in the Forest Reserves, and Muir told Pinchot that he wanted nothing to do with him again. The debate between the two men and their allies went on in various forms for decades, even after Muir's death in 1914. Muir's progressivism dictated eternal preservation of the Forest Reserves; Pinchot's statement of restricted sheep grazing in the reserves infuriated Muir.

John Muir was born in Scotland in 1838 and died in 1914 at the age of 76. In 1849, the family moved to a Wisconsin farm where he had a hard life as a farm boy with a harsh father who mentally and physically abused him and made him memorize the New Testament and most of the Old Testament of the Bible. At the age of twenty-two, he started school at the University of Wisconsin, but was never a serious student. He did not graduate, but through his talents, extreme interest in the natural world, and ability to draw attention from the academics, he became an *academic*.

He fled to Canada in 1864 to avoid the Civil War draft and met his brother who also had avoided the draft. He spent almost a year wandering the woods collecting plants. At the end of the Civil War, he returned to the U.S. where he was employed for a year, the longest employment of his life, and was seriously injured. After the injury, he determined to be true to himself and follow his dream of exploration and plant study. His exploration centered at Yosemite which he described as "the grandest of all special Temples of Nature". He only took very temporary employment work to sustain his early studies. He wrote and lectured as he wandered and became noted as a "premier naturalist". Many of his fellow intellects and politicians visited him in his Temple of Nature by walking and camping with him in the outdoors.

In 1871, Ralph Waldo Emerson offered him a teaching position at Harvard, which he turned down, as it would take him away from the outdoors. Muir married well and had a financial base to continue his work. Marriage further enabled his activism. He continued writing, traveling, and lobbying for preservation.

He co-founded the Sierra Club in 1892 and was its president for twenty-two years. Since then, it has become an all-powerful lobby for preservation and a model for a multitude of similar groups that became active preservationists, now labeled *environmentalists*. Muir and the Sierra Club's first big victory was the federalization of California's Yosemite National Park. Americans want to preserve the significant features in this country — but Muir wasn't satisfied with the 150 million acres of forest reserves that were put in place at the end of Teddy Roosevelt's administration. He told Pinchot that 150 million acres should be preserved, and he wanted much more.

Muir had published innumerable publications, and had honors heaped on him, including trails that bear his name. He believed that the plants and animals in the wilderness come straight from the hand of God, uncorrupted by civilization and domestication. His motto, "wild is superior", is still carried on by millions of people.

This scripture is contrary to the old Oregon Country settlers and our American heritage, a group who adapted and used nature to serve the needs of humans. In doing so, our heritage created a civilization where people had the luxury to leisurely pursue esoteric academics, while the rank and file Americans continue to produce food and services to enable the Muirs of the country to lecture and dream among the trees.

Muir fled to Canada in 1864 to avoid the military draft and collected plant specimens while romanticizing about nature's wonders. At the same time, my great grandfather was a volunteer in a Wisconsin Regiment in the Civil War and "fled" with his regiment to war to die (if need be) to further the American dream. His regiment participated in the Battle of the Wilderness in Virginia and stormed the Confederate defenses. Repulsed, Grandfather fell and lay on the battlefield all night while his regiment regrouped to storm the defenses again the next day, when they found their comrade in arms incapacitated. They carried him to the surgeon who prepared to remove his leg. The surgeon was paid according to the number of limbs amputated. Grandfather persuaded the surgeon to desist, and he returned to his farm in Wisconsin.

From Wisconsin he soon traveled to the Skagit Valley in Washington to purchase a farm and raise a family. His progeny moderately flourished because of an aggressive use of the region's natural resources, forest resources that were made useful by entrepreneurs like Mr. Weyerhaeuser.

Much of the public domain regressed to forest reserves, then to national forests, by means of strong central federal control that usurped the local influences. The western interests had to fight to get concessions, like a share of revenues from the federal forest. Adam Smith's 1776 remark became appropriate for the reality in the West. He said in part, referring to the British administration of the American colonies, "Plenty of good land and the liberty to manage their own affairs their own way seem to be the two causes of American prosperity."

Fortunately, private land and the national forest lands have been managed to support the western communities and the jobs for the common folks. In the 1990s, the preservationists prevailed and government land was largely limited to scenery and wildlife. The forest communities that were near large government land holdings lost their vitality.

An undocumented and concealed case to the point: an eastern Oregon community lost its historic timber harvest and grazing on the surrounding national forest and appealed to the Department of Agriculture. A mid-level federal bureaucrat visited the community and told them their "historic rights" were invalidated for the better good, as visualized by the Washington DC bureaucracy. The community's fathers offered to buy the national forest, to the amazement of the bureaucrat. He said the community couldn't afford such an expense, but the fathers had the plan and financial numbers to buy the forest. It could be operated on Pinchot's sustain yield plan (growth equals timber harvest) and grazing.

The revenues from their plan would furnish the leverage to raise the capital to finance the purchase of the national forest. Recreation would be increased, since road abandonment would be eliminated. The needed roads for the resources would access the land to the old and handicapped. And, wildlife and water quality would not suffer.

Further, a dying forest would be vitalized by removing the dying and dead trees (about a third of the existing trees were dead or near-death), and an aggressive regeneration plan would be in place. Finally, fire protection would be enhanced with a private wood-wise work force equipped with big tractors, pump trucks, and the proper equipment available for immediate action.

The bureaucrats laughed at the community leaders and went back to Washington. Another part our American heritage was throttled by John Muir, that is, the suppression of an agriculture and forest community!

HOW FORESTS ARE DEFILED

It is academic to speak only of the conversion of much of the public domain to forest reserves that were soon converted to national forests. It is more meaningful to examine how it worked in a national forest. Fortunately, Chris Morgenroth wrote in his autobiography of his experiences as one of the first to be employed as a Forest Ranger in Clallam and Jefferson Counties in Washington State.

Morgenroth was born in Germany in 1871 into a very modest family and fled his home to land in New York City in 1886 after working in the engine room of a German ship. He jumped ship with neither documentation nor the English language and, after working in several menial capacities, the adventuresome boy came west with an acquaintance in 1890.

In Seattle, Morgenroth met another adventurer, a prospector named Gus. The two went farther west by boat to Port Crescent where they found employment for a while building the breakwater to protect Crescent Bay. When the project and the town shut down, Chris and Gus decided to go farther west with the small stake they had earned. They boarded a steamer at Port Crescent to travel 25 miles to Pysht. With mail to deliver, they went ashore in a rowboat to deliver it to the postmaster. They were invited to stay at the postmaster's house, where they met two pioneers who had settled on the Forks Prairie along with about 20 other families in the vicinity. Chris and Gus were briefed about the trail, and the next day they started their journey with 75-pound packs. They traveled eight miles and crossed the Pysht River 14 times, sometimes hip deep in water in the first eight miles along the 40-mile trail to Forks.

Irresponsibly, Gus brought along a bottle of whiskey; when he had finished off most of it, he was in no shape to continue. Chris left him sheltered and hiked towards Forks, reaching a trapper's cabin just before dark. He rested while two trappers with lanterns went back down the trail to succor Gus. The next morning Chris and Gus continued on to Forks, where they stayed with a settler to obtain information in preparation to go deeper into the wilderness. They learned the Bogachiel River south of Forks had some homestead sites; however, there was no trail to the Bogachiel.

Chris and Gus hiked to the lower Bogachiel and fought through the brush along the river to the vacant bottom land. Chris located a claim in a small clearing along the river, surrounded by trees as large as 11 feet in diameter at the base. Chris settled on the north side of the river, and the two men laid the foundation for a cabin. Chris posted a claim description with his name and date on a tree, and then the two men forded the river to the south side and repeated the process for Gus. The posted claim gave Chris squatters' rights for six months. It was May of 1890. Chris was almost 19 years old, and the posting symbolically made him a part of America.

The two men went to the trading post at La Push on the coast, 28 miles downstream, where they purchased 700 pounds of supplies for their new farms. They purchased a canoe and paddled it up the treacherous river to their homesteads. Pooling their labor, they built each a cabin and planted potatoes, carrots, and turnips. They had become part of the American dream.

However, it was a hard dream on the northwest Olympic Peninsula during that era. Transportation was on foot over primitive trails or by dugout canoe, or a combination of both. Later, pack and riding horses made life easier; still later wagon roads made it even easier. Early farms were small due to huge crowded trees on the land. The disposal of trees with ax, saw, fire, and hand labor took time. The removal of the trees slowly enlarged the clearings around the settlers' houses and out build-ings. The clearings were cultivated and a garden was the first priority, while pastures or hay fields soon followed.

Cattle were the economic mainstay. The herds were necessarily small as only a few animals could be sustained somewhat on underbrush, weeds, and grasses along river bottoms and benches. There was no feed for cattle between the crowded trees. The cattle herds increased as pas-tures and hay fields were carved from the forest for the cattle. But, there was no ready market for farm produce or cattle. The nearest market was in Port Townsend. A few cattle could on occasion be driven to the town.

Settlers supplemented their income by trapping fur-bearing ani-mals and collecting bounty on predators, mostly wolves and cougars. But, the "big income" was by working away from home periodically. In the 1890s, Port Crescent's logging was the nearest opportunity for Chris, a long journey. The foot journey started at his homestead on the Bogachiel River where he took the trail he helped build to Forks. An Indian trail from the town took him to Fairhome on Lake Crescent. There he would hire an Indian to canoe him across the lake to Piedmont, and then hike 12 miles to Port Crescent and a logging camp.

Eventually Chris no longer had to go to Port Crescent to supplement his farm income. A land survey contract was implemented on two-and-one-half townships of land centered near his homestead. Forty years after the Surveyor General drove the cedar stake in the ground west of Portland and the government started its survey of the Oregon Country, the survey crews reached the Bogachiel area. The survey contractor hired two crews of five men to do the work. Chris was hired as a chain man at $40 per month. A chain is a steel tape of about two chains long (each chain being 66 feet long. There are 80 chains in a mile.) Chris pulled a chain around countless miles of sections (each section at 640 acres) noting the distances and land features, such as streams and ridgelines crossed.

In addition to this good salary, Chris learned the surveying trade. In 1901, Chris surveyed a 160-acre timber claim and blazed trees with his ax to mark the property lines for a settler friend. With his Jacob staff and compass, he ran a compass line around the 40-chain-square timber claim. Chris also left the woods briefly to go to sea after seals, but found the pay meager and the life dangerously hard.

Besides locating and starting the farm, the pioneers' priority was transportation, that is, foot trails in the 1890s. Chris gathered several neighbors and they located and built a trail from Forks to The Bogachiel. Then they extended the trail to the Hoh River and farther south to the Queets River.

Chris obtained his citizenship papers in Seattle in 1896 and a short time later was sworn in as a Constable of Western Jefferson County for six years. The constable responsibility did not interfere much with his other activities, but the position was not gratifying.

Chris always found time for exploring, hunting, and fishing. His most noteworthy exploration was to the source of the Bogachiel River in 1892 — the river he had watched run by his homestead for two years. He and a settler friend hiked through the brush upriver, making about six miles a day for three days before coming to the alpine meadows, where they preceded to climb a mountain they named the Bogachiel Peak, which afforded a 360-degree view of the Olympic Mountains, out into the Pacific Ocean. Chris recognized the ridge that separated the Bogachiel source from the other rivers and named the ridge the High Divide. He and his friend also explored the Seven Lakes Basin below Bogachiel Peak. They were perhaps the first whites to view this part of the Olympics, although some settlers, miners, and trappers had already set foot deep into the region.

Inadvertently, Chris had trained himself to fill a then modern need as a forest ranger. In 1903, the government was seeking experienced woodsmen to become Reserve Rangers to administer the newly formed Forest Reserves. Unlike today, the government was looking for people who were experienced in woods work, knew the territory, and the people. Chris wanted to explore the wilderness, build trails, and interface with people. Rangers were paid $60 per month to do the work he loved.

So, he applied for the Forest Ranger position and was accepted and paid for his recreation.

One of the first tasks for Chris was to locate and construct a trail from Sappho (just north of Forks) around the south side of Lake Crescent. Other rangers and even the superintendent helped with the construction. Besides the trail building, he often fire patrolled on foot 15 to 20 miles a day, repaired trails, cruised timber, and issued permits.

The Forest Reserves became national forests in 1905 led by Chief Forester Gifford Pinchot. National forests, Pinchot believed, were for the "people". Chris disagreed and, in a paper presented to the Forest Service in 1917, tells how discouraged the local settlers were with the creation of the Reserves.

He wrote in part: "In 1897, President Cleveland ordered most of the Olympic Peninsula set aside as a Forest Reserve with no further settlement. This meant county revenue would never increase to sufficiently fund roads, schools, and other necessary improvements. About 90 percent of the settlers became panic stricken and began to pull up stakes. The few existing trails which connected settlements and constituted the only artery of transportation soon deteriorated as there was no county aid, and voluntary upkeep was too much for the few who remained. The feeling and antagonism of the remaining settlers towards the Forest Reserve action was intense, and Reserve officers and rangers were looked upon with suspicion and as a common enemy."

Later the extent of the forest reserve on the Olympic Peninsula was reduced considerably to the angst of Pinchot and his progressive friends. Most of the area occupied by the exited settlers reverted to the public domain. However, it was too late for the financially stressed and those settlers who had left; they were quickly replaced by eager newcomers. The ugly feeling towards President Cleveland's action and the progressives still prevails by many who live on the Olympic Peninsula.

Chris went on to write how the reverted reserves were repopulated by happy people because the county revenue had increased (circa 1917) to provide new roads and "hundreds of miles of trails along which telephone wires were strung, connecting every settler with civilization." Chris documents a booming industrial expansion in Clallam County. Port Angeles had the biggest sawmill in the world and a railroad that connected Port Townsend with Joyce and beyond. The private sector timber harvest and agriculture were bountiful, resulting in a tax base that would produce the services the county required; the federal government influence was confined largely to the local national forest.

Nevertheless, Chris and his peers worked hard with the community. They improved the national forest by improving and building trails with added telephone lines for fire communication, initiating fire lookouts, adding fire patrols/guards, and game management. Above all, they educated the public about fire prevention.

The greatest challenge for Chris and the local Forest Service was the Sol Duc Burn of 1907. A land clearing fire got out of control and burned forty acres before the ranchers could control it. An unobserved log smoldered for two months, then burst forth, encouraged by an east wind. It took Chris and his two men nearly a week to get to the fire, located just west of Lake Crescent in the Sol Duc Valley. By then the fire was about a mile square, and his small crew was no match against the out-of-control blaze.

Chris sent for help from Port Angeles. It took eight men a day and a half traveling from Port Angeles by stage, boat, and on foot to get to the fire. The settlers near the fire contributed tools, and Chris was able to recruit a few more people to build fire line and a back fire to control the main fire, plus suppress the spot fires that started ahead of the main fire. Still, the fire burned 12,800 acres and, at one time, traveled eleven miles in five hours.

Chris averted a near catastrophe when he sent one of his firefighters to warn two settler families to flee from the rush of the flames. The families, unable to outrun the fire, took shelter in a root cellar located in an open field. The fire roared around them, sparing the family and the rescuer. Finally the wind died down, and the fire subsided until the rains came in September. But, a multitude of wildlife was found dead and injured. The screams heard from wildlife as a fire kills, are horrible. Chris observed burning tree limbs five inches in diameter sucked into the hot air, exploding and shooting fire in every direction, a monster that is impossible to stop until the wind abates.

The trees were mostly standing to become white snags that I marveled at in the 1930s driving on Highway 101 through the burn. Ironically, Chris paid for the firefighting from his own funds; it took two years before he was reimbursed.

Primitive conditions existing in 1907, particularly transportation, contributed to the catastrophic fire. The firefighters' adage is to catch the fires when they are small. That adage couldn't be followed by primitive transportation in those days. Chris had the whole responsibility of the fire, it seemed, with little support from his organization. He had to beg and borrow many of his tools and recruit many of his firefighters. He was sent eight men from Port Angeles, a town of several thousand men, to fight a project fire. Chris complained there were no trained men to fight fires. Still, just north across the ridge, Michael Earles employed hundreds of loggers who were trained and organized woodsmen. Perhaps the lumbermen were unapproachable, but the literature suggests the Forest Service under Pinchot's leadership didn't ask for cooperation during fire emergencies.

Commendably, the Forest Service started reforestation efforts on the burn in the fall of 1910 by broadcast seeding Douglas fir. It was a failure; the wildlife ate the seeds. It wasn't until years later that broadcast seeding could be successful when the seed was treated with Endrin, a pesticide. In 1919, the planting of Douglas fir seedlings began, and the entire burn was completely planted after several planting seasons.

Another man-caused fire burned over one-third of the reforested area in 1924. In the 1930s, the CCC "boys" felled most of the snags in the re-burn to "fireproof" the area, and planted Douglas fir seedlings to re-create a new forest.

In hindsight, it was ironic that Pinchot, the ultimate role model for American forestry who continually lectured the private timber owners and the public on responsible American forest management, could not or would not reforest the Sol Duc burn. It took over a decade for the government to do the right thing by planting trees to reforest it. He had the resources of the American government behind him. Perhaps, tree planting was not economical at that time, but surely a visionary could see the future when economics would change.

Pinchot would not sponsor legislation, but instead fought legislation that would bring the government together with the private sector to combat the fire menace. A predecessor defied Pinchot to do so with his sponsor of the Clark/McNary Act in 1927 and other programs. The Clarke-McNary Act encouraged the cooperation between the nation and the states in forest fire protection and tree planting, among other positive cooperative forestry projects.

In September 1951, another forest fire blew up, mostly on Forest Service land in the Sol Duc (sometimes spelled *Soleduck*) watershed. It burned 35,000 acres and almost the town of Forks. Again, the fire started from a previous fire when a residual hidden fire in the forest floor exploded. The fire traveled eight miles in two-and-a-half hours and had gone 17 miles in eight hours. My grandparents' house was burned, along with others in Forks. However, the community resources were marshaled, and hundreds of firefighters saved much of the town and adjacent forestland. Loggers with tractors built 25 miles of wide fire trails that removed the fuel, that exposed mineral soil to keep the fire contained until the fall rains put it out. What a contrast that was to the Sol Duc Burn of 1907, fought solely by the federal government, that is, Chris and a few men, mostly borrowed hand tools, and crippled by foot and horse transportation and no communication. The 1951 Forks Fire was a community effort by hundreds of firefighters with pump trucks, pumps, tractors, radios, and telephones.

Time has brought us new technology. But more importantly, it brought us forest communities who know how to bring their resources together to save their communities. There have been three major fires in the Sol Duc watershed in the last century, on or near Forest Service lands, which the government's technology, combined with its education policy, have failed to prevent. Government technology in today's world has put the emphasis on eliminating tractor-built fire trails, eliminating fire access roads, preserving fire-throwing snags and, more significantly, it is believed that small fires in the forests are inoffensive in many cases. Arguably, the new government policy has endangered the forest communities, while its reduction of commercial products from government lands has greatly reduced the communities' ability to protect themselves from fire.

The greatest forest devastation on the north Olympic Peninsula was the January 1921 windstorm, with a wind velocity well over 100 miles per hour. The event was commonly called "The 1921 Blowdown". At 6:30 p.m. the wind hit Forks — a wind that affected about 1,000 square miles, destroying trees in its path. The destruction varied from broken topped trees, occasional wind-thrown trees, and islands of trees completely blown down to mostly undamaged areas. In places there were walls of fallen trees 30 feet high.

Lack of infrastructure (mostly roads) precluded salvage logging, so most of the trees were left in place to rot. About eight billion board feet of wood lay rotting, enough wood to build 600,000 homes. There were no deaths, but families were isolated by trees fallen across roads and trails, while the wind damage to the dwellings was considerable. The biggest danger was from forest fires, as the dead trees were tinder dry and ready to explode with the first spark. Most of the land affected by the windstorm was private and state owned. The local people had the practical experience to know the fire danger, since the community had almost lost two families in the Sole Duc Burn. Today's academics and progressives ignore the fire danger created by dead timber.

Emergency fire regulations were implemented in 1921 almost immediately. Anyone entering the storm area was required to register and be informed of the regulations. Smoking and camp fires were prohibited except in safe places. Fire equipment and water pump trucks were cached at strategic sites along the roads and in the woods. The area also had foot and road fire patrols.

The blowdown area largely encompassed a hemlock forest, along with some interspersed Douglas fir and spruce. The area receives over 100 inches of rain a year. Hemlock is a prolific seeder and, along with the moisture of heavy rains, does not require exposed mineral soil to regenerate as other tree species do. Hemlock seed can germinate on a rotting log or stump and thrive. More importantly though, there were scattered trees throughout the blow down to furnish seed for regeneration. Fortunately Chris could report that 15 years later, the wind-damaged area was naturally regenerated, and a young forest was growing up between the rotted windfalls. The fire danger was also moderated by the hemlock's lack of durability, allied with heavy moisture that quickly returned the wood to the soil — contrary to the white Douglas fir snags in the Sol Duc Burn that persisted for decades.

Unlike the 1921 blowdown disaster, the Sol Duc fire had no standing live trees in the burn. Trees on the perimeter were too far away to adequately reseed the area. A mineral seedbed was there, but no seed.

The public domain was transferred to the people of the country in an erratic but generally effective manner until the late 1800s. At that time the progressives led by Pinchot and Muir returned much of the public domain to the government through the implementation of the Forest Reserves. Both Pinchot and Muir's agenda dictated a strong central government that subverted the local pioneers to the preservationist's interpretations of the better good. Pinchot's plan would put in place highly trained "scientists", who were educated in mostly eastern and European universities, to dictate central policy.

Chris Morgenroth again documents in his writings what really happened initially. In his presentation to a U.S. Forest Supervisors meeting in 1917, he said: "The responsibility of the Forest Service to serve the local communities and forest users is of the greatest importance. Co-operation is the key in solving existing and new problems as they continue to arise."

He ended his remarks: "We have gained the confidence and support of the public, and as long as this exists, we can count on the public for their co-operation and support of any fair policy or regulations."

When Chris uses the word *public*, the emphasis is on the local *public*, whose livelihood largely depends on the national forests' multiple use.

Chris was chosen as a pioneer Forest Ranger because he had lived with the people in and near what became the Olympic National Forest and knew the forest from living and working there, plus he was intelligent. In 1909, about four years after becoming a Forest Ranger, Chris was enrolled in a new Special Short Course in Forestry at the University of Washington for three months. The training Pinchot deemed mandatory for his forest rangers was paid for by the government. This was a shocking concept for that time. The course was taught by Associate Professor Hugo T. Winkenwerder. He was the future dean at the college (to who I paid homage monthly years later). The course included many guest lecturers who probably learned their forestry mostly from The Europeans. After all, the Chief Forester Pinchot didn't understand Douglas fir regeneration potentials.

Chris and his peers took their education and common sense and worked very hard at doing the right thing, that is, making the local people partners in developing the national forests. Chris reported in the early 1900s how the "timber barons" deserve some credit for making the Olympics accessible. In 1907 Chris, as a Forest Ranger, with his crew built a trail up the Skokomish River that was funded by Alfred H. Anderson, who funded Anderson Hall, the home of the College of Forestry at the University of Washington.

Chris and his party located a trail from Lake Crescent to the Olympic Hot Springs in 1908, and forest camping facilities located nearby. Further, he and his crew built a trail to tie the Sol Duc and Olympic Hot Springs together, making the beauty of the Olympics accessible to the publics — a quasi-cooperative venture between the government and resort entrepreneurs. In 1927 there was a cooperative Forest Service/County road built from the Elwha Ranger Station to the Olympic Hot Springs.

In the early 1900s, Chris and his peers worked hard to make the Forest Service part of the forest community. Today the Forest Service and other government agencies largely ignore the needs of the local forest communities for the "better good" as defined by John Muir's disciples. The disciples ignore Adam Smith's observation to the peril of the American standard of living and the environmental health of the land.

The term, Olympic Peninsula Rape, was applied by the preservationists to the more than two centuries of devastation by the so-called timber barons. It is only fitting that the vulgar rape label should be applied to the progressives who destroyed the forest communities. Chris describes that rape in his 1917 paper, where he tells of people fleeing the peninsula upon the implementation of the Reserves in 1897.

PORT ANGELES MATURATION

Port Angeles began a rapid change in the 1890s from a piecemeal settlement of Victor Smith's dream for his self-enrichment and the Puget Sound Cooperative Colony's dream of a Utopian new world order. These dreams were mixed in with struggling settlers and rudimentary business people battling to survive.

Town leadership began to emerge to create the infrastructure and order that would convert a disorganized forest community into a civilized town or city. The infrastructure slowly emerged under leadership of people with their own self-interest, but also with an emotional need to turn a wilderness into a thriving community with industry and jobs that contributed to a successful America. Here leaders with impractical visions mixed with the movers and shakers.

Six men came to Port Angeles in the 1890s to heavily influence the maturation of the city. Norman Smith, James Coolican, and M.J. Carrigan were part promoters and part scoundrels. Their influence was relatively short lived. G.M. Lauridsen, Thomas T. Aldwell, and Kron O. Erickson were respected businessmen who lived out their lives through the 1940s in Port Angles. All six men and their peers had a deep-seated reverence for the scenic beauty of the land, blended with a vision of the potential of the area's natural resources and people. They worked for themselves as well as for the betterment of the people of Clallam County.

Norman R. Smith, son of Victor Smith who brought the port of entry to Port Angeles in the 1860s, came to Port Angeles to become a political force. Through friends in Washington DC, he was instrumental in making the city a sub-port of entry. He became the city's mayor in 1892 for two terms and participated in city politics for many years. He traveled the world to bring investors to the city and, for a short time, sold shares in his dream of a mill that soon went broke.

All communities in the West were fighting for a railroad, and Port Angeles was no exception. There were 14 separate railroad promotions in a 27-year period before Port Angeles got its railroad just before World War I. Smith believed a railroad must come north from Grays Harbor to the city via the south shore of Lake Crescent. So in 1890 he built a railroad line on a critical pass on a rock bluff where a real railroad would have to pass to get to Port Angeles. The railroad track had two rails, 15 feet long, spiked to about a dozen railroad ties — a lot of work and some expense. But any real railroad would have to pay dearly to purchase Smith's rail line. Ironically, the spruce railroad during World War I was constructed on the north shore of Lake Crescent.

In 1903, Smith built a real railroad that was operational for three miles from the Port Angeles waterfront south up Tumwater Creek. Smith had interested eastern investors in financing a timber enterprise. The investors bought timber tributary to the city in Indian and Eden Valleys and along Little River. They also took an option on a mill site on the Port Angeles waterfront.

Smith now had the money to start building a railroad from the mill site into the timber holdings. He formed his own construction company and began laying track; in due time a locomotive was shipped into town — the *Norman No.1*. The townspeople went wild over an operational locomotive in their town. To celebrate the event, Smith loaded some 50 of his friends on a rail car and steam-drove them to the end of the three-mile railroad.

Then in October 1903, the railroad became just another dream as the investors took their money and fled to the East. The investors had sent a representative with a bank draft to further their investment, but also to examine the finances of Smith's construction company. The representative found some of the transactions of Smith's company faulty.

The investors lost over $100,000 on their investment and Port Angeles lost a railroad and a mill. G.M. Lauredsen, a Port Angeles businessman, writes that the complete story of the lost railroad would not be flattering to certain local people.

An associate of Norman Smith and a promoter was Colonel James Coolican. He was a professional developer who was a smooth talker and formal dresser who had offices in Seattle, Portland, San Francisco, and Port Angeles. He traveled extensively throughout the country selling Port Angeles. His motivation was clear when he obtained control of 880 acres on the west side of Port Angeles and additional acres around the community. He was in business to sell property. In 1891, the colonel formed a Citizens Association to sell the city and published a brochure titled "Port Angeles Illustrated".

In June the following year, the colonel wrote that he had rounded up a group of investors representing $50 million for a visit to Port Angles. The colonel and Smith spent time and money visiting Washington DC and other eastern cities to sell Port Angeles. Coolican was the president of M.J. Carrigan's Board of Trade that complemented his real estate corporation. The colonel combined his office with the Board's and decorated them to impress potential buyers.

In early 1896, a party of investors came to Port Angeles to complain that Colonel Coolican and his associate, a man named Cain, had misrepresented the sale of 40 acres. A mass citizens' meeting was held, and a resolution was passed condemning the two men. Carrigan was almost included in the condemnation. The three men were called the "Three Cs" because of their close association. The Three Cs called a citizens' meeting and passed a counter resolution. Nevertheless, the town's citizens seemed to favor the condemnation of the three men.

Shortly thereafter, the real estate business became depressed. The colonel took his last group of potential customers in an open stage to Lakes Crescent and Sutherland in the usual tour to impress outsiders of the beauty of the area. The nasty weather and the depressed market didn't sell the prospects that day, thus speeding the failure of the colonel's business endeavors.

The next day the colonel and his wife left for Chicago. He died on the train; his friends knew he had died of a broken heart. His last request was that his ashes be committed to the Port Angeles Bay — and they were by his many friends. The colonel's thoughts and last wishes reflected those of most of the people on the north Olympic Peninsula. They loved the serene beauty of the country and made many pilgrimages, similar to those trips to the lakes. It was their heritage.

The other principal of the Three Cs, M. J. "Mike" Carrigan, or just M.J., came to Port Crescent in 1891 from Ohio where he had worked on two newspapers. He too was taken with the beauty of the area and was under contract to produce a newspaper for the developers of Port Crescent. Carrigan, in the summer of 1892, moved his newspaper to Port Angeles and soon after sold it. He then took on the secretarial position for the Port Angeles Board of Trade.

In 1884, Smith had brought an experienced coal-driller to town and tried to raise money to drill for coal. The citizens were not interested in funding the project. Later two citizens took up the drilling cause and failed. The townspeople soon came to believe if they could find coal, a railroad would soon be theirs. Carrigan charged into the fray with other investors to form a company for drilling. He raised $10,000 from the citizens, and ordered a diamond drill capable of boring 4,000 feet to be shipped to Port Angeles. The people made drilling a community project as a "small army" of volunteers helped move the drill into place in the Tumwater Valley. Meanwhile, the women were in the Board of Trade rooms preparing an elegant luncheon for the workers. After lunch there were speeches by seven people, including several women. The toastmaster was the loquacious Colonel Coolican who also spoke of "Port Angeles without coal".

The drill reached a depth of 600 feet through sand, clay and gravel before it was moved five miles west of Port Angeles to Dry Creek. After drilling 1,000 feet through solid rock, no coal was found, and the town moved on to another dream. Sequim also drilled for coal in 1894 without success. In 1903, a citizen in Freshwater Bay, about eight miles west of Port Angeles, also drilled several hundred feet for coal without success.

Carrigan's forte was obviously not the evaluation of the coal potential in the area, but in public relations and organizing public events. M.J. brought the navy to Port Angeles in 1895. In his frequent trips to Washington DC he became aware of the naval establishment in the capital city. He opened the Navy door to make his pitch: Port Angeles has a fine harbor that would facilitate naval operations on the west coast. He also embellished the town by calling it the "Second National City". Of course, the Navy people replied that Port Angeles was a village that would be overwhelmed with a thousand or more sailors. Carrigan assured them that the village would do just fine, and invited them to "come and find out".

So, in October 1895, the U.S. Cruiser *Philadelphia* with Admiral Leslie Beardslee aboard sailed into Port Angeles harbor. For three weeks M.J. and the town hosted the admiral and crew. Of course, the first priority was Lake Crescent and fishing. The admiral caught fish. In fact, a trout native to the lake is now named the Beardslee trout. The next year, the admiral brought himself and the Pacific fleet into Port Angeles — and every year thereafter until well into the 1930s.

With the fleet in town, Carrigan didn't only take the admiral on the standard tour to the lakes with a banquet or two, he organized the whole community to host the Navy. He organized the first Clallam County Fair to coincide with the admiral's arrival. The fair was held in the Opera House for three days. The Opera House exhibits were impressive, while livestock filled stalls and pens just outside. The events were climaxed with a Harvest Home Ball, with the admiral's band providing the music.

The next year when the fleet arrived, Carrigan put out a county-wide request for provisions. He even offered cash at the Board of Trade for produce, seafood, and beef. He was flooded with food. The local farmers and business people were happy with the fleet; they had a new market. Nevertheless, like the tourist spike to an economy, this was short-term income. The city needed a productive economy and jobs that employed people every day. In Clallam County the forest was and is its natural resource that fuels a robust economy.

Undoubtedly, the man in Port Angeles who lent stability, integrity, and vision to the maturation of Port Angeles was G.M. Lauridsen. A poster was printed in 1892 claiming Port Angeles embraced the best harbor on the Pacific Coast. Gregers Marius Lauridsen came to Port Angeles because of the magic of the country as presented by the poster. He was a Dane who had been a small-time merchant in the East and wanted to improve himself; the poster suggested an opportunity. He bought a lot unseen in Port Angeles. He also purchased wholesale groceries from Seattle to stock a modest store (shack) on his lot. On reaching Port Angeles, Lauridsen was appalled at his real estate purchase and "beautiful Port Angeles". His lot was near tidewater, and the incoming tide brought sewage and its stench to his doorsteps. The streets of the village were occupied by cows (with their droppings) near the numerous saloons and worse diversions.

There seemed no future in the town until a passerby needed a grocery item. Lauridsen picked an item from his meager stock and sold it just above wholesale cost. The customer was amazed at the bargain, and the Dane realized there was a business opportunity in Port Angeles. He accumulated a financial surplus with low prices (relative to the other merchants), along with honesty and trust. In that era, people bought their groceries on credit, which worked only with trust between the merchant and customer. The credit system lasted into the 1930s.

My folks bought their groceries on credit, paying the bill at the end of the month (super markets were in their infancy). My folks religiously paid their bill in cash after the pulp mill check was cashed. The grocery owner gave me, a seven year-old, five cents worth of candy. The merchant/customer relationship was sacred, and Lauridsen built up a sacred relationship with most of the community. Lauridsen knew the community, and the community knew him.

In 1893 the only bank in Port Angeles failed, and local businessmen were forced to carry out bank functions. There was virtually no federal currency in circulation. The only money in town was from the sale of shingles and the military G.A.R. pension checks. Lauridsen by default was the local shingle mill's broker. He marketed their shingles to the lumber export towns. And, there was a 90- to 180-day waiting period before payment from the mill exporters. Shingle mills could not wait the 180 days for their money and needed to borrow from him. In other words, he extended credit to the shingle mill owners and more importantly their employees. The shingle mill employees virtually could not feed their families without credit from the Lauridsen store.

Lauridsen was forced to keep exhaustive credit books, which were expensive; he was constantly challenged by his clients through ignorance or fear. So, Lauridsen *made* his own money. He could pay the shingle manufactures with his money and the manufacturers could in turn pay their people with Lauridsen's money that was good at his store. And, he would be paid eventually by the export mills — that is, within several months.

Lauridsen *money* became the official currency for about ten years in Clallam County. Everyone in the county and beyond honored it because his integrity stood behind it. Then, a naïve woman tried to buy postage stamps from the U.S. government. The government would not honor the currency and forced him to discontinue his money but, in their benevolence, didn't prosecute him for producing unlawful currency.

In 1893 a local paper wrote this about the merchant: "G.M. Lauridsen evidently intends to keep up his reputation for selling groceries cheap. He has cards up in his store offering for cash: 11 pounds of beans for 25 cents; 11 pounds of rolled oats for 25 cents; 7 pounds of raisins for 25 cents per sack. Who can say that provisions are high in Port Angeles?" Coffee sold for 25 cents a pound, but little was sold as people roasted wheat or rye in sheets in lieu of expensive coffee. The paper also noted that in 1893 the road supervisor opened a road from Port Angeles to Lake Sutherland, and a four-horse stage made a trip one day and returned the next day.

In 1896 the local newspaper noted one of the most important real estate transactions of the year when Lauridsen bought property west of Laurel Street and moved his store from his old location near the Valley Creek. Many years later, he described life in the 1890s: "It was a time in our city's existence when a job for a head of a family was cherished, and held onto. No W.P.A. Everybody knew it was a case of *root, hog, or die.* Everybody was willing to work, and extreme poverty was unknown. In our meager circumstances we learned to love and respect our fellow man; we got along fine."

In 1912 a railroad proposition came to the forefront again as initiated by Michael Earles. He showed the Milwaukee Railroad that there was a wealth of timber to be moved from his timberland west of the Elwha River and beyond to Port Angeles. Earles and the railroad got the interest of a construction company owned by C.J. Erickson. Erickson had everything he needed to start construction except the rights-of way, a tedious and lengthy process that meant negotiations with a multitude of landowners. As president of the Commercial Club in Port Angeles, Lauridsen took the responsibility of obtaining the right-of-ways.

The Commercial Club solicited $72,000 in the form of notes from the local citizens to fund a lawyer and an engineer. They proceeded to locate the right-of-ways and furnish the legal descriptions of the property to be purchased for the railroad. Lauridsen and his associates spent a year and a half obtaining the easements. Many property owners gave their land for the railroad; a few others forced condemnation proceedings. More than 300 deeds were obtained, and 181 people were paid in cash for them. It was in good faith when Erickson started clearing the right-of-ways before all the deeds were finalized in 1914.

Obtaining the right-of-ways was only part of the challenge for Lauridsen. In 1913 the Industrial Workers of the World (I.W.W.), a militant union, drove off Erickson's workmen with threats of bodily harm.

They had demonstrated elsewhere that their threats were not idle. They had a couple of agitators stationed in Port Angeles to confront any workmen bound to the railroad construction site. Erickson was ready to give up on the railroad project.

Lauridsen called a meeting of the Commercial Club. The members were outraged that two agitators could stop a railroad that the people in Port Angeles had worked 25 years to obtain. The solution was simple, a committee of three "stalwarts" was appointed to speak to the agitators. The confrontations led to physically transporting the agitators to the steamer leaving for Seattle. The walk to the wharf was followed by a jubilant crowd of citizens. The committee chairman bought the tickets for the agitators and instructed them: "God be with you as long as you keep going, but God pity you if you ever come back."

But that was not the end of the affair; the I.W.W. brought a lawsuit for $25,000 in damages against Lauridsen and his transport committee. His lawyer suggested there could be no damage by giving free transportation out of town to two loafers. The jury of mostly farmers agreed and rendered a verdict of not guilty.

Lauridsen was a busy man, but found time for politics to further expand his public service. In 1908 he was a County Commissioner who was hosting a dignitary on a trip to the lakes. The dignitary believed the lakes would be great assets to Clallam County if a good road could be built to access the unique beauty of the lakes region. The first approach to Lake Crescent was a trail from Port Crescent to Piedmont on Lake Crescent. Still later, a road was constructed from the intersection of the Port Angeles/Port Crescent road over the mountain to Lake Sutherland. Finally, the Eden Valley road from the Port Angeles/Port Crescent road over the mountain was built. The dignitary suggested a road through Indian Valley would eliminate the steep mountain grades. Lauridsen started construction of the Indian Valley road that has been modernized as today's Highway 101.

In 1915 he built the G.M. Lauridsen building on Lincoln Street just north of Second Street, a building specifically designed for publishing a newspaper. The *Port Angeles Evening News* was published in that building for years and I, as a newspaper boy, picked up my papers there every afternoon (except Sunday) in 1941 to start building my college fund.

Lauridsen left the grocery business and became a banker. In 1903 the Citizens National Bank came into existence, and sometime later he became its president. He continued in the banking business until he retired in the mid-1920s. It was reported that he amassed nearly half a million dollars by his death in 1940. And, most citizens believed he earned every penny of his small fortune. Nevertheless, the G.M. Lauridsen Trust Fund was set up after his death and funds are still available for loans to the unfortunate and needy in Port Angeles. He continues to contribute to the city and county he devoted his life to.

Ironically, as a boy I lived on Lauridsen Boulevard for years and didn't know why my street had such an awkward name.

Arguably, Thomas T. Aldwell is the unrecognized father of Port Angeles. He traveled from Canada with a few hundred dollars in his pocket to better himself and later a family. Aldwell visited Seattle and Port Townsend to find them too prosperous and civilized, so he went on to Port Angeles, "The Last Frontier". He arrived in Port Angeles in 1890 to find sixteen saloons, a small newspaper, and about 1300 people. It took only a few minutes to walk from one end of town to the other with muddy streets, saloons, stores, the Opera House, and a few framed houses or cabins. He then walked to the top of the bluff to view the harbor where he dreamed of the harbor rimmed with vital industry with expanding payrolls and houses, but more importantly, a place to raise a family. So, he stayed.

Soon after he arrived, he joined the squatters that planned to take the government reservation. He squatted on two lots, each 50'x140', covered with virgin timber which the squatters started to clear and build on. In 1891 he proved up on his lots and paid five dollars for each one.

Tom Aldwell was born into a wealthy family in 1868 in Toronto. His father died when he was a young boy, and the family became almost destitute while he was educated in an English style boarding school.

There the boys competed vigorously and physically with each other, and he learned to fight. In his later teens he became a teller in Canadian banks, but found the work boring and confining. At age 22 he came west to improve himself.

Aldwell found a rent-free room on the upper floor of a Port Angeles hotel, furnished with a mattress on floorboards and a chest of drawers. He was happy with his sleeping arrangements for more than a year as it saved money to fund business opportunities. Then he started to make friends by doing what the pioneers on the frontier did, work hard and be honest with people. He went from job to job and tried several small business ventures.

One of his first jobs was to work for the Dry Creek Lumber and Shingle Mill Company for a dollar a day. He piled lumber and was the timekeeper. He bunked and ate at the mill and was charged for his room and board. He also accounted for the crew's meal charges, which were even made during times the men weren't working. One Sunday, he went to a saloon for a bucket of beer to take out. There a mill worker hassled him because of the unfair meal charges he was believed to be responsible for. The mill worker called Aldwell a name that was intolerable and Aldwell called the mill worker outside to settle the matter physically. The mill worker didn't want the conflict, but a bystander accosted Aldwell as he was taking off his coat, and bit his ear. Aldwell decked him with one punch. Following his demonstration of boxing, the sawmill workers treated Aldwell with respect.

In 1892 Aldwell found a business that would further his learning about opportunities in the growing community. He bought a cigar store and built it up into a lucrative business while giving him time to put his energy into other ventures.

In the early 1890s county voters decided the county seat should be moved from Dungeness to Port Angeles. Still, possession was nine points of the law, so one night the young men of Port Angeles decided to go to Dungeness for the records. Aldwell was one of them. They started from Port Angeles in the middle of the night with a wagon and an elected leader, well armed. One man drove the wagon and the rest were on horseback.

As they approached Dungeness, their captain warned them they were entering enemy territory and to move quietly. They expected an army of townspeople and farmers to meet them ready to fight. Instead, the County Auditor met them cordially and helped them load the records into the wagon. This event illustrates the mind-set of the people in that era and is a continuation of the raucous and well-armed frontiersmen who crossed the Allegany Mountains after the Revolutionary War. The verve, emotion, and initiation of people almost always prevailed swiftly with justice and no harm or injuries.

While still operating the cigar store, Aldwell moved rapidly to other endeavors. He advertised himself and became a public accountant, eventually developed a farm south of town, became an assistant manager of a weekly newspaper, and a city editor and treasurer of another. With a shortage of cash, one newspaper advertised that a subscription could be paid for with ducks, chickens, eggs, turkeys, butter, potatoes, cabbage, hay and grain.

Nevertheless, his business activities didn't interfere with physical workouts. He swam vigorously at Lake Crescent and in the Straits. He was even written up in a Seattle newspaper in 1902 for saving two men from drowning. It happened in the Port Angeles Harbor. Two men in a small boat were approaching a dock when the violent wind-driven water overturned their small boat. The athletic Aldwell swam to their rescue, righted the boat, and helped the exhausted boatmen to shore.

In the mid-1890s the Port Angeles people were entertaining the naval officers (the fleet was in) and Aldwell was in a group traveling from town to Lake Crescent when a young lieutenant wanted to finish the journey by running from the lower Elwha River to the lake. Aldwell joined the officer in his run of about nine miles.

Aldwell was drafted into politics in 1894 that engaged him for the next sixteen years. A would-be state senator asked Aldwell to manage his campaign because of his many friends in the area. Aldwell reluctantly accepted the challenge, and the senator won the election. The political experience captivated him. He decided if he could elect a friend, he could certainly stand a chance in winning votes for himself, so he ran for County Auditor as a Republican — the minority party — and won. He followed up his election by becoming a leader in his party. Also in 1894 he became an active party organizer in the Republican Party.

In that era, almost everyone belonged to a party — Republican, Democrat, or Progressive. The voters were divided into precincts in the Republican Party. A leader or committeeman was elected by precinct delegates at a County Convention. The County Convention was followed by a State Convention. Aldwell wrote that all Republican candidates were honest as validated by their past activities. They put the Party first before their personal ambitions. Aldwell believed honesty, a friendly attitude, and hard work were the keys to get elected. When he ran for the auditor's office, he traveled to the Lake Ozette precinct, occupied by Scandinavians who favored the Scandinavian running against him. He walked from Quallayute to Lake Ozette, paddled from one end of the lake to the other, stayed at a friend's house, and walked by trail to Clallam Bay, which was a distance of thirty-five miles. He carried a bottle of liquor and a box of cigars in his pack to treat every man he met on the trail. He called the men who took more than one swallow from his bottle "the gurglers". No one from Ozette voted for him, but his gentle association with the Ozette men between elections carried the precinct for him in his second election.

Aldwell's action towards dishonest opponents was also very direct. The editor of the local newspaper wrote a story that stated gambling was practiced in his cigar store. He warned the editor he wouldn't be responsible for his actions if another lying story was published. The next day the newspaper stated Aldwell had visited the editor to buy him off. The second newspaper in Port Angeles carried a story the next day that their rival's newspaper was closed, as the editor wondered what hit him. The editor chose to sue Aldwell for damages of $10,000.

The jury awarded the editor $20 for compensation as the paper was closed several days. The judge felt Aldwell had no right to take the law into his own hands. But, the editor told no more Aldwell lies, nor probably anyone else's perceived lies.

In 1897 while Aldwell was County Auditor, the Forest Reserve became a reality and much of Clallam County was included. Many people in Clallam County fled. Aldwell, the County Auditor, documented the damage to the county: a county depopulated. The County Engineer prepared a map showing the voters in 1896 and the number remaining in 1897. The map also showed the road and school districts and the county obligations (debt) in that area. The obligations were secured by the timber and land that was taken from the county for reserves. It pointed out that many widows with children had purchased securities that were now in jeopardy. There were certified statements to support the map. The county (along with other counties) asked the federal government to eliminate at least part of their county from the new Forest Reserves. Two eliminations were made in Clallam County: one in 1900 of 248,000 acres and one in 1901 of 92,949 acres. Neighboring Jefferson county eliminations were much smaller, so Aldwell asked their U.S. Senator why Clallam County was more successful. The senator suggested that Clallam County's documentation was better.

An insignificant County Auditor had thwarted the academics in the Forestry Commission of the National Academy of Science who sponsored the Forest Reserves. Gifford Pinchot a member of the Commission undoubtedly could not understand how a few settlers could prevail over the desires of the academic elites. Aldwell saved Clallam County for a while from becoming another federal government's landed estate dedicated to the preservationist. After that, the substantial Forest Reserves were returned to the public domain. The citizens repopulated the area rapidly seeking land to build forest communities.

Aldwell and three of his friends located timber claims in what had been forest reserves near Lake Ozette. The four men were attending their claims when a fire got away from them and they spent several days fighting the fire day and night with success, preventing a big forest fire. Some would claim that Aldwell profited by influencing the government to return the land to the citizens of the county — but Aldwell was following the legal process of obtaining and purchasing timber claims to get the land into the private sector. His action suggests that the citizens used the timber claims to further their financial future.

The system wasn't exclusively a tool of the timber barons as preservationists have portrayed. Eventually much of the timber claims were consolidated into blocks. Entrepreneurial groups purchased individual claims at a normal profit for the small owner to make possible timber holdings large enough to justify railroads, locomotives, logging equipment, and camps for the work force. The entrepreneurial group had the talent and the resources to develop the county rapidly, a task the federal government could and would not do.

The Ozette Logging Company was created to utilize the timber to generate a profit for the entrepreneurs who consolidated a timber ownership and inadvertently produced jobs for the people in Clallam County. Their logging operation created a few hundred jobs, and their logs partially fueled several mills who employed hundreds of Clallam County mill workers. It also helped businesses in the forest communities — mostly Forks and Port Angeles.

My maternal grandfather's Freshwater Bay dairy farm was made uneconomical by local government regulations, and he found menial work at the Ozette logging camp for several years in the late 1930s to keep his idle farm and wife alive. My paternal grandfather was at Forks in the 1940s, and his logging employment was also on Forest Reserve land returned to Clallam County. My family thrived only because the Forest Reserves were eliminated there, thus made available to the Ozette Timber Company and their peers.

However, The Forestry Commission studied the flora and fauna in a natural setting in recommending millions of acres of Forest Reserves in the late 1800s and ignoring the human factor. They didn't care about my grandparents and similar families or even knew they existed. Their followers today still ignore the forest workers. They have set up the timber barons as the villains of the forest and conveniently ignored the people who depend upon the timber industries, who employ a host of ordinary Americans. Meanwhile, the federal government ownership in Clallam County is expanding and is off-limits to producing fiber (trees). It is dedicated to northern spotted owls and other critters. Spotted owls are being displaced by barred owls that migrated from the east. The preservationists now wish to destroy the barred owl as they nearly destroyed the heritage of Clallam County and the livelihood of those who have labored in the forest and mills — a forest that is renewable to furnish sustainable fiber to build America and provide habitat for wildlife.

In 1914 Aldwell left politics, even though the Republicans asked him to run for the state senate. His interest was in real estate, where he could create wealth for himself and take up the challenge of developing his chosen homeland, Clallam County. When he arrived in the 1890s, Clallam County was largely a wilderness. With his peers, he was determined to create a vibrant American community.

His first significant real estate transaction occurred in 1901 when he took advantage of the public domain via homestead legislation. He listened to the "boys" in town talk about the claims they should have had — so he decided he would not *talk* but *take* one. A friend showed him his claim on the Elwha River, seven miles from town, and Aldwell offered him three hundred dollars for it. He bought the site for the beauty of the Elwha gorge. Later he learned he owned a power dam location. A 16'x18' cabin was on the claim with a spring nearby. There was no wagon road from Port Angeles to the site. Other settlers packed to their homesteads with horses while Aldwell packed everything on his back. When he reached the river, he had to raft or canoe across the river, and, on occasion, swim across it.

Aldwell bought lots and property around the county and three-quarters of a mile of waterfront on Lake Crescent. He had agents traveling the country to advertise his property and the area. By 1948 when he retired, he had bought and sold over 1,100 pieces of property. In

1906, he built a two-story building in the center of Port Angeles at First and Laurel Streets. To support local businesses, he built it of Tumwater Valley sandstone that was quarried nearby.

Aldwell protected his property, in particular, his homestead ranch on the Elwha River. The land was not surveyed at his homestead site, and Aldwell had only squatter's rights (claim) until the government survey was completed. One day he found four men (claim jumpers) on his ranch ready to build a cabin that would give them a basis to contest Aldwell's claim. Needing help, he went to town and recruited two "spectacular men" who carried long knives in their belts. Early the next morning, Aldwell, armed with his rifle and his recruits, returned to his claim to find the jumpers still building a cabin. He quietly told the four jumpers he didn't believe any jury in the county would convict a man for shooting a jumper — and the jumpers hurried on their way.

Shortly thereafter 20 well-armed Indians came to Aldwell and a neighbor friend for help in protecting a fellow Indian's claim. Aldwell, with a friend plus the Indians, knocked on the door of the Indians' cabin occupied by jumpers. Aldwell told the jumpers that the land office always favors Indians over jumpers. With 20 Indians with guns pointed at them, the jumpers hurried off to town to pay the Indian "owner" a couple of hundred dollars for a quit-claim deed to the claim.

In 1894 Aldwell discovered his beautiful ranch had more than beauty when a pulp mill developer happened into his office. The developer suggested that industry needed power, and Aldwell took him to his ranch on the Elwha. The two men saw that the Elwha site was suitable for a dam and hydroelectric power that would bring industry and civilization to the area. So a plan was put in place. The first step was to acquire the land three miles upriver from the ranch, now the dam site, for the reservoir. The reservoir would become Lake Aldwell. The reason for purchasing the property had to be kept secret to keep the land value from inflating. It took twelve years to acquire the land needed for the Elwha River dam project. The pulp mill developer furnished the capital for purchasing the land and Aldwell furnished the labor to purchase it including his ranch. The dam itself was built on the ranch. The pulp mill developer and Aldwell each had half interests in the agreement.

In 1908 George A. Glines bought out Aldwell's partner, and the project became a Glines/Aldwell project. Glines was a wealthy Canadian real estate operator who was eager to go ahead with the dam, but he needed financing. First he formed the Olympic Power and Development Company with a board of directors of wealthy men who bought stock in the company. To get complete financing, the new company had to get power franchises to demonstrate the dam project could deliver power and thus income to pay the investors. Aldwell got franchises from Port Angeles, Port Townsend, Western Steel near Port Townsend and the Bremerton Navy Yard. It was not easy to get the franchises, but he prevailed.

Then Aldwell and Glines went to Chicago to Peabody, Houghteling for bonds to finance the construction. Glines talked to the firm initially and was turned away, until Aldwell arrived to reopen the discussion by showing pictures of Clallam County. The pictures of the Elwha River, Lake Crescent, and Lake Sutherland were common selling points for promotion of Clallam County then and into the future. Peabody, Houghteling financed the project. The Olympic Power and Development Company became the Olympic Power Company — but Aldwell was still busy negotiating financing terms and selling stock. He was not finished; he visited Seattle and local papers to get publicity without cost so he could continue his efforts to sell stock and raise money. He made this effort with risk to his own personal finances, because a failure of the dam project probably would have ruined him financially. The bonds for construction were executed October 1, 1910.

He was the General Manager for the construction of the dam, but it was only an advisory position, as Peabody, Houghteling controlled the construction through their engineering company. The costs ran over budget, and construction was slow. Aldwell had to raise more money. The power would not be on line as promised to contracted users, but worse yet, he believed the dam was not built on bedrock and would blow out. For his efforts to correct the failings of the project, the engineering firm attempted to remove him. The foundation blew out on October 31, 1912.

The Navy decided in 1913 not to contract for Elwha power, and Aldwell went to Washington DC to change their minds. He stated that without the contract, the dam would not be completed. The Olympic Peninsula would remain an undeveloped wilderness rather than a developed area that would contribute to a war effort. The Navy agreed and gave Aldwell the contract to develop the Peninsula. (It wasn't until after the second World War, that he believed his 1913 statement to the Navy had been verified.)

Aldwell coolly continued to make the dam a reality by repairing the damage. On December 12, 1913 power from the Elwha dam was available, thanks to him.

In verification of Aldwell's confidence in the dam, an associate of Peabody, Houghteling suggested to the Zellerbach officials that they locate in Port Angeles. The officials were briefed and shown the Clallam County resources. The Elwha power plant brought them to Port Angeles. The pulp mill they built in Port Angeles was still in operation in 2011.

The Crescent Boxboard Company located in Port Angeles in 1918, a company that became Fibreboard Products Incorporated in 1927. This firm was the one that employed my uncle in the early 1940s. Fibreboard had tried to locate in the city, but there was no site available on the waterfront. Aldwell wanted another power purchaser for the Elwha facility and industry in Port Angeles. So, he communicated with the necessary people to make reserved property available to Fibreboard. Initially, it employed 235 people in the mill and 90 in the woods.

World War I brought the need for spruce lumber for airplane construction, and the greatest supply was at the west end of Clallam and Jefferson Counties, an inaccessible area. Grays Harbors wanted a railroad built from its location into the spruce, and so did Clallam County. Aldwell got a letter from an influential friend working for the War College Division of the Army asking for information about spruce. He sent him the pertinent information. The friend was in Portland to accelerate the building of the railroad in Clallam County. Apparently, Aldwell was influential in getting the Army railroad for Clallam County. The Army had its railroad, but there was no mill available to turn the logs into lumber for the airplanes.

The Port of Port Angeles Chamber of Commerce appointed Aldwell Chairman of a committee to obtain the mill for Port Angeles at the mouth of Ennis Creek near the east end of the Harbor. Mill owners in the area did not want another mill built, so they claimed the wind would preclude dockage. This was not true. Aldwell had affidavits from twelve Colony mill men who stated that the wind never disturbed their mill dockage or log booms at the Ennis Creek site. The mill was built and was never operated, because the war ended before it could become operational.

The Army was going to scrap the mill. The Chamber of commerce sent Aldwell and another man to Portland to save it for future use, and the mill was saved. Again, Aldwell's associate from Peabody, Houghteling was looking for a mill site. The Olympic Forest Products' pulp mill was built on the army site and went into operation in 1930. The mill was merged with Rayonier Corporation to produce acetate rayon from wood cellulose.

Finally, in 1941, a group of plywood men were looking for a location and were discouraged by local mill men because they thought there was a lack of timber on the Peninsula to merit another mill. Aldwell had the timber data to convince the plywood men there was enough timber available and hoped timberlands would be transferred from the Park Service to the U.S. Forest Service. He was always optimistic in believing that most people wanted to convert wilderness into civilized forest communities. The plywood mill was operating part-time in 2011, while the Park has expanded. Conversely, the Forest Service is smaller in size and produces little wood resources for processing in the community. These factors play a part in taking the Peninsula back to the poverty they experienced in the Clallam County wilderness of the 1800s.

One of the Port Angeles city fathers represents the American dream as presented to youth of America in the early 20th Century — K. O. Erickson. In 1910 he moved from the Quillayute Country to Port Angeles to engage in real estate, insurance, and the banking business. In 1918 he was part of the creation of the Washington Bank and soon became its vice-president. He founded the Port Angeles Savings and Loan Association in 1923. He financed some of the city's largest buildings, contributed to numerous good causes, received many marks of honor, and was made an honorary chief the Quileute Indians.

Erickson's grandson was my classmate in high school, a fact that never occurred to me or that I cared about when we were in school. Another classmate lived close to Erickson's home and casually observed the boy's grandfather. We gossiped about his elderly actions in driving through the neighborhood without knowing or caring about his station in life.

Erickson was born into a poor family in Sweden on a sustenance farm. The family's principal food was bread mixed with bark, moss, or straw. He had a few years of formal schooling where he excelled. The family's poverty made him dream of riches that might help better himself. From the stories circulating in Sweden, he read of the gold fields in Australia and was determined to go there and dig up a fortune.

Family and neighbors listened to the boy's dream of gold and ridiculed him. How would he even pay for a voyage to Australia? Erickson believed he could get there as a sailor and be paid for his work. Reluctantly his mother frugally outfitted him. Accompanied by his older sister, he traveled to a Swedish seaport to find a ship. His sometimes drunken father considered his leaving was one less mouth to feed.

A Danish sea captain thought the 12-year-old boy was too young to go to sea, but his sister insisted he was intelligent, hardworking, and could be useful. The captain relented and brought Erickson aboard as a cabin boy at one dollar a month. The boy performed his cabin duties well and ambitiously followed the sailors in their tasks to slowly learn the sailor's trade and help out. He was appreciated by the captain and crew.

The Danish ship docked in England, nowhere near Australia, so Erickson looked for another ship. But first, he had to get off the ship. He had to conquer a high stone wall surrounding the harbor. In addition, the ship's crew held him captive on the ship because English authorities on shore were on the lookout for deserting sailors.

Nevertheless, he accompanied a sailor ashore and was able to make arrangements to stay at a sailors' boarding house, similar to the houses in Port Townsend. The boarding house owner found Erickson an ordinary seaman's berth on an English ship bound for Africa and possibly to Australia. The berth was an education for the young sailor. He was on watch with the chief mate who took an interest in him, lent him books, taught him English, and gave him badly needed clothes. He had become a bona fide English-speaking sailor.

Erickson worked his way to Australia, where he found the gold fields played out. He worked at a sheep ranch for a time, then returned to the sea and finally headed for San Francisco. He found the gold fields on the Sacramento River were played out too. Destitute, he took a job in a furniture store, working on coastal steamers in the summers between San Francisco and other west coast ports.

By the spring of 1888, Erickson was walking the streets of Seattle. When he was there years earlier, in 1881, it was a town of stumps, sawdust covered streets, and very primitive. By 1888, it was a growing bustling city with railroads, shipping, a variety of manufacturing plants, and multi-storied business houses. The streets were covered with fir planks. The very spirit of the people was exciting and refreshing in this vitalized town. His routine of furniture labor and working on coastal steamers was boring and financially depressing. Seattle was a model for him to emulate. He could dream of a new town of his own and grow with his community.

He had to find a place with mostly vacant land. He made inquiries of real estate people and the government land office. The only land available appeared to be in Quillayute Country that was timbered and mostly vacant. He applied for a 160-acre homestead at the government land office in Seattle. The only requisite he made was that it be located as close to the ocean and the Indian reservation as possible. He now had the land claim and had to find how to get there. He was told only that there were no roads or trails and only Indians living in the vicinity of his new claim.

He bought a map of the Olympic Peninsula and a compass, as well as enough supplies that he could carry on his back. His supplies included an ax, file, shovel, pick, blanket, extra pair of overalls, frying pan, tin plate, tin mug, spoon, fish line and hooks, matches, five pounds of bread, five pounds of flour, five pounds of bacon, one can of pepper and two pounds of salt. He also carried his sailor's sheath knit and a pocket knife.

Erickson boarded the side-wheeler *Discovery* in Seattle as it was bound for Neah Bay. The captain informed him that people traveling to the Quillayute disembarked at Pysht. He was rowed ashore during the evening, camped beneath a large spruce tree, and rolled into his blanket to sleep the night away. At the first break of light the next morning, he studied his map and determined the Pysht River pointed straight to his destination, the Quillayute River. Six days of arduous packing up the Pysht River, over a low mountain pass and down to the Quillayute River drainage brought him to his destination. The trip was made wading in water to his waist for several hours in the Pysht River, detouring around windfall trees, some over six feet in diameter, over-around boulders, and through thick brush. On his homestead, he explored his land and noted the Indian canoes beached across the river, but he kept his silence and avoided his Indian neighbors.

He located a small clearing for his cabin surrounded by giant trees. The trees varied from two to ten feet in diameter, most too big for cabin building. Nearby though, he found smaller trees to build the walls of his home. A young sailor in his youthful vigor had no experience with an ax or in constructing a cabin. Nevertheless, with only an ax, he felled the trees, cut logs, and dragged the heavy logs to his cabin site for walls. He used the tops of fallen trees for roof beams. He had neither nails nor hammer, nor did he have saw and tools to make shakes. The roof beams were covered with bark from the trees and held down by rocks. There was no way to build a chimney for a fireplace, so he made a central fire pit with an opening in the roof for the smoke to escape. It took him two weeks to build his primitive cabin with only an ax and file. In today's world, we marvel when several men with modern equipment build a cabin.

While working inside the cabin, Erikson heard voices. Stepping outside, he was faced with a crowd of Indians with old guns, knives, bows and arrows. The speech their leader gave was not friendly, but Erickson didn't understand a word the leader spoke, and, they didn't appear to understand him. He showed the Indians his receipt for the money paid to the United States Land Office for his homestead.

After the Indians had an apparent angry discussion among themselves, they departed. The white man wanted to be friendly, but had not the language to pacify the Indians or even know what their concerns might be. Nevertheless, he was not afraid, for he was confident of his right to this land. He exemplified the American pioneer spirit that brought our country from the east to the west coast, our American heritage.

Erickson sustained himself with fish and berries while developing his property. He had hoarded most of his provisions that he packed from Pysht. His hoarded provisions enabled him to explore. He wanted to evaluate the land north of his homestead to the Straits of Juan de Fuca. Explore he did, and found an endless forest devoid of people, with large tracts of land suitable for agriculture. The trees on the land were the largest and most beautiful specimens he had ever seen. It appeared the agricultural land would support thousands of families.

When his provisions were about exhausted, he returned to Seattle where he talked to anyone who would listen to him about the wonderful opportunities awaiting them in the Quillayute Country. The response was negative because there was plenty of land available near Seattle where railroads and county roads were prominent.

Then Erickson found a convert, a young Norwegian sailor who was employed in a Seattle factory. The two decided to become neighbors on the Quillayute. The Norwegian filed for a homestead adjacent to Erickson. It was fall and too late in the year to travel and work their claims during the harsh winter. In spring they would travel together to their homesteads.

Instead, Erickson worked out his passage on a ship to San Francisco to labor again in the furniture factory. He worked for five months saving as much money as possible while dreaming of his homestead. In the spring of 1889, he wrote to his soon-to-be neighbor and returned to Seattle. His new neighbor had purchased the necessary supplies for their homesteads — adding two axes, two saws, two shovels, one adz, and a tool for splitting boards and shakes from spruce and cedar trees to the supplies that Erickson had packed to the Quillayute the previous year.

The two sailors retraced Erickson's boat trip and trek through the forest to arrive at their homesteads on the Quillayute. They found Erickson's cabin torn down and partly burned. They assumed the Indians had destroyed the cabin, but that didn't daunt them. They immediately started to build their two cabins, working together. This time they had the tools to build more sophisticated homes. They found a hollow windfall spruce. The spruce trees for the most part were too big for their four-foot cross-cut saw, but a hollowed centered windfall tree they found enabled them to use the saw on the shell of the tree to cut blocks that were then split into planks. The cabin walls were constructed with logs; the floor, roof, and door with split planks. Crude furniture was made from planks. With their shovels, pick, and saws, they built a fireplace with chimney of stone and clay. The cabins were constructed without nails.

During the sailors' miserable trek, loaded with heavy packs from the Straits to their homesteads, they longed for a boat to carry their loads. While building their cabins, they took a break to walk the beaches and discovered a plethora of materials washed up from wrecked ships. They salvaged some planed boards. Then they discovered a wrecked lifeboat. They began to repair the craft, determined to make it sea worthy to furnish them with sea transportation and eliminate the need for back-breaking packing of supplies.

They debated the ownership of their craft, since it was on the Indian reservation; it probably belonged to the Indians. They went to the Indian village and to the most prestigious house (assuming it was the chief's). Without a common language, they somehow communicated to the chief their wishes. The Norwegian partner held up a silver dollar, and the boat was theirs.

They salvaged metal and wood from the beach, and even built a crude forge to make other tools. The Indians watched their boat work with friendly interest. They solved all the problems in repairing their boat, but one. They needed oil to fill the small cracks. Fortuitously, a whale washed up on the beach near the Indian village. The Indians offered the blubber to eat or process for oil — and their boat was finished

It was a calm and sunny day in May when the sailors launched their boat to return to Seattle for supplies. They waved to curious natives as they rowed away from the beach at La Push. The weather was calm, but the sailors remarked that if a storm blew in, they would not survive. Fortunately, there was no storm, and they rowed or sailed when the wind was favorable to Seattle. They caught fish and camped on the beach at night, to sleep and cook a meal of bacon and pancakes or freshly caught salmon.

The stay in Seattle was only long enough to buy more supplies, some in cash and some on credit. (It speaks volumes about the trust in the late 1800s when a merchant would sell goods on credit to near-destitute homesteaders living many miles distant from Seattle.) The sailors slept in their boat. They bought the usual provisions: household utensils, a seven-foot saw for tree falling, hoes, steel bars, picks, and other land-clearing tools. Their boat was so heavily loaded there was hardly room to row. It was seven days of rowing against the wind to return to La Push. Fortunately the seas were calm again. When they beached their boat, the Indians surrounded them, wishing to trade. They bartered some of their precious supplies for the Indians' furs. The Indians' eagerness to trade suggested a business to Erickson.

The summer was spent clearing their land of the thick forest, a mammoth job with trees sometimes having a 50-foot spread of roots. The two homesteaders worked together, cutting, grubbing, sawing, and burning from early mornings until late evenings. On occasion they would fish or pick berries. Hunting wasn't that necessary, as elk and deer could be shot from the cabin door. They worked for more than six months and had not seen a white man near their homesteads.

The two decided to go back to civilization to earn more money during the winter months, hoping to fund themselves through the next summer. The men returned to Seattle to find the town mostly destroyed by fire. They, of course, had no news of any kind beyond their homesteads. They temporally dissolved their partnership, and Erickson returned to San Francisco for another winter's work in the furniture factory.

His experience with the Indians had opened a whole new world for him. He anticipated that trade with the Indians would be interesting and financially satisfying. But, his boat was too small and slow for trading purposes. He would need a larger boat, a warehouse or store, and additional money to stock the store. His meager earnings could not finance the venture. When spring came, as he prepared to leave for his homestead, and knowing about the trading plan, his landlady offered to lend him $250 toward the venture. It was a good start to finance a trading business. On arriving in Seattle, Erickson deposited his loan in the Dexter Horton Bank, the famous pioneer banker in Seattle. Eventually he paid it back twice over.

Erickson and his old partner again returned to their homesteads to start building a small store/warehouse addition to Erickson's cabin. Then his dream of independent trading was shattered. A small two-mast schooner owned by the Washington Fur Company entered the

Pysht Harbor with trading supplies. Erickson knew he couldn't compete with a well-financed and established company. Fortunately he was offered work with the company and spent two years with them, where he learned the trading skills and the Chinook universal Indian language. More importantly, the Indians worked well with him.

Another kind of disaster struck in 1893; a depression closed much of the industry in the country. The settlers' routine was generally to work their homesteads in the spring, summer, and fall, then seek outside work for money to buy staples that would keep the homestead viable. Erickson was no exception, but relief was in sight.

Walter Ferguson, a settler nearby who exchanged work occasionally with Erickson, had a proposal. They would mine gold on the beach. The settler had lived in Alaska and had the mining skills. He was college educated, refined, and liked his liquor overly much.

Erickson's dream to dig for gold was about to become a reality. They staked two claims of 20 acres 16 miles north of their homesteads near Lake Ozette and on the beach. The two men salvaged lumber from the beach and built a cabin and a flumes/sluice box. They then took in a husky Irishman named Lester as a partner because of his ability with a shovel. The three men organized the Ozette Gold Mining Company and recorded the company in the county auditor's office in Port Angeles. Ferguson was the president who managed the gold, Erickson the treasurer, and the Irishman the secretary. Erickson and the Irishman shoveled gravel into the flume eagerly for the first week. They recovered three dollars' worth of gold. The partners continued their work for several months, earning the team three to five dollars a week. The fall storms began to bring an endless round of rain and fog, making mining impractical.

Erickson's gold mining days were finished, and his thoughts turned to trading. His landlady's loan would buy supplies, but the boat to carry the supplies was an obstacle. Erickson couldn't buy a boat, so he searched for one to charter. He finally found a captain with a small sloop who would leave the Straits and brave the ocean to La Push.

From there, Erickson went to the wholesalers to buy a cargo. But his money would purchase only a part of the merchandise he needed. He was forced to purchase more cargo on credit, which was reluctantly given. Erickson's enterprise was considered risky mostly because of the wild ocean between La Push and the Straits. One wholesaler gave him a ton of flour on credit. The voyage to Pysht was made without incident. Erickson hired the Indians to off-load the sloop and transport it by trail to his little store. The Indians were paid mostly with tobacco, sugar, and flour, as the Indians had little use for money. They used furs to purchase goods.

The traders came infrequently to La Push because of its isolation and the turbulent Pacific Ocean. The alternatives to ocean travel were the trails that were poorly built and maintained in the early days. The trading business was slow to start because of the poor business climate in the country, but with time it improved and more settlers came into the area to make Erickson's business flourish. He expanded his business into several locations in and around his original store near La Push. In 1894 Erickson was appointed postmaster of Mora, also the name of his Swedish home. His knowledge of the area brought prospective settlers and others to him for his insight.

In June of 1894 Erickson was appointed United States Commissioner at Mora. Now settlers did not have to make a two-week trip to Seattle to do business with the Land Office. A person had to file an application for a homestead or timber claim and later prove he had complied with the laws to obtain a deed to their claims.

Eventually the chartered schooner's captain decided the voyage from Seattle to La Push was too dangerous to continue. So Erickson purchased his own schooner to carry his freight, the *Sunbeam*. He was too busy to sail the boat himself, so he hired a skipper. His business was expanding fast and he needed to supply his stores. His skipper quit and he couldn't find another qualified person to run his schooner. Winter was coming and his merchandise supply was depleted. In desperation he took the schooner himself to Seattle for supplies, a time of year when most small schooners avoided the ocean. He got to Seattle and back nearly to Cape Flattery before a raging ocean storm approached. He considered and should have gone back to Neah Bay where he could ride out the storm. Instead he thought the storm would abate enough to allow him to reach La Push, so he sailed out into the ocean. Erickson was driven by his need for productivity, which would not allow him to lie idle in a safe harbor at Neah Bay waiting for the storm to pass through the area.

The storm increased in fury, with winds about 80 miles per hour. The waves were 30 to 40 feet high. He reached sight of La Push where the Indians observed his little schooner in trouble, but the Indian canoes couldn't get out of the La Push Bay, nor could the schooner get in. The wind was driving the schooner onto the rocks at La Push Point. Erickson worked the schooner around the point onto a sandy beach. It was a total wreck, and Erickson was found unconscious on the beach, barely alive. The Indians picked him from the beach and carried him unconscious to his wife.

Erickson was married in 1894 to a young woman from San Francisco, who he took to Mora. When they brought her husband home, she thought him dead. The nearest doctor was over a hundred miles away, so it was up to his wife alone to nurse him back to health. She did it in three weeks. She was so tired and discouraged with the Quillayute Country she asked that they return home to San Francisco. Erickson assured his wife things would improve and they continued to live at Mora.

The schooner and cargo were a total loss amounting to $3,000, and his business was curtailed for the winter. As soon as he was well, he went to Seattle to start up his business again. The Seattle merchants gave him credit for another full cargo of merchandise. He chartered a large boat with both sails and motor. However, he had to wait for his cargo until spring when a vessel could get into the La Push Bay. His reconstituted business soon allowed him to repay the Seattle merchants.

Erickson almost lost his life, and now he was about to have his business taken away by the federal government. In 1897 the government transferred the vacant land on the Olympic Peninsula to the Forest Reserves. Erickson believed the only land excluded was in the little towns like Port Angeles, Port Townsend, and Aberdeen. No road building was allowed and a person had to have a permit to enter the Forest Reserve. Erickson observed many settlers who had taken up and improved their homesteads quit their homes and move away. However, Erickson stayed and did what he could to reduce the Forest Reserve. The boundaries were moderated after four years of turmoil. Erickson and his peers then proceeded to turn the wilderness they were left with into productive land for Americans.

The pioneer citizens took back much of their county in 1906 and elected Erickson county commissioner to facilitate the development of western Clallam County. The greatest need was for better trails and roads. There was a complete lack of roads. Erickson served six years as commissioner. And, in that period, wagon roads were built around Pysht, and Clallam Bay, and between Mora and Forks. The Forest Reserve would prevent any road construction or development, but now with the Reserve gone, the settlers were building their small part of America.

The Ericksons lost two children because they couldn't get the children to a doctor in Port Angeles. Then in 1907 his wife died at 36, leaving him with a two-week-old baby girl and a three-year-old boy. He was alone in the wilderness with little children. He struggled to raise them with the help of an Indian woman to do the menial work. She didn't have any formal education to start the children's education. The closest adequate schooling was in Port Angles. The business burden was a full-time-job, and with the responsibility of the children, he was almost overwhelmed. He struggled for three years with his exhausting challenge, then sold his business and moved to Port Angeles. Here his children got help, and Erickson became another force in the growth of the town.

The maturation of Port Angeles began in the 1890s with men who took on the Olympic Peninsula wilderness and converted some of it into thriving American communities. Aldwell on arriving in Port Angeles in 1890 climbed the bluff to overlook the harbor. There he dreamed of the harbor rimmed with vital industry and expanding payrolls, a place to raise a family. Later in the 1890s, Lauridsen observed: "Everybody knew it was a case of 'root, hog, or die'. Everybody was willing to work and no extreme poverty was known. In our meager circumstances, we learned to love and respect our fellow man and we got along fine."

The Port Angeles city fathers of the 1890s were a continuation of the first Europeans who crossed the Atlantic to form the original Thirteen Colonies. The colonies, with American spirit, expanded across the continent to the Pacific Ocean. Port Angeles was "The Last Frontier". These men expanded our American Heritage and created a Port Angeles harbor rimmed with industry. Clallam County was converted from a wilderness into a community of Americans. Peninsula Americans created wealth with their productivity, enabled by the rich land that grew farm products and trees. Trees were turned into lumber, plywood, paper, and rayon. The wealth, combined with the counties throughout America, produced the greatest democracy the world has ever known.

The productivity created by our forebears continued through the 1960s. In 2011, the harbor was slowly converted into recreational facilities; the productive Elwha dams were destroyed; and government regulations were curtailing the use of our land for growing farm products, trees, and extraction of minerals. The federal government is taking more land and resources from the county to expand new-age wildernesses, called *wild lands* and more. A multitude of government programs are revitalizing the Forest Reserves program that was objectionable to our city fathers.

Aldwell, Lauridsen, Erickson and other city fathers would be very distressed. Their progeny are angry at the threat to our American heritage.

MICHAEL EARLES' CRESCENT COUNTRY

Michael Earles came to Port Crescent and Clallam County in 1898 when the county had an economic development that created real wealth and jobs for the county, and that economy was developed by the organized utilization of the timber tributary to Crescent Bay.

The first white people to come to Crescent Bay came by canoe from British Columbia to trap for furs in the 1860s. The trappers and others settled in the Crescent area, followed by the early exploration of the interior by the trappers. Concurrent with the settlers, a few loggers operated along the shores with their oxen.

In 1880 a Dungeness logger set up a logging camp on the bay with his twelve oxen. He walked the beach between his Dungeness home and the bay in his infrequent trips to his home. The logs were yarded by oxen to the bay and rafted for the tugs that towed them to the Discovery Bay sawmill. A store near the bay was also established at that time, where the settlers from nearby Freshwater Bay and Eden Valley traded after a trek by trail to the store.

Then in 1889 the land developers or speculators formed the Port Crescent Improvement Company and bought most of the land on the west side of the bay from an early settler. The developers surveyed a town of 166 blocks and named it "Port Crescent". They justified the town on the basis of plans to make it the terminus of a railroad that would originate in Grays Harbor County where the Northern Pacific Railroad would connect them to the interior of the country. Also, the railroad would be extended into British Columbia via ferries.

Port Crescent's plan was completed and construction begun. The Improvement Company and the pioneers built a county road from Port Crescent to Lake Crescent that would begin to serve the perceived extensive farming communities in the area. A wharf was built on the bay, and boats regularly connected the town with other ports on the Strait and Puget Sound. While a breakwater was started to make the port more useable, the cost and practicality doomed the endeavor. The town had two hotels, two saloons, a cobbler shop, a small sawmill, and a schoolhouse, with about thirty residents and the usual amenities of a small town.

Most important of all, the town had a newspaper, the *Port Crescent Leader*. The *Leader* reported the activities and the sense of success with stories, such as that of a farmer who located near the Lyre River on February 19, 1891. The farmer reported a harvest of three tons of hay, potatoes of 300 to 400 bushels per acre, a plentiful harvest of carrots, parsnips, and cabbage weighing 24 pounds. The farmer optimistically stated that after the sale of his timber, he still had a valuable asset in the rich loamy soil. He felt that he soon could sell both logs and farm products easily at a prosperous Port Crescent. The farmer's optimism was repeated by the settlers, loggers, business people, and developers in the area.

The Crescent Country extended from the Elwha River to the east, to the Lyre River in the west and the Indian/Soleduck Valleys to the south. At the height of optimism, Port Crescent made a bid to become the county seat of Clallam County, in competition with Port Angeles and the existing county seat at Dungeness. Port Angeles had a larger population and therefore the votes to win the competition.

Then the depression of 1893 brought disaster to Port Crescent. After surveys were completed for the railroad from Port Crescent to Grays Harbor, the railroad folks withdrew their plans. In the middle of the 1890s, the Port Crescent Improvement Company failed, and the town hibernated — until Michael Earles arrived in 1898.

Earles had started at the bottom of the food chain. In his earlier years, he held a drill (a steel rod) for a striker in a mine. The striker needed some skill and strength to swing a sledge hammer to drill into rock. Earles soon moved from holding a steel rod to working in Wisconsin logging camps and then to construction of the Great Northern Railroad as a contractor grading the road bed.

By 1893, he had accumulated enough wealth to build a small mill at Clallam Bay with the necessary logging to support the mill. After the mill burned down, a disgusted Earles left for Maple Valley in King County to continue to use his talents. Then he moved on with a partner to Whatcom County (Bellingham) to build an export sawmill complemented with logging operations.

Earles and his Puget Sound Mills and Timber Company bought a tract of timber in 1897 to the south of Port Crescent from a Port Crescent Improvement Company investor. In the spirit of the pioneers of the west, Earles purchased most of Port Crescent's infrastructure. A year later, he moved in a team of mules and a primitive railroad locomotive carried on wooden rails strapped with iron strips that enabled the start of logging on the bluffs above the town.

The area tributary to Port Crescent was well populated with homesteaders and others who owned land, people much like the farmer on the Lyre River who had visions of a farm that would make him and his family comfortable. The settlers' aspirations complemented Earles' vision: a homesteader could sell either land or timber to Earles. As the homesteaders' land increased in value, county tax revenues could better fund schools and roads. Earles began a land and timber purchase program to encompass the Crescent Country.

Next, Earles had to upgrade his logging operation. First, he designed an efficient system to get the logs to the log booming grounds at Port Crescent for transportation by water to his Bellingham sawmills. He designed a railroad system out of Port Crescent into the timber, and a mainline railroad to Joyce, extending it east to the Elwha River and west to the Lyre River and beyond. Temporary railroads could then log north and south of the mainline. Earles' foresight that led to a complex operation seems amazing without modern tools to work with.

With his extensive plan in view, Earles had to upgrade the logging. First, it was to acquire the technology and the capital to design the railroads with steel rails. Next he acquired seven modern locomotives to run the rails and deliver the logs to Port Crescent for rafting and towing to his sawmills in Bellingham. He also purchased "donkeys" to yard and to deliver the logs to the railroad. A donkey was a steam boiler attached to a sled with log runners that powered a drum (a spool of steel cable). A cable, when attached to a log at a distance from the donkey, would draw the log to the donkey.

The donkeys, as well as the steam-driven locomotives, were generated by a boiler fired with cordwood. This fuel was labor intensive as logs had to be bucked (sawed) in short lengths and hand split to be stacked in front of the boilers. The donkeys were sited next to the railroad tracks to bring the logs via steel cable to the railroad cars. The cars would be loaded and moved to the water by the steam driven locomotives. The cable would be extended more or less a thousand feet from the tracks, making it necessary to design a temporary railroad to grid a logging area on about two thousand feet — an engineering challenge.

Initially, Earles' operation had to integrate a horse with the donkey. Along with the boiler, the donkey had a drum of steel cable which had to be pulled from the drum out into the bucked logs (setting). Several logs were attached to the cable (mainline) by side cables or chokers. The donkey powered the logs into the the railroad. Then, a horse and rider returned the cable to the setting, over and over again. This was a slow and tedious process that confined logging to gentle topography that a horse could traverse — almost flat land; logging debris also impeded the horse. Earles and other loggers finally eliminated the horse by adapting the power in the donkey to bring in the mainline and return it to the setting.

This primitive logging system was named "ground lead" logging. The logs were dragged along the ground and the lead, or end of the log coming into the donkey, would hang up. That is, it would dig into the ground. Stumps or debris stalled the donkey, which required the loggers to improvise. Later the loggers used a spar tree; using blocks, the cable from the donkey traveled up the spar tree (a tree limbed and topped) beside the donkey and out into the setting. This arrangement lifted the end of the log coming to the donkey from the ground and reduced hang-ups.

However, with wood-fired boilers in the locomotives and in the donkeys, sparks sometimes filled the air, or the bearings in the locomotives and railroad cars heated and threw hot material into the woods. Fire in the woods was always a danger for the trees, equipment, and even human safety.

By 1905, Port Crescent and Earles were in full swing. People were optimistic about furthering their American dream. The Markam Hotel in Port Crescent was the headquarters for Earles' Puget Sound Mill and Timber Company, as well as providing living quarters for the company management. Houses were provided for married men and the manager, and company bunkhouses for the single men. There were 200 men in the logging camps; the total employment was about 300 — almost all white Americans.

Many homesteaders were located between Crescent Bay and the Elwha River, a diverse mixture of European emigrants and Americans. They all traded at Port Crescent. Before a wagon road was constructed, it took a long time to get to Port Angeles. From Joyce, they had to walk to the Elwha River and, unless the river was low, hire the Indians to ferry them across. Then it was a long walk to Port Angeles.

In lieu of a bridge, the county hired a ferry to transport citizens across the Elwha River. Joe Sampson, with his canoe, was contracted to move the citizens across the river. It was 1913, and he was paid $40, then $50 a month until a bridge was constructed in 1914. The settlers used Port Crescent to do their business. At the peak of the town's boom, Port Crescent had more trade than Port Angeles. Michael Earles created the boom that Port Crescent developers could never have accomplished by themselves — that is, Earles the producer of goods, versus a promoter with nothing to offer but talk.

The people at Port Crescent worked long hours. Loggers worked eleven hours a day, six days a week, and most homesteaders worked longer hours. Nevertheless, Sunday was a day to rest and have some fun; fun that was simple relative to today's costly entertainment. Almost every Sunday, the community gathered at Agate Beach. Dances were held at the Markham Hotel, and fishing trips planned at Salt Creek.

The loggers sang hymns at a private home as single men and women gathered at a friendly neighbor's house. There was blackberry picking in season, clam feeds on the beach, and, above all for the men, a 'coon hunt. And there was serious saloon drinking for some of the loggers.

Earles was the driving force in development of the community between the Elwha River and Twin, and from the Straits to Lake Crescent and beyond to the upper Sol Duc River. When he started the development, he was a wealthy man who drove himself in work and play, as well as driving the people around him. He spent much of his time at his Seattle office; but when he was on the ground with his people at Port Crescent, he dressed informally, even somewhat slovenly. He was of Irish descent with a stocky build and medium height and sported a modest mustache to match dark features. He was a dedicated poker player who played on the boat when traveling from Seattle to Port Crescent, and often didn't depart at Port Crescent so as to continue a poker game as the boat continued on to Neah Bay. The poker game often went on all night, with Earles departing the boat when it returned from Neah Bay to Port Crescent.

The Crescent Country ranch settled in the 1860s by woodsman John Everett, and adjacent the second forest created by clearcut in the early 1900s by Michael Earles.

Contrary to the common portrayal of an aloof and absent timber baron of that era, Earles married the school teacher at

Port Crescent, a Miss Joyce, and built a modest house (for a man of his wealth) in the village of Joyce, a village whose name was derived from the school teacher's brother; Earles partnered with his brother-in-law in business around Joyce.

Earles' timber empire was intermingled with the community of settlers, independent loggers, and shingle mills. He was active in instructing his staff to treat their neighbors fairly, a staff that in that era was commonly overly aggressive in their dealings with neighbors.

Besides timber and land purchases, there were railroad right-of-ways over the neighbor's property to be obtained, fences to mend when trees crushed them, as well as cleaning up after moving trains that killed cows. Although his main objective was to operate his business, he found time to create good will between neighbors. Earles was a hands-on man who corrected his staff when he believed they were too aggressive. It was common for a train to destroy a cow that was slow to move away from a steaming oncoming train that couldn't stop. A settler would demand compensation for the cow at twice the value of the cow. Naturally Earles' employees would be enraged in dealing with the settler, so Earles, a hands-on owner, was be the one to placate the settler.

Earles also cooperated with the federal forest rangers by making his logging camps available for their use, as well as the use of his horses and mules. His sense of fairness could be touched with devilry. At his Sol Duc Hot Springs facilities, his people cut a few Forest Service trees. When the Forest Service brought suit for damages, Mike objected. Finally the suit was settled out of court for the *huge* sum of $30. But, the forest supervisor had to visit Mike's office in Seattle four times before Earles was available to remit the money to the Forest Service.

Of course, the Forest Service people believed Earles was a tyrant and cheap, in spite of him making his organization available to house and facilitate the Forest Service work crews who traveled to work. On the other hand, Earles believed the Forest Service was petty and should have ignored the $30 damage to "their" resources. After all, the man could have charged many times that for his help to the Forest Service or made it difficult for them to move across his land. Perhaps, it was the start of a rigid bureaucracy dealing with a man whose first priority was to produce the needs of America — in this case lumber.

Earles didn't confine himself to producing lumber. He and his bother-in-law Joyce built a shingle mill near the village of Joyce and started to raise rice just north of it. They even brought two Japanese farmers on board to show them the rice paddy techniques. However, rice was a product that could not be adapted to Joyce's climate, soils, or topography. Earles was a more successful farmer by designing and operating a farm at the mouth of Salt Creek and near Joyce to produce food for his logging camps and his mills' boarding houses. Uniquely, he free-ranged several hundred head of cattle over the lands after he had harvested the trees. The cattle ranged from the Elwha River to beyond the Lyre River to feed on the scant grass and herbs between the stumps. The cattle were rounded up once a year and a portion slaughtered to furnish meat to his hungry loggers and mill hands.

Earles was taking the trees off the land and converting the land from a static forest to useful farmland. Apparently he thought the small farmers could utilize the land more profitably than a huge "corporate farm", for he subdivided much of his new farmland into 10- and 20-acre dairy farm lots and advertised them for sale at a nominal price. This effort was only moderately successful.

Then, Michael Earles discovered the health benefits of the Sol Duc Hot Springs. In 1903 he and eleven others visited the springs to discover for themselves this unique feature. Unfortunately for Earles and perhaps Clallam County, shortly after his visit to the springs, his doctor told him he was dying and should move to a healthier climate. After another examination that suggested he didn't have time to move, he listened to stories of the Indians as well as whites who thought the hot mineral water was healing.

The hot springs were first made known to the settlers by Theodore Moritz who had befriended an Indian with a broken leg who he had housed until the Indian recovered. To reward Moritz, the Indian guided him to the Indians' magical waters adjacent to the upper Sol Duc River. In the early 1880s, Moritz filed a homestead claim on the land surrounding the hot springs and constructed a horse trail from the Springs to Fairholme, a village located on the west end of Lake Crescent. He also eventually added to his pioneer cabin a primitive bathhouse, wood-floored tents, and a rudimentary dining room. Moritz's facility soon attracted visitors to the springs' supposedly curative waters.

Earles and his party, like others before them, traveled from Port Angeles via a hazardous two-day trip by wagon, lake scow boat, and trail to bathe in the hot sulfur-smelly mineral water contained in carved cedar log tubs. Besides bathing in the mineral water, the water also had to be ingested to complete the therapy. Earles believed the therapy cured him and allowed him to continue in his business. He believed he should make an effort to make the therapy available to a wider range of people — therapy he believed would save lives.

In 1909 Moritz passed away and Earles formed a company to develop the Sol Duc Hot Springs. The first step was to buy the property from Moritz's heirs, which followed soon after the man's death. The company then coordinated with the Forest Service on the company's plan to build a wagon road from Fairholme on Lake Crescent to the springs. When the 14-mile road was finished in 1910, a sawmill and shingle mill were hauled over the road and soon were producing two million board-feet of lumber and three-quarters-of-a-million shingles for the buildings. Two hundred men worked on the resort that soon became the leading resort on the West Coast, hosting 10,000 guests in its peak year from across America and Europe. The cost of the resort was $500,000.

The resort was built around a top-of-the line hotel whose furnishings were done by the Frederick and Nelson Department Store in Seattle, supervising decorations. The hotel stood four stories high and featured rooms with balconies on one floor. It featured hot and cold running water, telephones, steam heat, and many private baths. The bathhouse was the main attraction of the resort, but there was also a large reservoir of mineral water, circled with seating.

The working facilities included a power house that generated electricity and steam for heating, an ice plant, ice house, a steam laundry, and a building to house the workers. For the guests, there was a gymnasium, a ballroom, a sanatorium, the hotel or cabins/camping areas, as well as fishing tackle for enjoying the nearby river and lakes.

The sanatorium was a three-story building between the hotel and the bathhouse, which was perhaps the best in the west. It had an operating room, surgical instruments, a laboratory and X-ray equipment, as well as beds for 100 patients, all tended by nurses, a medical superintendent and resident physician. Massages were available to the guests. This facility was definitely better equipped than most of the towns in the area.

A visiting Danish landscaping professional remarked that the grounds harmonized with the building and were the most beautiful he had ever seen. Incorporated in harmony were golf links, tennis courts, croquet grounds, bowling alleys, and theater, as well as billiard and card rooms.

Probably unique to an elite resort (past or present) was the resort's dairy and garden which furnished much of the food for the guests. The local water was used for everything, both fresh and mineral water. The temperature of the mineral water was 130 degrees Fahrenheit and contained gases plus minerals. The mineral water was thought to alleviate a multitude of health problems. It certainly eased my sore muscles after hiking. The mineral water was ingested fresh at the spa and bottled to take home.

Modern writers would think a resort that was built by a "timber baron" would cater only to the rich and famous. Not so, cabins and tents were available for the less fortunate that enabled them to share Earles' magical cure alongside the rich and famous. The hotel rates were three dollars a day or more. Baths were fifty cents and up. Customers who couldn't afford a tent could camp out under the stars. The resort could arrange transportation for their guests at $7.50 from Port Angeles, $11 from Seattle, and special rates from other cities.

However, the trip would be considered long and uncomfortable for most modern travelers. The Seattle folks boarded a steamer at the Colman Dock at four a.m. and steamed to Port Angeles. There they boarded an open red Stanley Steamer to begin a 19½-mile ride to Lake Crescent's East Beach, a rough road in autos with rigid springs. Stanley Steamers gave no protection against the rain, snow, heat, dust, or bugs and, unfortunately, the ride always featured several of these uncomfortable factors. Of course, the cars often had mechanical problems that left passengers stuck under a tree until the mechanical problem was solved.

The passengers underwent a sea voyage, an archaic car ride, and their Lake Crescent slow boat voyage for 12 miles across the lake to Fairholme. The last stage of the journey incorporated the red Stanley Steamers, with their slow and bumpy ride, that delivered them to the Sol Duc Spa.

Passengers represented a part of our American heritage, that is, both women and men who worked from daylight until dark, the men in some workplace and the women usually raising four or more children. When in public, like on Stanley Steamers, women were *properly* gowned and wore hats; the men wore coats, vests, gold-chained watches, and ties to tell the world they were successful Americans. Earles' Sol Duc Hot Springs was the talk of the West Coast and far beyond. It was the place to go for health and recreation by both rich and poor. Then the disaster occurred.

On May 26, 1916, sparks from a defective roof flue fired the shingles of the main hotel. Most of the resort was destroyed by the ensuing fire. There was little insurance, and the Sol Duc resort became just another common resort up to the present time. Clallam County mourned the passing of an icon: the Sol Duc Resort that was created by Michael Earles. When Mike died in 1919, he was almost forgotten. Furthermore, his empire had disintegrated. If Mike had lived a decade longer or left a strong heir, would the resort have been rebuilt and brought from the ashes again to be the world-class spa that would bring people from around the world to the Sol Duc Hot Springs? We will never know.

Around 1909 Earles thought his operation would be more efficient with a new sawmill in Port Angeles, only a few miles from his timber in the county. He was converting the timber into logs and finally into lumber to build America. Earles never shared his reasons for wanting a new mill, but logic provides some insight. His timber extended from the Elwha River west to the town of Twin and was criss-crossed with his logging railroad. The logs were loaded on railroad cars and dumped into water at Port Crescent to be rafted and towed to his mill in Bellingham, a mill that could not be supplied with enough logs from the Bellingham area. It would be more efficient to take the loaded railroad cars from Clallam County directly to a mill across the Elwha River and into Port Angeles

So, Earles started to lobby the politicians to facilitate his plan to benefit himself and the county. First, he asked the county to reduce taxes on his timberland and potential mill site. The county hierarchy wanted to help him, but was fearful of a lawsuit. Rightly so, the traditional law of America has mandated that property taxes must not be differentiated based on a property owners' income or any other reason. Property taxes are assessed strictly on property value.

County officials were powerless to furnish Earles with an incentive to build his mill in Port Angeles. However, the merchants and other citizens of the county were not limited by government bureaucracy. A mill employing several hundred people would fill the stores with customers and raise property values in the town. In addition, it would be a source of jobs for the city's young people. Earles reasoned that his mill would enrich the citizens of Port Angeles; therefore, he should receive some compensation from the citizens. So, the citizens by subscription (donations) funded the purchase of a mill site at the east end of the Port Angeles harbor. In turn, Earles built the biggest (arguably) sawmill in the world operating at Port Angeles in 1914 as opposed to Bellingham or elsewhere. The local name for Earles' mill was the "Big Mill".

Mike Earles was the superintendent of the state-of-the-art mill. It was a long mill that could cut timbers up to 150 feet long and cut lumber to fit the customers' needs as well as to make boxes. A shingle mill to complemented it. Three hundred men worked in the mill and were provided accommodations that included a bunkhouse, cookhouse, store, and butcher shop. A wharf could handle three oceangoing ships at once. Steamers and windjammers delivered Earles' wood products all over the world.

A year after he got the Big Mill up and running, he sold it to the Charles D. Nelson Company; the year was 1915. The Charles Nelson Company ran the mill until 1930, when it closed and soon after was scrapped. The closure was attributed to economics of the Great Depression. My father was working at the mill until the end of its operation, the year I was born. Fortunately, Zellerbach's pulp mill was operating next door to the Big Mill; after several months of knocking on their door every morning, Dad was hired to eliminate the nuisance of having him around their office every morning.

Earles' 1909 vision for the Big Mill also included a railroad to tie his logging operation to industrial Port Angeles. So, he worked with the community to accomplish his goal. He led the Chicago, Milwaukee, and St. Paul Railroad general traffic agent through his operations to interest him in developing a railroad on the Peninsula. Earles had dressed formally earlier to tour John Rockefeller Jr. and his entourage through his operations. The railroad agent probably also had a well-dressed Earles as a tour guide. The agent didn't volunteer to start constructing a railroad, but he was interested in the commercial potential of the area.

Earles brought C. J. Erickson to the Peninsula to undertake the construction of the railroad. Erickson had just made considerable money by building the Bremerton Navy Yard, and Earles talked him into constructing a railroad from the Port Townsend Southern line at the head of Discovery Bay to Port Angeles and west 20 miles to connect with Earles' logging railroad.

First, there was a problem in obtaining the right-of-ways. The Port Angeles Commercial Club, led by Lauridsen, had the task of accomplishing this. The club raised money by subscription for the project. This massive task took more than a year.

Before all the right-of-ways were procured, Erickson started construction. During the tedious process of obtaining right-of-ways, there were companies involved in the railroad to be liquidated, plus identities to be dealt with. Undoubtedly Earles furnished funds to expedite construction, and his business aggressiveness built a railroad. The railroad was completed in 1914 and sold to the Milwaukee Road, the people who had the experience and capital to operate a railroad successfully.

On July 21, 1916, a host of local business people took a train ride to the west end of the track seven miles west of the Lyre River. In 1916 the first regular passenger train made two round trips a day from the town of Twin at the western terminus of the line to Port Townsend, where passengers could take a ferry to Seattle. The average train had three coaches, and the passenger fare was $2.25. Passenger service was not the mainstay of the railroad; the movement of timber made the line profitable. The railroad freighted 95 percent timber and 5 per cent farm products. Commercially the railroad was a complete success, and for the people in the north Peninsula, it facilitated their movement around the country.

The railroad's success was an example of how communities could work together to better their lives without the help and interference of federal or local governments. The citizens, particularly the more affluent citizens, risked their hard-earned wealth to further improve their livelihood in their part of the country.

The railroad and the movement of logs brought changes from the Elwha River to Joyce. The forest had been mostly removed and a new forest started to emerge, enabled by seed cast by the older trees that geminated and started to grow in the rich forest soil. Scattered farms started to emerge from the wilderness along with small businesses. With a solid tax base, the county could fund a county road from Port Angeles to the Lyre River. The citizens in the area could then readily access the rest of the country and get their farm products to the market expeditiously. The logging camps moved farther west to Twin and Deep Creek. The logs west of Port Angeles were transported by train and not to the water, no longer needing to be towed to mills out of Clallam County.

Port Crescent soon became a ghost town and disappeared entirely by the late 1920s. The Port Crescent community was physically moved to Joyce. The Port Crescent store was moved there to be on the railroad line, as was the post office. Most of the goods and people came into the area by train not water. In the past, people traveled by boat to the Peninsula; now they came mostly by ferry and train. Joyce replaced Port Crescent as the small commercial center of the Crescent Country.

Prior to the railroad, there were Port Crescent's homesteaders plus primitive logging to the Straits where logs were rafted and towed to mills down the Straits. Gettysburg and Twin were two of the small logging and farming communities in the area.

Gettysburg was founded by Robert N. Getty who turned his homestead into a village on land a half mile east of the mouth of the Lyre River. The Port Crescent Leader described Getty as "the good looking papa of Gettysburg, a hustler from the tall timber". He built a store, hotel, boathouse and warehouse. In partnership with the loggers in the area, a breakwater was built to protect the log rafts from the turbulent water of the Straits.

Getty was also the postmaster. His village served the loggers and homesteaders in the area. Before 1908, the pioneers' only way to the nearest town, Port Crescent, was a walk on the beach or an upland rough trail. A canoe or rowboat would also get them to Port Crescent. The nearest commercial boat landing was at Port Crescent, and the mail had to be carried over a trail to Gettysburg and Twin. Later, someone had to row into the Straits to meet the passing steamer to collect mail.

More importantly, whiskey was packed on the mail trail, and often the eager loggers would meet the whiskey packer half way at Whiskey Creek for an early drink, hence the name Whiskey Creek.

Getty served the local homesteaders and loggers. The homesteaders were proud of their vigorous vegetables and oats that reportedly grew seven feet tall. The first logging outfit logged on two of the homesteads, more than welcome by the homesteaders as it cleared away the trees for their agricultural endeavors. The logs were yarded by oxen to the water and rafted behind the Gettysburg breakwater. Twenty loggers were employed.

Then Hall and Bishop started logging on their homesteads and expanded by buying timber from adjacent homesteaders. They were so successful they expanded their operation to include a three-mile logging railroad that enabled them to reach the interior for logs, a feat that was impossible for those confined to logging with oxen. In 1893 Hall and Bishop were contracted to furnish 100-foot logs that were 24 inches at the top for the Chicago's World Fair. Then in 1914, Michael Earles' logging railroad reached the outskirts of Gettysburg, which turned Gettysburg into a ghost town.

In 1890, eighty people took claims in the Twin area. The settlers cleared their land slowly and had a few beef cattle to sell to the local loggers. The nearest store and amenities took a hard eight-mile walk east on the beach and a winding trail through the woods to Gettysburg. For the bulk of their supplies, an order was sent to Port Crescent by steamer, and the order was picked up by a passing steamer. Of course, the pioneer had to row to the steamer sailing up the Straits. Besides the settlers, there were two logging outfits that logged near the beach, at first with oxen and then with steam donkeys.

Michael Earles' railroad and the Milwaukee railroad had provided passenger and freight service to the pioneers, and Earles' two large logging camps had brought jobs and civilization to the area. In 1921 the logging camps closed, the Milwaukee Railroad pulled its tracks, and Twin became very quiet.

The railroad made it possible to expand other businesses into the interior of the Crescent Country, that is, the shingle mills. Prior to the railroad, the shingle mills had to be located close to water, as water transportation was vital to getting the shingles to market.

The Goodwin family settled in the lower Elwha Valley in the early 1870s and expanded their farm to include a shingle mill that was run by water power. The shingles were loaded on scows from the beach, and the scows were then towed by tug to market. Loading the scows was hazardous and was often interrupted by high seas.

Goodwin soon moved his shingle mill several miles west to Freshwater Bay. The bay had a sheltered cove that afforded a quiet anchorage for the scows. The mill was up-graded to incorporate steam for power and to operate a dry kiln. Kiln-dried shingles would demand a better price than Goodwin's Elwha green shingles. At that time numerous shingle mills sat close to water.

Shortly after the railroad was expanded from Port Angeles to Twin, the Rayment Shingle mill was built at Ramapo, a family operation; a family picture taken in 1919 show 22 family members in working clothes, in front of their ancient truck and mill. The family members ranged from Grandpa (the owner) to babies in arms. Even the young boys and the women contributed to the manufacturing of the shingles.

Ramapo was located about two miles east of Joyce near where Salt Creek crosses the present Highway 112. The Ramapo School District was established in 1895, and a log schoolhouse was built on a settler's donated land. A "modern" school was built in 1915, and the Ramapo Grange was organized in 1916. The grange was built on acreage also donated by a settler, and the hall was later used for the seventh and eighth grades of the Crescent Consolidated School District until a brick school was built at Joyce.

In 1912, a two-store general story was built that included a post office. The second story was used for dances for local folks. Two years later, a settler purchased 20 acres from Michael Earles and built a small sawmill on the property. In 1919 the railroad was just north of the highway.

My paternal grandfather was related to the Rayment family and was asked to join the operation in about 1919. My father was a boy of ten years of age. My grandfather stayed with the Rayments for several years, then went to Port Angeles, later to put together a logging operation at Black Diamond in the foothills south of Port Angeles until the second World War. Then he worked in the woods for another independent logger near Forks.

When my grandfather arrived at Ramapo, it was a thriving community whose people were looking to further their American dream for a better life. The community was surrounded by old stumps. The high cedar stumps were a resource that fueled the Rayment shingle mill that employed my grandfather. The loggers cut the trees high (high stumps) because they thought the base of the trees were crossed grained, pitchy, defective, or the flared butt required more labor. A big cedar was invariably hollow at the base of the tree and unusable for lumber, so stumps were 15 feet high or higher. The fallers used spring boards (a steel tipped board that could be jammed into notches cut from the ground up the tree) allowing fallers to "ladder" up and stand on, to make the under and back cut in dropping the tree. A felled cedar tree also partially shattered into pieces too small for lumber. And finally, the market generally would not accept lumber with knots; logs with surface knots were left in the woods.

The process for making cedar shingles lent itself to utilizing high cedar stumps. Shingle bolts of wood were fed to the saws of a shingle mill. The bolts were a couple of feet long and sized in width to be handled by a man. One or two men could walk through the hollow stumps, cutting bolts to trim the cedar stumps to near ground level. Then a truck or horse drawn wagon made its way to the bolts to be loaded and delivered to the shingle mill. Fortunately, the ground was level around Ramapo facilitating the use of wagons or trucks. The manufactured shingles would be delivered to the market place by train, which eliminated the risk of water and tide on the Straits, making more cedar available for manufacture from inland cedar resources.

My father was a young boy who went to school and played in and around Ramapo for several years until the family moved to Port

Angeles. He and his older brother's favorite pastime was to play and fish in Salt Creek, a very small creek near the mill. Amazingly, their biggest thrill was gaffing salmon at the Salt Creek waterfalls during the salmon run. They had access to unlimited fish and would have undoubtedly wasted many, as boys do. This sport was practiced every year that the boys lived in Ramapo.

Forest area similar to Salt Creek surround a past clearcut of the South Fork of the Sol Duc River.

By modern standards, this historic fish run should have been decimated and nonexistent because of the massive logging in and around the creek. Undoubtedly many trees had been felled in and across the creek, the logs dragged up, down, and across the stream. Cattle used the creek indiscriminately. For over a decade the only forest cover or erosion controls were the stumps. The stream was not shaded, which caused its temperature to elevate. This stream was almost bare of trees when my father pulled salmon out of it. It appears logging might have enhanced streams productivity, but I'm sure the fish biologists can rationalize this unique phenomena. Almost thirty years later, my high school friend caught twenty-five steelhead fish at the Salt Creek falls and released most of them. At that time, the second growth Douglas fir and alder had shaded the creek. Salt Creek is not as productive as in the past. The only variable is the Indian netting across the mouth of Salt Creek in recent times.

In the 1880s, the Crescent Country was mostly a primeval forest that many worship, but the settlers and Michael Earles, among other loggers and shingle mills, converted the land into an American community. By

1920, the primeval forest was gone and a new forest was created, interspersed with small farms and housing. Against most modern thinking, the forest regenerated itself as a natural phenomenon, made possible because massive wild fires did not visit the area. The second growth has mostly been harvested and a third forest is now growing.

In the late 1930s, my maternal grandparents purchased a 40-acre dairy farm in Crescent Country at Freshwater Bay. I was about nine year old and loved the farm. The Crescent Country was interspersed with small farms and a vigorous new forest of Douglas fir. I helped my grandfather cut wood for the family's wood stoves in this new forest and was enthralled with the useful forest resource. I walked from the farm to Freshwater Bay and unknowingly through the site of the Goodwin shingle mill, wandering at their mill pond. Today, I drive through Ramapo and think of my father and his fishing. Crescent Country is a part of my heritage, and I'm thankful my forefathers fought and defeated the progressives' attempt to exclude my family via the forest reserves from my heritage.

Michael Earles started his Crescent Country logging in the late 1800s. An entry about the country by a modern author states: "The loggers took up their axes to lay waste to the bigger and better forests of Clallam County." My grandparents would describe Michael Earles' entry into Crescent Country as a wonderful endeavor that cleared the way for their dream home and established a structure that provided a livelihood for them and their progeny. My grandparents would be thankful the primeval forest was not preserved as dreamed by the aristocrats who could have destroyed the modern Crescent Country.

THE GLORY DAYS OF LOGGING

President Franklin D. Roosevelt toured the Olympic Peninsula in 1937 to observe a timber harvested area — or in the common vernacular of the day a "logged area". In his ignorance, or more likely his bias, he said, "I hope the son-of-a bitch who logged this is roasting in hell!" Of course, he purposely made this statement for the media who would propagandize it to the American people.

Further, he used the common propaganda of the preservationists to blame a greedy timber baron who they perceived was enriching himself to the detriment of the human race. However, there were also hundreds of loggers nearby he was *condemning to hell*, along with the forest communities in the area who depended on timber for their existence. The nation depended on the lumber that came from people's labor and the renewable forest.

Stan Fouts, of Forks WA, stands beside the stump of one of the first trees harvested in the Sol Duc Valley.

A sensitive man does not denigrate honest labor. Each man working in the woods takes great pride in his work. The fallers of big timber, as late as the 1940s, took hours to fall a mammoth tree. Two fallers on each side of the tree used their axes in a continuous motion to shave an undercut/wedge to direct the tree's fall. The wedge extended almost a quarter of the way into the tree. The wood chips from the ax blows were three to five inches square and covered the ground. Opposite the undercut at the back of the tree, the cross-cut saw was moved in continuous motion to cut almost to the undercut, and the tree fell naturally. Sometimes wedges were driven with a maul into the saw cut to lift the tree towards a predetermined path. Sometimes the fallers put a stake in the path of the tree to test their skill and almost always drove the stake into the ground with the tree.

Then, a bucker cut the tree into log lengths, running a six-foot or longer saw almost continuously for eight hours with care. These lumbermen understand the stress in the tree that could bind up a saw or shatter a log, thus endangering the bucker.

The next step was to get the logs to the railroad for loading onto railroad cars. A high climber spurred up a giant tree, limbing the spar tree up to about 150 feet, topped it with saw and ax, displaying a sense of pride that sometimes demanded a victory dance on the severed tree top. The climber, with a rigging crew below, rigged the tree with cable guy lines that ran from near the top of the spar to the stumps on the ground to strengthen the spar. Giant blocks were attached near the top that carried cable lines from the yarder powering the cables, moving the logs from the woods to the yarder. Initially the rigging crew had to take the line and block out to the edge of the bucked logs, usually 800 feet or more over steep, debris-littered ground.

The rigging crew had to attached cables (choke) to every log that was yarded to the railroad, where it was loaded onto rail cars. The rigging crew and their supporting people took great pride in putting out many carloads of logs a day. They compared their production to other operations, and competition between operations was stiff. The cynics say the bosses set the goals — and they do — but most loggers want to excel and set their own goals too.

A simplified view of the loggers' work has been stated in order to neutralize the view by many who think of loggers as rowdy, uncaring, or dare devils. Besides the basic logging, a support group plans and locates the transportation system and the logging units.

In fact, the loggers are innovative, hardworking, competitive, and are family men or have aspirations to become family men. The majority of the loggers in the early 20th Century were single men living with single men for long periods in the logging camps. Like single men today isolated from families, they occasionally blew off steam in town, much like college students on spring break on the Florida beaches. Of course, their antics in town have been glamorized to sell books. Also, their primitive town playgrounds were salted with bad and lawless people who sometimes could turn their play into tragedy.

The debris after logging is assumed by the uneducated to be a waste of the resource and a creation of a wasteland that will never return to the beauty of the forest. Visionaries know otherwise. Mr. Fredrick Weyerhauser bought 900,000 acres of timberland in the Northwest in the early 1900s and stated, "Not for us, nor for our children, but for our grandchildren." A few years later, his northwest manager remarked that the forest is renewable, made in reference to natural regeneration. Even as a young boy watching the Douglas fir seedlings pop up in my grandfather's pasture, I concluded that only humans could stop the forest from intruding on civilization by clearing them for farms and cities.

World War I began and Sitka spruce was deemed to be critical to winning the war. Sitka spruce was usually found close to the coast of Washington and Oregon. This almost forgotten tree was the only wood considered fit for the structure of the airplanes of the era. The Allies didn't have enough spruce to build an air fleet strong enough to defeat the Germans in the air.

Early in the war, an Italian military office called *spruce*, "a wood… which is consecrated by the Creator to insure liberty of the world and is the harbinger of peace and good will among mankind." Somewhat later, it was believed that the entire war effort hinged on spruce. Three allied pilots arrived in Aberdeen — one Italian, one English and one French — to meet with sawmill owners to implore them to increase their production of blemish-free spruce lumber.

The mills obtained most of their logs from the forests that were primarily Douglas fir. A whole new transportation infrastructure would have to be built to increase the production of spruce. And even then, there were few forests composed primarily of spruce; most of the spruce trees were intermingled with other species.

The timber industry wanted to produce more spruce for the war effort, and a combination of political structures was implemented to expedite the process. However, there seemed to be two insurmountable problems. The first was access of the spruce to railroads, logging the trees and converting them into wood for the aircraft frames. The second problem was the labor to solve the first problem. The war had reduced the labor pool of men, and the remaining labor was striking (walking off the job), deliberately slowing down production.

Industry and the government tried to overcome these obstacles without success until the government gave authority and the resources of the army to produce the spruce lumber. Colonel Brice Disque was assigned to lead the effort to produce the needed trees, and he did!

The Sol Duc Valley railroad grade was converted to a forest road, clear-cut in the 1930s. The Fork's Burn of 1951 destroyed many of the trees, but was replanted in 1964.

An army spruce division was formed of 30,000 men who were led by Colonel Disque. The colonel quickly made peace with the timber industry and labor to direct the spruce production. He immediately started to build railroads, mills, and logging activities by combining the soldiers with civilian labor, paying soldiers at the rate of their civilian co-workers. The division undertook thirteen railroad projects, built 130 miles of track, and cleared 80 miles of right-of-ways. The cost averaged $30,000 per mile of railroad constructed by the army versus the private construction of $750 per mile before the war.

On the Olympic Peninsula, 45 miles of mainline railroad were built and 20 miles of spur track laid. Merrill and Ring built a road from their Pysht headquarters to Clallam Bay in cooperation with the army. Alex Polson in the Quinault area also built a railroad in cooperation with the army.

The main effort on the north peninsula was the construction of a mainline railroad from Lake Pleasant near Forks to the Milwaukee Road near Joyce. This new construction accessed the spruce from the west end of Clallam County. The spruce logs were hauled by rail to Port Angeles. At Port Angles, the Spruce Division began to build a sawmill to process the spruce logs from the Forks area.

The Siems-Carey-H. S. Kerbaugh Corporation was given a cost-plus contract to build the 37-mile spruce railroad from the Milwaukee line near Joyce to Lake Pleasant. The corporation also had the contract to build the Port Angeles mill and the logging of spruce in the Forks area. The contract specified that the new railroad move 300 cars of logs, provisions, fuel, and supplies for the logging camps daily. Lake Pleasant was the terminus for the mainline railroad, and facilities were constructed to serve 10 trains, as well as facilities for the labor force of trainmen and loggers.

Port Angeles became a thriving city with the activity of the Spruce Division, and tiny Joyce became a town with hundreds using the post office and other facilities there. At Lake Pleasant, 6,000 "sprucers" began to cut spruce trees. Transportation to accommodate this horde of people as the railroad was being built was a challenge.

Supplies were transported via the Milwaukee Railroad to Joyce, off loaded to army solid-tire trucks that traveled to Lake Crescent, and ferried across the lake to a primitive road to Lake Pleasant. There were only two small ferries on the lake that could handle the traffic of the army and the civilians. Civilians were excluded from the ferries, forcing them to use the trail around Lake Crescent. County roads became a quagmire of mud and almost impassable. But, there were roads and railroads to further Disque's effort to win a war for freedom because of the pioneers like Tom Aldwell who fought off the preservationists in the federal government, those that would make Clallam County a Forest Reserve.

When the production of spruce seemed inadequate, Douglas fir was found to be as good as spruce for airplane frames. There was an adequate supply of Douglas fir immediately available. Of course, both spruce and fir had to be free of defects and fine-grained wood (probably more than eight growth rings per inch), qualities of wood found only in old growth trees. Finally, only a small percentage of the trees were useable for plane frames. The rest of the tree was left in the forest or used for construction lumber. Hence, there was a lot of waste left after logging, a waste that was constantly decried by the preservationists.

Ironically — or fortunately, depending upon your view — the spruce railroad and the Port Angeles mill were never used, as WW I ended before the facilities were completed. The spruce railroad was completed on November 30, 1918. Perhaps the greatest benefit brought to society from the spruce program was to bring relative peace and reform to labor in the Northwest forests.

The Sol Duc Valley railroad grade was converted to a forest road, clearcut in the 1930s. The Fork's Burn of 1951 destroyed many of the trees, but was replanted in 1964.

In July 1917 The I.W.W. had gone out on strike to close most of the logging and mills in western Washington. The isolated mills at Gamble and Ludlow, and the Grays Harbor Commercial Company at Cosmopolis continued to operate. The Cosmopolis mill operated only because it was protected by an electric fence and fierce security people.

Colonel Disque's priority was to bring spruce to the war effort, which was impossible in view of this labor unrest.

The I.W.W. was a militant union whose goal was to destroy the American capitalists to enable workers to prevail in the nation. Leaders denied they were Marxists. However, their principal leader fled to the U.S.S.R. to escape prosecution in the U.S., and was eventually buried in the Kremlin.

The I.W.W., an acronym for the International Workers of the World, were commonly called *Wobblies* or *Wobs*. Their labor disruptions were harsh and violent; their tactics were returned by the recipients. It was almost a war or revolution in the early 1900s. The Wobblies made a strategic mistake by ignoring the general citizens. They thought in terms of only two classes of people, capitalists and workers. The general public in the cities, towns, and rural areas generally rejected their tactics and banned and deported them from their communities — sometimes unlawfully and violently. Certainly the capitalists (mill owners) supported the citizens and tried to protect their property.

On the other hand, the nation was moving toward an eight-hour workday and sanitary working conditions; large timber companies were moving in that direction too. It made economic sense, but they resisted what they felt was blackmail by a union whose stated goal was to destroy them.

Colonel Disque came to the rescue. In short, he implemented an eight-hour workday, and sanitary working conditions. Just as important, he formed a new union, the Loyal Legion of Loggers and Lumberman, or 4-L. The 4-L brought management and labor together in the logging camps and mills to discuss common issues. Spruce continued to move from the forest to the mills and into airplanes and off to war. The I.W.W. continued its agitation after WW I, but the eight-hour workday issue was gone, and the union drifted into oblivion, to be replaced by the modern unions of today.

World War I fortunately interrupted movement of the forest industry from chaos and moved it into its glory years. Working conditions were brought to 20th Century modern standards, and the equipment was improved to enable logs and lumber to be mass produced. Mass production was a boon for the consumer as it produced plentiful lumber at a low cost to build America. The elitist and preservationists were terrified with what they thought was the irretrievable destruction of "their" forests.

Port Angeles and Clallam County expected great economic growth, funded by the federal government via the army's spruce division. Alas, the war ended and the army abandoned the spruce railroad and mill. Port Angeles felt abandoned too. But, Port Angeles still had the undeveloped timber resource tributary to their town and the "Big Three Logging Companies": Merrill and Ring, Bloedal Donovan, and the Crescent Logging Company.

The companies had the capital, the talent, and modern equipment to develop the private timber in the county to enrich the county, the state, the country, as well as themselves. Technology in logging railroads and logging equipment enabled a quick utilization of the resources. In particular, the old steam donkey was replaced with modern donkeys, now called *yarders* and *skidders*, which could bring logs (yard) from distances of well over 1,000 feet from the railroads. The new yarders brought the logs to the railroad quickly, overpowering any obstruction. The slow steam donkeys of 1900 were replaced by Big Bertha cannons of massive steel transported by railroad to the logging site.

Merrill and Ring was a Michigan company that had been investing in Olympic Peninsula land and timber for decades, that is, buying from a variety of landowners. By 1900, the company's holdings exceeded 25,000 acres near Pysht, a block of timber that would justify a logging venture.

In mid-1915 Harry Hall boarded a steamer at the Coleman dock in Seattle for the voyage along the Strait of Juan de Fuca to Pysht. Merrill and Ring sent him to start building their logging camp on a homestead there, purchased by the company. When Hall arrived at the campsite, several tents already were established. He moved in with the German foreman.

Hall helped put up more tents and a foot bridge over the small Pysht River to facilitate the work of about 40 swampers who would clear the campsite. He then worked with the engineers laying out the campsite and the railroad.

There was recreation. About once a month, a dance was held at Clallam Bay or Forks, bringing everybody in the area to town. The dance started about nine in the evening and paused at midnight for a big dinner. After dinner the dance continued until six in the morning, when breakfast was served. Transportation was by Reo, Model-T Ford, or other vehicle over primitive roads often blocked by falling trees, limbs, or washouts.

Late in 1916 logs were being railed out of the woods to be dumped into booming grounds at the mouth of the Pysht River. There the logs were rafted and towed to the mills to the east where they were sold.

Hall writes that the company personnel at Pysht was a stable contented group of people. I can attest to Hall's statement. The father of my aunt (by marriage) worked in logging for Merrill and Ring for several years in the late 1930s. He stayed in camp during the week and came home to our family in Port Angeles on weekends.

In 2011 Merrill and Ring was still growing and harvesting trees on its Pysht forest. In fact, they were growing a third forest. The transformation of Clallam County from a wilderness to a civilized community with a modern road system has made logging railroads and camps unnecessary. The modern road system, trucks, and equipment have permanently accessed most of the private timber holdings, allowing the labor force to be home with their families.

Bloedal Donovan Lumber Mill became interested in investing in the Olympic Peninsula in 1919 when the Spruce Division mill and railroad were being deposed by the government. The Port Angeles people believed their economic salvation was at hand. Bloedel and Donovan and another partner had founded a logging company near Bellingham in 1898. J.H. Bloedel and J.J. Donovan were two young engineers who met near Bellingham, took a timber claim and a partner, and started logging. This company then evolved into the Bloedel Donovan Lumber Mills in 1913 with Bloedel and Donovan the principal owners. They operated three sawmills, two shingle mills and two logging camps. Their employees numbered 1,000. More important to Port Angeles, their mills needed timber to continue to operate. Between 1921 and 1924 Bloedal Donovan purchased 32,000 acres that was mostly tributary to the spruce railroad that reached to the Lake Pleasant/Forks area. The government wanted $1 million for the railroad and demanded the railroad be a common carrier. Bloedel Donovan stated it could access its timberlands at less than a million dollars and they didn't want a railroad for others to use and the government to regulate. (A common carrier was obligated to transport the public's freight.)

No deal! The government couldn't allow one company to have the only access to most of the timber in the western half of Clallam County. It wasn't until 1922 that a road was finally constructed around Lake Crescent, between Forks and Port Angeles. All heavy freight prior to this had to be transported by rail or water.

A speculator, Lyon, Hill and Company of Portland, Oregon, became aware of the spruce railroad's potential and purchased the railroad and other assets for $1 million. After all, the timber in the West End had to come over its railroad. The asking price was $3 million for potential buyers.

Bloedel Donovan built its own railroad. It had purchased the Goodyear Logging Company at Sekui in 1914. In turn, Goodyear had purchased the Robinson Logging Company who developed the Sekui operation in 1898. Robinson started building a railroad south towards the Sol Duc Valley and Forks/Lake Pleasant. They built one of the tallest wooden railroad trestles in 1904. So, Bloedel Donovan bought a booming ground for log dumping at Sekiu and 15,000 acres of timberland partly cutover. Most importantly the company bought a railroad aimed at the terminus of the old spruce railroad, then owned by its competitors.

They also owned much of the timber tributary to their mainline railroad to Lake Pleasant and beyond. The railroad paralleled the old spruce railroad for several miles. Bloedel Donovan had the biggest logging operation in Clallam County. During 20 years of logging, it built 100 miles of railroad. In the peak years of 1928 and 1929, it employed 1,500 men. One of the sections of timber contained more than 160,000 board-feet per acre. A current Douglas fir forest ready for harvest at 50 years old would contain only about 50,000 board-feet per acre. Sadly for Port Angeles, the logs were rafted and towed to Bloedel Donovan's mills in the Bellingham area.

In 1927, the Crescent Logging Company was formed with stockholders who owned timberland in Clallam County. The stockholders included the Polson Logging Company; Merrill, of Merrill and Ring; and William Boeing, of Boeing airplane fame. The Crescent Logging Company was formed from restructuring the Irving-Hartley Logging Company, which had logged north of Lake Crescent.

Petrus Pearson was a stockholder and managed the company. He had come from Sweden at the age of 16 to work for a logger/mill as a timekeeper. His menial timekeeper position gave him the training to move upward in the logging business, eventually to become manager of the Irving-Hartley Logging Company. The Crescent Logging Company's first camp was at Piedmont, located at the north end of Lake Crescent.

The Crescent stockholders had timber holdings in the Sol Duc Valley and obviously were interested in purchasing the spruce railroad from the present owner, Lyon, Hill and Company. The stockholders and other interested parties bonded together to form the Sol Duc Investment Company. The spruce railroad became the Port Angeles Western. The Crescent Logging Company moved its operations mostly into the Sol Duc Valley between Lake Crescent and Forks, intermingling operations with Bloedel Donovan. They were in competition in every way, especially bidding for timber from private owners. In 1940 Pearson purchased the inoperative Carlsburg sawmill to operate it on logs from the Crescent

Logging Company. The Crescent logs were processed in Clallam County, the only company in The Big Three Companies to do so.

The tradition of logging is built around log production measured by the number of railcars or trucks loaded in an eight-hour day by a crew. A crew is built around yarders and loaders that yard logs and load them for transportation to a mill or processing center. The tradition, started in the Northwest in the 1850s, has continued to the present day.

In 2011 the Axe Men TV show produced a program that matched logging companies against each other based on the number of truckloads of logs they produced over several months, recreating a sense of how it has been done for decades.

In the early 1930s, The Big Three Companies began an extemporaneous competition. The Crescent logging crew of 18 loaded 65 loads in a day and was praised in the Port Angeles newspaper. Over the next year, the Big Three tried to beat that goal, and did it five times. The last competition was won by the Bloedel Donovan crew that produced 93 loads, a record that was thought to be a record over more than a century of logging. Sadly, in today's America, few other groups can match the verve and productivity of the loggers. On the contrary, they are viewed as *archaic and quaint* by the elite.

The Port Angeles Western log trains crossed the Freshwater road frequently in my youth. As we crossed the tracks on the way to my grandfather's farm, it was a thrill to watch the smoking train puff and snort through the valley. The train represented the work ethic of Clallam County. In 1951 the train stopped running, and shortly the tracks were removed. It was near an end of an era, the era of the "Glory Days of Logging".

The Big Three Logging Companies finally ceased operations. The Crescent Logging Company was purchased by Fibreboard in 1944 and in turn was liquidated. Merrill and Ring pulled its railroad tracks up at Pysht in 1944 to convert the property into a sustainable forest adapted to modern forestry and logging technology. Bloedel Donovan was purchased by Rayonier in 1945.

I stayed at Rayonier's Sappho camp in 1954, where I cruised timber in the rain for two months. It was one of the last railroad logging shows in the country. A speeder transported me over the rails from camp to the woods where I legged it into the woods for eight hours. (A speeder is a small and improvised gas-powered rail car used to carry a few men or light freight.) Rayonier soon closed its camps and converted its operations into a modern sustainable commercial forestry endeavor.

At the peak of the glory days of railroad logging, there were 460 railroads, more than 6,700 miles of track, and about 1,230 locomotives. The wooden trestles were sometimes works of art and sometimes rickety piles of sticks that somehow carried the trains. The Baird Creek trestle near Longview was almost a quarter-mile long. The wood to build that bridge today would require a tree harvest of about five acres to furnish the timbers for the trestle. A trestle near Aberdeen cost about $1 million. These structures were high fire and flood risks.

By the 1960s, the Glory Days of Logging were history, to be replaced by more mundane forest enterprises. Life was easier, but the heritage of the people carried through to the present day, that is, the ethic of productive hard work and the satisfaction of contributing wood fiber to better our lives. The naysayers of the past were wrong. The so-called destructive forest practices in reality converted dying forests into vibrant young forests that we see today on the lands dedicated to growing trees. Today's hard-working loggers are now logging the forests that their predecessors created in the Glory Days of Logging.

WEST END PIONEERS

Western Clallam and Jefferson Counties on the north Olympic Peninsula have been referred to as the "West End" by the local folks for more than a century. The West End has been isolated from the eastern part of the Peninsula by the Olympic Mountains and rough coastal hills south of the Strait of Juan de Fuca. This wilderness region is the farthest western part of the 48 contiguous states, and was the last to be civilized by the American pioneers.

In the middle 1930s, my Port Angeles family frequently talked about the West End as if it were "Camelot". I soon discovered my maternal grandparents operated a 160-acre dairy farm on the Forks Prairie, where they were milking about 30 wonderful dairy cows.

My folks began frequent car trips to Forks from Port Angeles, about 60 miles, from our house on Lauridsen Boulevard to Highway 101, west through an enchanted countryside. On such trips, we drove past the city limits, across the highway fills, and over Valley and Tumwater Creeks choked with young green trees.

The creeks were the streams I fished in later, at about nine years old. Two or three of my peers and I would grab our fishing poles, jump on our bicycles, and pedal to Valley Creek, just over a mile from my house and about 1,000 feet past the city limits. The limit on trout was 21, and we usually took about six for each of us. We cleaned the fish, which our mothers reluctantly cooked for us. We believed we were adding to the family's larder.

Valley Creek had experienced the debris flow in the 1860s that flooded Victor Smith's Customs House into Port Angeles Harbor.

Undoubtedly, all the vegetation 100-or-so feet on each side of the creek washed downstream, a factor that suggests the creek was permanently destroyed by the flood. But, the creek naturally rehabilitated quickly, and we had the trout to prove it.

Valley Creek was not good enough for us. It was too close to town and over-fished, we thought. Tumwater Creek was just a couple of thousand feet down the highway beyond Valley Creek. As we grew older and wanted more fish, we went on to Tumwater Creek where we doubled our catch. We marveled at a wooden bridge type structure in the middle of the creek, several feet above creek level, old and covered with moss.

Much later, logic and history suggested this was Norman Smith's three-mile railroad he built in 1903 up the creek from the Port Angeles waterfront. The construction denuded the vegetation on both sides of the creek as earth was moved through and across the creek to finish the railroad grade. Like Valley Creek, Tumwater Creek suffered no short-or-long-term destruction.

The next few miles past the creeks presented small cattle farms with modest houses and outbuildings — a view of a productive pastoral scene. Next, the Elwha River crossing was exciting. The south end of Lake Aldwell could just be discerned, and I thought of my uncle working at the dam on the other end of the lake. In 1942 the thrill for a youngster was viewing the gun emplacement on a bluff overlooking the bridge; our *enemy* could never cross that bridge. On the other side, our car motored through Indian Valley forested with young trees. The highway ran above the Lake Sutherland, source of Indian Creek. Looking down, the lake shimmered like a jewel among the forested hills, hills that had been clear-cut periodically and renewed naturally. My dream of swimming and playing in the lake was realized later.

A short distance from Lake Sutherland, the highway burst through a pass in the hills to view beautiful Lake Crescent. The highway curved at water level around the lake for several miles; on occasion there were small roadside resorts and stores to serve the public. It was exciting to motor past a fish hatchery that enhanced the lake for the sports fisherman. The lake seemed alive with beauty and human activity.

By 2011 the hatchery was gone; the fishing was poor; most of the public amenities were gone, and, water skiing had stopped. There are few people playing on the lake; the Park Service is well on the way to converting a recreation lake into a wilderness lake. At the end of the lake, the road started up the Fairhome grade, a grade surrounded by over-mature timber and notoriously difficult for motorists in inclement weather.

At the top, we were in the Sol Duc River Valley. A road junction to the left was the road to the Sol Duc Hot Springs where I later learned to swim. Beyond the junction, the highway travels straight and level through the 1907 Sol Duc Burn for several miles. This burn was characterized with young Douglas fir and white snags, the remnants of the so-called *ancient forest*. I was informed of the history of the area, which generated my dream of Camelot. I wanted to be a part of creating a forest.

Continuing down the valley and looking north up the ridge, I could see a fire lookout, the Klose Nanich, that looked down on the romantic valley. Just past it, the highway is routed next to the rushing boulder-filled Sol Duc River, a river view that has not changed to the present time.

Next to the river we saw a beehive of activity at the Snider Ranger Station. These were the people who created the new forest in the Sol Duc Burn. How exciting! Later, I learned my uncle was there with the CCCs (Civilian Conservation Corp) and fought forest fires at $30 per month, to preserve our forest. Even more exciting, he hitchhiked to Port Angeles to see his family periodically.

The family motored past the Snider Ranger Station to a recent clear-cut logging site and almost to the Forks' farm. We stopped to pick the trailing wild blackberries (Riubus ursinus), a blackberry for the purist because of its flavor, unsurpassed by the other contrived blackberries, especially the introduced weed — the Himalayan blackberry. I was too young to pick berries, so I sat on a stump while my parents filled a half-gallon container with berries in an hour — to be made into my grandmother's pies. I marveled at vegetation that interfered with the berry picking and the bees (yellow jackets) that attacked my mother.

The area had been logged only about three years, but already had a host of vegetation, including Douglas fir seedlings. Later when the family visited the Sol Duc Hot Springs, I asked why we didn't pick berries. I was told there were no blackberries in the old forest, nor many bees, because there were few flowering plants for the bees. Later in life, I was to learn of the evolving forest characteristics. The early succession of the forest's vegetation composition is dramatically different from the late succession forest of older trees. On most current federal forests, I can no longer pick blackberries or enjoy the honey-producing fireweed, because timber harvest has been curtailed greatly.

Our journey ended with our entrance to the economic center of the West End — Forks. My grandmother was pleased with the berries, but the young grandson and his eagerness for the productive farm dominated the visit.

To a youngster from the "big city" of Port Angeles, Forks seemed unique, an earthy community dedicated to achieving a livelihood from the soil. I needed to understand the history of the forest and the farms.

Grandfather Rue farmed the Peterson homestead on the Forks Prairie during the 1930s. I was seven-to ten-years-old and wanted to journey from my home in Port Angeles and help my grandfather farm for the rest of my life. He milked thirty cows by hand with the aid of a hired hand on 160 acres. The hired hand lived in the loft of a one-bedroom family house. The cows had to be milked twice a day, which meant very early in the morning and late in the afternoon.

The primary marketable product was cream, which was sold to the dairy a couple of blocks away. The farm had a milk house where the cream was separated from the milk with a hand cranked "separator". The skim milk was fed to the hogs. The farm's existence was based on cream, supplemented by hogs fed mostly on skim milk, chickens managed by my grandmother, an orchard, and a huge garden.

The three-person business took all day, seven days a week. The summer involved a haying crew to transport the hay with horse-drawn wagons to the barn from the fields. The hay was the winter feed for the cows and the team of horses. After the haying, the crew repeated the process with the oats that were thrashed on the farm by a machine to separate the oats from the stalks. Grandmother fed the crews, preserved the products from the garden and orchard, processed the eggs, and did the normal household chores, all without modern work savers.

Leisure time was confined to a quarter-mile drive to Forks (two blocks small) for a movie or weekly shopping. Once a month, they took a trip to Port Angeles (60 miles away) to visit their grandchildren. After all, the cows had to be milked. And, the highlight of my grandfather's day was one hour on the radio to listen to "Amos 'n Andy" and the news.

Forks Prairie was small relative to the extensive rich farms in the Dungeness Valley. The prairie could support only a few 160-acre homesteads. But the prairie had deep rich soil and was almost devoid of trees. A farmer could plant a crop immediately, contrasted to homesteading in the deep forests that surrounded the prairie. The nearest Native American village, the Quileutes, was located at the mouth of the Quillayute River 15 miles to the west. The village had a difficult harbor that could be used only by small boats during calm weather. And calm weather was rare in the winter.

The Quileutes used the prairie for hunting, an Indian trail connecting the village to the prairie. With difficulty, canoes could traverse up the rivers between Forks and the Quileute village, traveling the Quillayute to the Bogachiel and finally the Calawah Rivers to reach Forks. The town of Forks was so named because it was located between the Calawah and the Bogachiel Rivers.

Prior to the American settlement, the prairie was maintained by the Quileutes for hunting by periodic burning to maintain the grass that attracted the deer and elk. The old forest surrounding the prairie became almost devoid of the lush grass needed to maintain healthy numbers of animals. However, the numerous meandering streams in the area provided good habitation in the flood plains for grazing animals, second only to the temporary openings created by clear-cut logging that mimicked the prairies.

The first white men to reach Forks were undoubtedly Hudson Bay traders and trappers. In 1850, a canoe of traders landed at Pysht on the Straits of Juan de Fuca and spread out across the countryside. Some of these traders arrived at the Quileute village where they found a bonanza of furs. The tribe included great whalers, sealers, and hunters who accumulate a plentitude of furs to trade for the white man's goods. A Hudson Bay Company boat from Victoria traded at the village periodically until the Americans took control of the area.

In the early 1850s, two Hudson Bay hunters and trappers settled on the Peninsula. John Everett took a claim on Freshwater Bay and John Sutherland took a claim at Forks. The two men had "discovered" Lakes Crescent and Sutherland, but only Lake Sutherland retains the name of the explorers. In addition to their discoveries, the two men became well known on the north Peninsula for their skills in the woods. A career hunter and trapper also built a cabin on the prairie in 1860, which he used intermittently for years, marketing wild meat and furs in Victoria, Canada. In the modern world, it is hard to visualize a one-man entrepreneur who could collect wild goods and create a market in far-off Victoria. The transportation of goods, probably by canoe north on the wild Pacific Ocean and through the Straits, was a Herculean task.

The West End's potential was circulated to the Dungeness and Port Townsend communities that were as cosmopolitan as any in America. In 1867, a group of Dungeness pioneers explored the Forks area to improve themselves with free land. In 1868, they returned via Pysht on the Straits. They blazed and cleared a trail from Pysht to Forks and re-discovered the Forks and Quillayute Prairies, grasslands waiting to be farmed.

The group filed claims and even obtained from the territorial legislature the designation of a new county, Quillayute County. However, the new county failed to have enough residents even to fill the offices of a legitimate county, and collapsed. In addition, the new residences of Quillayute County soon became discouraged and returned to Dungeness. The land was rich, but their goods could not be transported economically to the markets in the east. Today with highways, the people in Forks can travel to Port Townsend in less than two hours; in the 1860s, it took days.

The next significant move to transform a wilderness into American communities came with the arrival of Dan Pullen in about 1872. Pullen was thought to have given the Quileute Village the name of La Push, derived from the Chinook jargon. About the same time, several other people settled near La Push and the nearby Quillayute Prairie.

Dan Pullen, born in Maine, quickly became a sailor at the age of 14. He left the sea as a young man to become a logger around Puget Sound. He wanted to better his fortunes, and his obvious frugality made possible the purchase of a small trading schooner. The trading rewarded him with a small fortune before he settled at La Push, where he was joined by two brothers. The brothers took up preemption and homestead claims and added to their land holdings by purchasing other settlers' claims.

Pullen became one of the wealthiest men in Clallam County, wealth that was created by his trading and land holdings. His primary property was a 160-acre claim among the Quileutes at the mouth of the Quillayute River. He built a house on the headland of his claim that was perhaps the most pretentious house in the county, a small mansion located alone in the wilderness West End.

Pullen started trading immediately at La Push, but the Washington Fur Company of Seattle was already established in the area. So, he sold out his trading business and became the La Push manager for the company. The trade was centered around seal skins, with a report of 8,000 seals taken in one season from the vicinity. In 1880, sealskins were purchased for $10 each. Later Pullen and the fur company separated, with hard feelings exhibited by both parties. Still later, the fur company went out of business.

In 1878, Pullen showed Luther Ford the Forks Prairie, sometimes called Big Prairie or Indian Prairie. Ford selected a homestead and brought his family to the site. When he located on the prairie there were only three men there, all single trappers and hunters. Ford was the first family there and had the first white child born on the prairie. He was a leader in the pioneer settlement because of his personality and farming leadership. However, the area was so isolated that a six months' supply of essentials had to be purchased from the traders at La Push to economically farm the prairie.

Pullen was a leader in the minute pioneer effort in the Quillayute Country. He was located on the only harbor tributary to the area with trading facilities that furnished goods to the community. He directed many settlers like Ford to claims.

He also formed a self-defense force when necessary. The Quileute Tribe was isolated from a reservation and had no federal government infrastructure to provide direction. According to the treaty of 1856, the tribe was to move to the Quinault Reservation far to the south. But, most of the tribe stayed at the historic Quileute Village, without a schoolteacher or other agencies folks. Finally after many years, the Makah Agency sent out a schoolteacher, who had to teach elementary details like dress codes and sitting in chairs. The children and parents revolted at times and finally threatened to kill the teacher. The only protection the teacher had was Pullen, since the government was far away on the Makah Reservation. At one point, Pullen brought armed settlers to La Push, all he could contact, probably fewer than ten. A show of force demonstrated to the natives the consequences of murder.

Pullen's endeavors went beyond trading and arguably "public service". The Pullen brothers made the first cattle drive from the prairies of the Quillayute to Port Townsend. They drove 150 cattle to Port Townsend in six weeks. The greatest aid to the drive was "an elaborate vocabulary". It was reported they swam the cattle across the mouth of Discovery Bay. The beaches were utilized for the drive, but in many places the beaches were inaccessible and the cattle had to be moved through the almost impregnable forests. Later the trails were improved and cattle were driven to the Straits and loaded on vessels or barges. Even then, some 9-to-12-feet diameter windfalls survived, to be climbed over or avoided.

Pullen could be credited with enabling the settlement of the West End. Unfortunately, his life swirled with controversy. He had filed a pre-emption claim in 1882 and a timber claim in 1883. The Quileutes didn't move south and believed Pullen's claim was an incursion into their historic village. Pullen was adamant in thinking that his claim was valid since he followed the letter of the law. Further, he thought the government was remiss in not moving the natives off his land.

Pullen was the trader, all powerful because he strongly influenced the economic life of the village. He was also a strong man who had achieved his success through the hard life of a seaman and logger, where leadership was many times enforced by harsh means. He was surrounded by a lot of Indians who had a history of violence.

Contrary to the threatened schoolteacher, Pullen could face groups of threatening natives with a steel bar swinging, guns blazing, or both. Quileutes complained to the Makah Indian Agency of mistreatment. The response by one Indian agent was that he was surprised that the Quileutes did not take the matter into their own hands; if they did, they would be justified. The government wouldn't control the situation. Undoubtedly, the settlers would take control of the situation if murder was committed in their country, and smart Quileutes were aware of this.

Still, the Indian agent's prediction soon became a reality. Obi, an influential Indian, went to Pullen concerning damages to his fence and garden. Pullen followed Obi to his house to view the damage and was pulled into the house where three Indians tried to beat him to death. The village chief broke down the door and pulled a bloody Pullen to safety. Obi was taken into custody and transported to Steilacoom for trial. When he told Pullen he would be the second white man to be killed by him, the Quileutes confirmed the killing. Obi sealed his fate by killing his cellmate, an Indian boy, he thought to please his captors.

Finally on February 18, 1889, President Grover Cleveland by executive order, gave the Quileutes one square mile encompassing their village and Pullen's claim. In the fall of 1889, as was their tradition, the Quileutes canoed to the Puyallup area to pick hops. While they were gone, their village was burned to the ground. History and the Indians blamed Pullen without proof.

In 1891, the court handed down a decision that the Indians had precedence over the white settlers. Pullen continued to drag the matter through the courts to lose his "fortune"; he died a broken man. Ironically, the victors, the Indians, were treated as heroes; the victim, Pullen was treated as a villain. Nevertheless, the Quileutes have an obscure village, while Pullen has the legacy of making a significant contribution in converting a wilderness into American communities.

Pullen, Ford, and others started the communities in the West End, but getting agricultural products to market was almost insurmountable for decades. During the summer, supply boats could enter the La Push harbor but could not carry bulky farm produce. The rich soil grew hay, oats, grain, and garden produce. The only practical market was the Indians who traded white man's goods for fur. Cattle were a partial solution because they were mobile, but a cattle drive to Port Townsend was uneconomical. The West End needed railroads or, more importantly, all-weather roads to the markets in eastern Clallam and Jefferson Counties.

Transportation came slowly to the outside world. The Clallam Bay road construction was started from the Strait to Forks. Thirty-five miles of road composed of mud, ruts, and puncheon, were completed in 1892. In lieu of cash, the construction was accomplished mostly by settlers who worked out their county tax liability. The road was hardly adequate to move heavy farm products to market. In the late 1890s, a foot trail was available from Forks up the Sol Duc Valley and across the divide to Lake Crescent. At the lake, an individual hired a canoe to cross the lake where another trail led to Crescent Bay and a steamer to the east. Roads and trails were improved until the spruce railroad became functional after World War I. More importantly, in 1922 a road was constructed around Lake Crescent to take autos and trucks quickly from Forks to Port Angeles. The West End had become accessible to the world markets.

The Forks town site was laid out in 1912 with a couple of stores, a post office, and a little log schoolhouse. Forks didn't grow significantly until the town had a railroad nearby and a good road to the outside world.

In other words, the commercial aspects of the West End didn't flourish until transportation in the 1920s opened up the markets to the east. However, optimistic Americans and soon-to-be Americans kept coming into the West End to claim free land. They had confidence that America would continue to grow westward, and this growth would stop only at the West End ocean front.

One of those men who created the American dream was John Huelsdonk, who became a legend matching the likes of Daniel Boone, Davey Crockett, and a host of other American woodsmen and pioneers. Huelsdonk epitomized Thomas Jefferson's American ideal: "A sturdy yeomanry, possessed of land and firearms and respect for education, a populace independent of great cities, cooperative but self-reliant."

His work ethic and vision were typical of the West End pioneers. However, his strength separated him from the ordinary. He became "The Iron Man of the Hoh". It happened on the day he made his routine 22-mile trek on the trail from Forks to his homestead on the Hoh River. He periodically had to pack household staples to his Hoh ranch. That day he was stopped on the trail by his settler neighbor, Chris Morgenroth, for the usual chat between friends. He was asked if the cook stove on his back was too heavy. The Iron Man remarked quietly,

"No, but the 50-pound sack of sugar keeps shifting in the oven and aggravatingly throws me off balance."

Other reports said it was 100 pounds of flour. Morgenroth identified the stove as being a #7 cast iron stove that weighed about 110 pounds. A cook stove of that era is described as: a huge cast-iron/steel monster supported by short legs, a rectangular monster that encompassed a large oven alongside a firebox that housed burning wood. This box was topped with a half-inch-thick plate of heavy iron. The stove had a steel back two feet above the steel stove cap, that had a compartment to keep food warm. My grandmother had such a stove, and it weighed much more than 110 pounds.

Many stories of that trek circulated throughout the Peninsula. It is possible the Iron Man met several parties on the trail that day, resulting in different versions. However, the feat is documented well. The only part to debate is whether it was 50 pounds of sugar or 100 pounds of flour along with the weight of the stove. The Iron Man was humble and would not even confide to his family the weight of the pack or the gossip revolving around the event.

The Iron Man at times worked for the government and private parties packing supplies to their work crews. On one occasion, he asked if he could obtain double pay if he carried the loads of two men. The boss laughingly agreed, expecting he would walk a few dozen steps and collapse. He packed about 200 pounds day after day.

Huelsdonk was born in 1867 on the lower Rhine in Germany. In 1880, he came to Iowa with his parents, grandparents, and six siblings. The family purchased a farm, and for almost the next decade, he helped work it. The older boys worked the farm, but yearned to go west. The Iowa sun blistered the boys in the summer; frequent lightning was disturbing; winters were cold and confining.

The farm finally was sold in exchange for a family store. Riding day after day behind a team of horses in the Iowa cornfields felt boring and lazy, and the family store was not appealing to a young active man who wanted to be outdoors. It was also obvious the future would be bleak sharing an inherited store with all of his siblings.

Elizabeth Huelsdonk Fletcher describes her father's journey to the West in the Iron Man's biography:

John was the first to leave Iowa to go west. He worked with a survey crew near the Snohomish River in Northwest Washington, then the Skagit River Valley to the north and finally Sequim on the Olympic Peninsula. The country was rich in good soil, trees, wildlife, scenery and a mild climate relative to Iowa. The region was not over-populated. He returned to Iowa and his two older brothers were anxious to join him to obtain free land in the west.

The three traveled to Lake Crescent where their wilderness trek began. They made a raft to cross the lake generally west to Fairhome, then up the hill to the divide into the Sol Duc River Valley. There they stumbled on a vacant new homestead. They stayed in the house three days to dry out, killed a deer and dug a few potatoes from the farmer's garden. It rained for three more days. In addition, they had no idea where they were going; instinct directed them south.

Before they left the homestead, John extended the farmer's drainage ditch to compensate him for the shelter and potatoes. A divide in the hills to the south was not apparent, so they followed the path of least resistance, west down the Sol Duc River to approximately Snider Creek. Huge trees obscured visibility to only a matter of feet in any direction, and they needed to look for a pass through the hills to the south.

To view a pass in the hills, they fell a sapling against a big tree and climbed the sapling onto the big tree. Their southerly trek took them to the Calawah River where they crossed on a foot log, a downed tree. Across the Calawah, they fell another sapling onto a big tree to view another pass that gave them access to the Bogachiel River. The brothers waded across the river and climbed over the next hill to the south and down to the Hoh River to find a settler's cabin. The settler informed them there were claims up and down the river, but none in the upper river above his homestead. This was good news; the brothers could settle close together.

John's two brothers started back to Iowa by going south to civilization instead of retracing their steps. It must have been a difficult journey for two Iowa farm boys to hike through a nearly uninhabited forest that was soaked with rain day after day, a trek unimaginable in today's world.

John stayed on the Hoh to develop his claim and to preclude others from preempting him. He rushed back to Iowa to propose to his boyhood sweetheart in early 1892. John and one of his brothers immediately returned to the Hoh to build a cabin on his brother's claim. It would be the newlywed's temporary home until a proper house could be constructed on their claim. The little cabin was made with saplings that grew close by; cracks between the logs were filled with moss. The bed frames were made of poles.

The brothers had brought their almost invalid grandfather with them to do the cooking, the washing, and keep a fire going. He could also advise the boys on gardening when they cleared enough vegetation to plant a garden. The brothers acquired a cow they could pasture among the alder trees and big leaf maple close to the river. Wild grass grew under the alder, but not in the deep forest. With a cow, it was necessary to cut the wild grass interspersed with the trees and build a small barn to store hay for winter feed.

The cabin was built; hay was in the barn; and the potatoes were harvested from the small garden. It was timely for John to return to Iowa and marry. Dora and John were married on October 15, 1892. They left Iowa immediately to avoid traveling in the winter weather, taking three weeks to get to the Hoh. They arrived at Pysht and were met by the brother and then proceeded to the Hoh, mostly in pouring rain. The bride rode a horse and the brothers walked. There were several overnight lodgings. Dora even helped with the cooking at some stops for the night. After they had traveled several miles past Forks, the bride was forced to walk. Her trunk was suspended from a pole. With a brother on each end of the pole, they trudged along the trail. The wet and muddy trail was blocked with mud slides in places, and the party had to detour through the salmonberry to continue on their way.

Finally, the newlyweds got to their temporary home. The river had flooded the night before, flooding the barn and house with several feet of water. The hay was ruined. During the flood, a brother carried his grandfather *out of the house. They slept under a large spruce tree all night around a roaring fire.*

The next day, the water had receded, and John and Dora arrived home to a silted house. The first chore was to level the silt on the dirt floor of the cabin to prepare for their first night at home. The sleeping arrangements were close. Two brothers slept in an upper bunk with grandfather in the lower bunk. The bride and groom slept in a pole bed separated from the family with a canvas.

John and one brother almost immediately started the newlyweds' house across the Hoh River because the couple was expecting a baby. They purchased a canoe from the Indians to enable the brothers to traverse the river that was so swift they used a pole to move the canoe rather than paddles. The Iron Man became an expert canoeist.

They built the house on a rise above the river near a spring. The bothers had learned a hard lesson about the flooding river that ran wild during the winter freshets, taking some settlers' houses and even their newly cleared land. In today's world, the raging Hoh River still is taking land that creates enormous sedimentation downstream, a phenomenon now that would be attributed to logging. And, today a small part of the lower Hoh River has been armored with rip-rap (rock) to save land adjacent to the river. The river's sedimentation is largely independent of human activity.

The brothers cleared ground for the house and immediately fell seven giant spruce trees. They knew a strong wind could blow the trees across the house, a fact that modern society often ignores. The house was to measure 14' x 20'. On the south (warm) side was the door and two sash widows. Saplings were utilized to construct log walls 13 feet in height to create a two-story house, with the downstairs room a normal eight feet high. The entire house, roof, and walls were covered with split shakes. The downstairs' floor was constructed of split planks about three inches thick and about six feet long. The green boards, on drying, shrank, causing big cracks between them. The couple and grandfather walked to their new home. Dora cared for the grandfather for the next seven years.

The baby was born shortly after they settled in the house. Fortunately, there was a homesteader doctor nearby who delivered the baby. The Iron Man learned the skill to deliver the next baby. Dora had her home, husband, and daughter to make her happy. But, she also had to contend with dirt and bugs, slinking wild animals, primitive manual labor, and cooking on a hot wood stove in the summer. The stove was inadequate to moderate the winter cold and dry sodden clothing. Perhaps, above all, there were no other women to share her feelings with.

Dora soon had more than bugs to contend with. The Iron Man was away from home often to Forks or down the Hoh in his canoe for supplies. An itinerant sailor with a small vessel would enter the mouth of the Hoh with supplies for the settlers, a feat that few would attempt, and settlers could canoe down river for supplies. (It was easier than the trail to Forks.) Poling back to their homesteads was difficult on the dangerous river. In addition, John's father's business in Iowa was ruined in the depression of 1893. The ailing father came to the Hoh to be cared for by Dora.

Dora's husband and his brother went down the river for supplies, leaving her with two very sick elderly men, a baby in a cradle, and a toddler at home. Evening set in and it was vital to milk the cow to feed the babies and sick men. She tied the toddler to a trunk. The baby was in a cradle with a rope attached to it and given to the grandfather in bed to rock the baby if necessary. Bucket in hand, she went out to find the cow that had wandered into the deep forest. After milking, she turned to return to the house and was lost. Her unflappable Native intelligence surfaced. Accompanied by the family dog, she scolded it and told him to go home. The dog would trot a few hundred feet and turn towards her. She scolded the dog all the way home.

At home, all was well. The toddler even enjoyed being tied, but still no husband or brother-in-law. They were long overdue from their trip on the dangerous river. What would the family do without her husband? At last, both men came through the door. Dora was a true Iron Woman of the Hoh.

When the Huelsdonk family came from Iowa to stay with John and Dora, there were fourteen people in the small house, and a small addition was added. Some of the family took homesteads for a while in the valley, but most left the Hoh eventually.

The family was fed from the local farm and from wild game. Occasionally money was earned from temporary government work like surveying. The highest priority was to clear the land for their ranch. Huge spruce were felled with a crosscut saw or burned by starting a fire at the roots of the tree, keeping the fire burning for weeks. Most of the big spruce trees were hollow, and a fire could be started in the interior of the trees. Only the straight-grained, knot-free, decay-free trees were useful for lumber or split shakes. The knotty tops of the trees were useless. On the ground, the big trees (logs) were burned with difficulty.

The Iron Man used a ship's auger to drill holes in the huge logs and charged the holes with hot coals. The understory (such as vine maple) was slashed, piled, and burned. It was useful to pile the slash against the big logs to burn. Twice the Iron Man's fires roared away from his homestead and through the forest. The forest fires were not major in extent and regenerated naturally to create a healthy forest. The hollow diseased trees were replaced by a healthy vigorously growing forest.

Early in the development of the Hoh homestead, the Iron Man needed cash to supplement the ranch's meager or non-existent earnings. He did what most homesteaders did; he went to the logging camps. The best opportunity was Michael Earles' operation headquartered at Port Crescent. It was a hike of 22 miles to Forks and up the Sol Duc Valley to Lake Crescent, a canoe voyage across the lake, and finally another hike to the vicinity of Port Crescent. The trek was much more than a day's outing. Earles' outfit only logged during the summer, which was probably more logging than most homesteaders wanted. The logging camp was a railroad camp just west of the Elwha River.

The first season John hurt his ankle, rode a horse home, and impatiently convalesced. The next season he caught his fingers in a block, which partially crippled his fingers on one hand. Logging was a dangerous way of life — but so was all life in that era.

Back in Iowa, the Iron Man's sister lost her husband in 1899. He had a sore toe and told his unbelieving wife, "Well Hanna, I have to die now." A few months later he died. The sister came to the Hoh to live with the family for a time.

The Huelsdonk family decided logging was too dangerous. But, the Iron Man had to seek an income until the ranch became sustainable. Income could be generated on the Hoh, through hunting and trapping. He soon excelled at his chosen craft. He was sensitive to the killing, but soon became at peace with his hunting and trapping because the animals were predators. Wildcats caught the chickens; cougars and bears ate the sheep; and wolves participated in wholesale slaughter. When the Huelsdonks arrived on the Hoh in 1892, elk were sparse. Later after the predator population was reduced, elk overpopulated the Hoh Country. The elk almost destroyed the understory vegetation, and the forest became more open to travel.

John's winter trapping routine was to go up the Hoh with his dogs for about five days at a time and camp, returning to his ranch to process the furs. Besides marten, mink, and other fur bearers, there was a bounty on cougars and wolves that paid well, about $50 for a cougar. He shot about ten cougars and ten bears a year. The family did not usually eat bear meat because the meat tasted too fishy, but they rendered 100 or more pounds of lard from one bear. They ate deer, elk, grouse, and lots of fish, mostly trout. Steelhead proved too big for their fishing tackle.

The Iron Man traveled light when hunting. Many times darkness forced him to sleep overnight. Often it was too wet for a fire and he sat with his dogs, his back against a tree and a slicker over his head. He had little trouble sleeping. He dressed in a cotton shirt and overalls and needed no wool underwear or stockings. He dropped a three-quarter-length oil slicker over his pack. In his hands he carried a gun and an ax.

Elk meat was a household food staple. In the early days on the Hoh, the elk were sparse and the Iron Man had to roam far. He carried the meat home on packboards, where the animal was quartered, each quarter weighing about 100 pounds. The quarters could be moved occasionally by packhorses if trails were nearby. Otherwise it took a man with a packboard to move the quarter sometimes miles to the house across broken and brush-tangled vegetation. Meat was never left in the woods no matter what the packing difficulty entailed. The meat was eaten fresh or preserved for later use by salting or smoking. Some years later, the elk population increased and the animals moved closer to the homestead.

The earlier scarcity of elk was attributed to over-hunting by wildlife predators, settlers, and Indians. The Indians lost their interest in the hunt, and the settlers eliminated most of the predators. Wolves no longer inhabit the Olympic Peninsulas. The elk became so plentiful they almost eliminated their food sources, such as elk fern and elderberry. Even the barbed-wire-like devils club was ravaged and the salmonberry endangered. They ate bark and the fungus-decayed wood of the sturdy cottonwood trees. The elk were starving, but the progressives were fighting to save the elk by preserving thousands of acres, particularly in the name of elk protection. The Iron Man was frustrated. The academics and their regulators would not go to the people who lived with the elk for solutions. It seemed it was beneath their dignity.

The Iron Man's frustration and vision went beyond elk. President Jefferson once suggested the American ideal was in American yeomanry. The Iron Man's vision mirrored that of millions of American yeomen who were subverted by the elites.

In the same era, the federal government asked the National Academy of Sciences, dominated by Yale University, to appoint a Commission to decide the fate of the Olympic Peninsula and hundreds of millions of acres in the West. The eastern Commission toured the area for a few weeks and never consulted with a yeoman. The commission attempted to take the Iron Man's homestead from him in the creation of the Forest Reserves, initially followed by more taking over the decades. Fortunately, the producers in the country moderated the eastern elites' plan for the settlers' future.

The Iron Man's frustration didn't interfere with his productivity to create forest communities for his family and others. When he heard that the Woodland Park Zoo in Seattle had cow elk, but no bulls, he decided the cow elk needed companions and he needed funds for his family. The zoo agreed to accept two bull elk. Two elk calves were captured easily, to be trained to accept his leadership. The pets were named Dewey and Bismarck, a yearling and a two-year-old when the Iron Man tied the elk to his saddle horn to lead them over the trails to Clallam Bay on the Strait. There a steamer crew slung the elk aboard the vessel, the elk joined their consorts at the zoo.

Sometime later one of Huelsdonk's daughters went into the live elk business. Daughter Dora was teaching school, but abandoned teaching to care for her now elderly parents (John and Dora) on the homestead. In addition, she wanted to be more productive. The Washington Department of Game asked her to collect elk to be delivered to Forks, paying her $100 for each elk delivered. An elk was worth more than a teacher's salary for a month.

The calving season came in late May and June when the elk grouped themselves in the river bottoms. A cow elk would generally walk away from its calf's hideout to draw Dora away with it. A calf could then be picked up without a struggle, a rope placed around its neck and led away to the homestead. There the new "mother" (Dora) fed the animal with a warm pail of milk. She would put her finger in the milk and then into the calf's mouth. A few revolutions with the finger and the infant would go to the pail. It took a five-gallon can of milk to feed the little herd of elk calves.

The calves grazed well in the fields with the cows, and were weaned in the fall. The tame calves followed the family around the homestead. In the fall they were driven by Dora and one of her sisters to Forks to be dispersed by the state throughout elk country where the elk population was non-existent or sparse. The calves were driven easily over the Forks/Hoh trail.

Dora had competition for the calves. Bears stalked the mothers and their calves. The mothers would run from the bears and the calves couldn't keep up. A well-known Olympic elk photographer came upon a bear eating a calf alive. The calf's ears were bitten off and it was crying pitifully for help. The elk also had to defend themselves from the wolves and cougars; the calves were especially vulnerable. Contrary to today's perception, nature is cruel and unforgiving.

The wild animals furnished food and income to the settlers that allowed them to survive in the forest until land could be cleared sufficiently to grow marketable farm products. Also, a transportation grid had to be constructed to economically get the goods to market. A road didn't reach the Huelsdonk's ranch until World War II.

John Huelsdonk vision was to see the valleys turned into farms paralleling President Jefferson's anticipation over a century earlier. The hills and ridges would grow a "crop" of trees as his farm produced grass, grains, vegetables and domestic animals. He had observed the abandoned homesteads quickly being reforested. It took less than ten years for ten foot or taller spruce trees to appear on the abandoned land. This observation by Yale educated Gifford Pinchot, the father of forestry, went unseen or ignored.

Removing the trees and brush took years to clear enough acreage to create a sustainable farm. The farms or ranches were primarily oriented to cattle, both beef and dairy. A pasture and hay fields were mandatory. A cabin and later a house was the first priority, a barn constructed immediately after the house. The cattle herd grew as the land was slowly cleared. A milk cow was the first animal brought to the homestead, especially for families with children.

Besides the land clearing, fences had to be constructed to control the cattle. Potatoes were grown in quantities for home use, trade, and a cash crop. A big garden was started immediately for peas, beans, turnips, rutabagas, beets, onions, and rhubarb. An orchard in some locations was added when cleared land was made available. The settlers' families spent all of their free time clearing land by slashing and burning.

The early clearing was converted to grass, timothy, and clover. As the clearing grew, oats were planted too. Before available threshing machines, oats were cut with scythes that had a cradle fastened to the handle. The cradle directed the fall of the oats. The stalks were grouped in sheaves and tied. The sheaves were stood upright, four to group.

When the grain had dried, the threshing began. The sheaves were spread on canvas and beat with a flail to separate the grain from the stalks. The flail was a hardwood board attached to a handle. The straw was separated from the grain and the grain sacked. The grain was fed to cattle and horses or sold. A hard working horse worked better when fed with grain. The new straw gratefully replaced the worn straw in the settlers' bedding.

As the ranches grew, the homesteaders overcame weather and wolves. The relationship between the settlers and the Hoh Indians was

friendly. The first settlers found Indian hunting shelters on the upper Hoh, and their canoe traffic on the river was frequent. The Indians shared their knowledge of the Hoh wilderness with the whites. The settlers in turn shared their knowledge and sometimes their vegetables and other goods. Both groups helped each other in the infrequent times there were emergencies. Above all, there was no attitude that "the only good Indian is a dead Indian", as suggested by modern writers when portraying the whites' negative attitude toward their Indian neighbors.

Upper Hoh River, where the Iron Man of the Hoh settled. This is his vision of the area, clear-cut in the 1930s, flourishing 70 years later.

A day of near-terror occurred in September of 1902. The Yacolt fire that burned thousands of acres near Vancouver raged, as did numerous other fires in western Washington. Day was turned into night on the Hoh by the smoke. Chickens were on the ground; they didn't have time to roost. Birds flew against windows.

Some people slept through the day, and settlers caught on the dark trails in the daytime couldn't move. They didn't carry the settlers' lantern, which was comprised of No. 2 or No 10 can. One side of the can was slit vertically and horizontally. The slit metal held the lighted candle, which projected light. A wire loop served as a handle.

Today the progressives continually tell us pollution is rampant. They even want to ban wood burning stoves. But, there has never been pollution in recent times as the people on the Hoh experienced in 1902, a pollution that was endemic through the 1920s or 1930s. Relative to those early years, we are pollution free.

In the late 1800s and early 1900s the academic progressives were politically active in forcing the government to take the land away from productive Americans who were using it to create the American dream. The country would have been better served if the academics had used their intellectual energy to incorporate the talents of all the people in the country.

The Iron Man and his neighbors had the vision that should have been incorporated in studies at Yale and beyond. Unfortunately for America, the so-called intellectuals and eastern politicians ignored "the people" who lived on the land, the people who gained knowledge through that use. The Iron Man and his neighbors struggled, worked the land, and educated their children while the federal government attempted to destroy their livelihood

The Iron Man concentrated on educating the children. The schoolhouse he built on his property was a small log cabin fitted with homemade furniture made with limber split from the resident big spruce trees. The pupils sat in a row on two benches, with a bench in front of them for a writing table. Paper was too expensive, so slates and slate pencils were used. The teacher had a desk near them. The school was started with four students, as were many schools in the area. The lack of transportation dictated the size and location of all schools. Schools were upgraded over the years with a fireplace, which was later replaced with a "modern" wood stove for heat.

The teacher was employed by the school district, which in turn was funded by local taxes. Taxes were raised mostly from the timber companies (the settlers had little or no money) who sometimes objected to the high cost of education. The teachers were certified and paid $40 to $60 per month. The school term began as a short three-month winter term that lengthened over the years. The only housing available to the teacher was in the homes of the local settlers.

The upper Hoh school teacher boarded with the Huelsdonk family, who received $20 a month for room and board. The Huelsdonk girls wore dresses to school. In the earlier years, the girls wore dresses at home. Their father believed overalls were more practical, so dresses were reluctantly put away. But, their mother dictated that dresses be worn in school, even though the school was only a short walk from the house. The children's education was supplemented with primitive home schooling.

After 17 years in the Hoh wilderness, Mother Dora Huelsdonk was to visit a city. Mother and children had not even seen the "big town" of Forks. They were to see the 1909 Alaska-Yukon-Pacific Exposition in Seattle and visit their grandmother in the city. To start the journey, the family — father, mother and four daughters — hiked 22 miles to Forks where the family stayed with a friend overnight. Mother rode a horse.

The daughters had never seen such a luxurious house. Early the next morning, a buckboard drawn by two horses took them 35 miles to Clallam Bay on the Strait. It took all day. Then, a steamer took them to Seattle, where they stayed in the grandmother's house. The girls had never seen an automobile, let alone the thrill of the exposition. A professional picture was taken showing the four daughters dressed in immaculate formal dresses of the era. Their grooming was perfect. The proud parents transformed the girls who had milked cows the week before into prim young ladies ready for ballroom dancing.

John Huelsdonk, The Iron Man of the Hoh, died in 1946, at 79. Dora passed away the next year. The myths of the Iron Man of the Hoh will be repeated for centuries. Unfortunately, history will write about a man who could carry a stove on his back and was a hunter/trapper in the quaint long-ago past. He was much more than that; he was and is our American Heritage, the man President Jefferson believed was the spirit of America.

The Iron Man was not unique on the Olympic Peninsula. Many others did as much, but were not publicized. These were the men and women who started with a wilderness on the east coast, civilized it, and took the civilization across the country to the wilderness of the west. They did it with aggressiveness to better themselves and their country, and many paid for it with their blood.

Perhaps the Huelsdonks' greatest heritage was their daughters. All four daughters graduated from college with an inherited productive drive to improve their forest community. They all came back to the West End to raise families because they loved the country, an emotion Yale academics will never know or recognize in others.

This emotion was demonstrated by daughter Elizabeth. In 1921-22, she was teaching in eastern Washington and came home to the Hoh for Christmas. She traveled to Forks. It was early afternoon when she started the 22-mile hike on the trail to the Hoh. She didn't take time to change clothes, just put on hiking boots. She walked 18 miles in the snow and was tired. She rested at a vacant settler's cabin and called her father on the Hoh River. (Some ranches had phones to report forest fires by then.) Her father immediately saddled a horse in the dark and brought his daughter home. A year later, the daughter married a settler's son and happily lived in the West End for the rest of her life.

Another daughter, Lena Huelsdonk Fletcher, furthered her father's vision by becoming a "champion of the rural landowner". She was a school teacher, farmer, writer, mother of six children and Justice of the Peace. She used the only communication available to her: she spoke out boldly and wrote letters continuously to newspapers and politicians. Lena died in 1985. Her last letter to the local newspaper urged "repeal of about half the state's restrictive and bureaucratic laws" and "let us return to constitutional law". Her statements are still being pleaded by rural communities, along with the producers in America. Unfortunately, the Congressman representing her district is elected by an urban majority, an urban community that cannot relate to rural concerns.

The Iron Man's granddaughter, Missy Barlow, resided in her later years alone on the Fletcher homestead at the mouth of the Hoh River until her death in 2010. There were few neighbors. She obtained a degree in botany from the University of Washington and spent most of her life near her heritage, the Iron Man's Hoh River.

I spent many afternoons on her ranch discussing the West End's natural resources and her grandfather's vision of building a vigorous forest community. She was a talented woman who produced oil paintings and a multitude of other art. She was a poet and writer and, above all, she was an unrecognized expert on the flora and fauna of the Olympic Peninsula. She killed her last elk in her late 50s and gave up the hunt then only because of "the crazy outside hunters".

Our discussions revolved around the underutilization of the peninsula's resources associated with the confiscation of the private land by the outsiders' federal government. The transient outsiders can never appreciate the Olympic Peninsula like the people who fought to transform a small portion of the wilderness into civilized communities. The stewardship of the land needs to be given to the Huelsdonks and their neighbors, not the Yale University academics and their peers. Until the stewardship is passed to the resident users of the land, our American Heritage and economic sustainability continues to be reduced.

I observed how the Iron Man's vision was almost brought to fruition in the middle 1930s, when farming and big logging was going on in the West End. The progress moved forward for decades.

By the mid-1990s, progress had slowed or even regressed. It started with President Teddy Roosevelt's creation of a National Park system and the progression of the federal government taking land from productive use to preserve it in a wilderness state. The Forest Service's sustained timber harvest no longer exists. Clear-cut harvest has been abandoned, while unreliable natural regeneration is all that is occurring. The little logging taking place is confined to a thinning that converts a Douglas fir forest into a hemlock forest, contrary to the laws of nature. A Douglas fir forest is renewed by catastrophes, such as fire or clear-cut logging. The federal government policy of eliminating regeneration harvests (clear cut) will create a climax forest composed of tree species exclusive of Douglas fir. The long list of new-age Forest Service practices on their land depresses the forest communities. The federal government continues to take private land for forest preservation, a practice that doesn't benefit the forest and suppresses the forest communities.

The federal government's progressive policies will destroy the West End forest communities, a decline that is already evident. The forest community depends on growing trees efficiently. Skeptics suggest tourism will fill the void. However, tree growing will not curtail the tourist trade and could even have a synergistic effect and enhance the trade. The skeptics tell the world that scenery and environment will be destroyed without federal protection. The record suggests the 1890s Port Angeles fathers were sensitive to the scenery before the academic east knew there was a Mount Olympus. The Iron Man and his peers understood the scenery and the ecosystem because they lived within it for years. There was no greed with these citizens.

Just before her death, the Iron Man's daughter, Lena Fletcher, identified the bureaucrats' attack on farming and tree growing as frivolous and unnecessary restrictions that reduce drastically the productivity of the farm and forest. Since 1985, these restrictions have more than doubled.

Finally, the Iron Man's vision for farming has been destroyed by government restrictions and changes in farm technology, combined with the economics of farming or ranching. The restriction on producing milk has almost eliminated an economic small dairy farm. Milk is now mostly mass-produced by huge cattle herds in feed lots; other farm animals have followed a similar format. Grain and hay is mass-produced on large farms that require huge investments in equipment.

The Peterson homestead that my grandfather farmed now is used to raise beef cattle, as are other homesteads that have not returned to the forest. The cattle business in the West End is marginal at best. Again, this business competes with cattle raised in feed lots and vast cattle ranges.

The West End began as a wilderness. Through the struggles of the pioneers and entrepreneurs, some of it became an American community of productive families. It is apparent the Iron Man's vision of farming and tree growing is partially correct. Modern technology has made most commercial farming uneconomical. Still, growing trees is very viable. Tree growing protects the environment and wildlife and creates employment in a host of industries and businesses.

The progressive/preservationists' goal is to preserve the landscape for some future generation to view, that is, millions of acres. The land in the West End along with the rest of the Olympic Peninsula is being taken away from the local people to preserve in a "natural" state dedicated by the federal government to academics and elites. The vibrant forest communities of my youth are deteriorating. The vibrancy can be returned and enhanced for the people and forest by simply returning to regeneration harvests across the forest lands of the region.

OLYMPIC NATIONAL PARK

A s America expanded west of the Allegany Mountains to the Pacific Coast, the government took control of most of the land that was identified as the public domain, owned and administrated by the government with the goal to transfer it to the citizens in an expedient manner. However in the 1890s, the government abrogated decades of American heritage and created the Forest Reserves. In 1897 President Grover Cleveland placed nearly two-thirds of the Peninsula in the Olympic Forest Reserve — that is, 2,188,800 acres — and people started to flee the Peninsula.

The battle for the Peninsula started that year and continues to this day. Fortunately for the citizens, the Reserve was quickly reduced and the Peninsula began to flourish, while The Reserve's primary purpose was to reserve the timber for future use. It soon turned into a nasty name-calling fight between elite preservationists and those people who wanted to utilize the natural resources.

The core of the Peninsula was, until the 1890s, an impenetrable mountainous wilderness, with Mt. Olympus at an elevation of nearly 8,000 feet dominating the core, surrounded by other peaks. The scenery in this mountainous core remains spectacular, with lakes, alpine meadows, rivers, glaciers, rocks, forests, and wildlife.

Around the core, the lowland was gentler and heavily forested. The openings, generally prairies, were small and few, while the lakes, rivers, creeks, and marshes were scattered throughout the forests. The Peninsula, was surrounded on three sides by salt water — the turbulent Pacific Ocean to the west, the Strait of Juan de Fuca on the north, and

Puget Sound on the east. Rain and water were plentiful. A combination of soil and water blessed this lowland with arguably the most fertile tree-growing region in the world. In the 1850s the lowland American settlers had started to convert this wilderness into civilized and democratic communities, but mostly ignored the less fertile core composed of the Olympic Mountain range.

Indians avoided the interior Olympics. First, there was little reason to challenge the rugged mountains when the salt water and rivers furnished easy canoe travel on waters that furnished the major source of their food. Second, superstition intimidated many of them. Even so, Indian legends spoke of the Sol Duc and Olympic Hot Springs, suggesting the hot springs originated from the hot breath and tears of two battling dragons. Unsubstantiated reports told of a coastal tribe crossing the mountains to gamble with a tribe on Hood Canal.

Undoubtedly, the trappers and the curious visited the area from time to time, but little was published of their adventures. Speculation on the character of the area was fanciful. In 1882 the army at Fort Townsend sent a unit to cut a trail into the Olympics, starting from the fort and extending to the Dungeness River west and south into the Olympic Mountains. After six months of strenuous labor in the summer, they came out of the foothills to the mountains and gave up the endeavor. The army considered the project too difficult for further action.

The army tried again in 1885 to penetrate the Olympics. Lieutenant Joseph O'Neil was assigned the task. O'Neil had been stationed at Fort Townsend earlier and was interested in exploring the mountains. He collected all the information he could over the several years he was stationed in the area at the Vancouver Barracks. He left in early July with six men and several pack mules to explore the mountains. Lacking information, he looked at a map and determined that Port Angeles was the closest community to the Olympics.

The O'Neil team arrived in Port Angeles on July 16 and set up headquarters in a hotel to make plans on the correct route to penetrate the mountains. They quizzed the citizens to direct their effort. Norman

Smith, the future mayor of Port Angeles, was the most vocal. Asserting that he had lived on the Peninsula for years and knew the backcountry, Smith joined the expedition for a while. He was a vocal politician with a hypothesis and little practical experience.

O'Neil planned to follow the Elwha River into the center of the mountains and exit the Quinault River that flowed generally southwest into Lake Quinault and civilization. It was thought this route would take them through the center of the unknown mountains, and rightly so. The men left Port Angeles to travel on a roughly cleared county right-of-way. They were then forced to use an Indian trail that shortly vanished. They moved ahead at about a mile in an hour and a half until they came upon an impossible marsh. They had to cut windfalls and brush to make a trail that would give access for the pack mules. The windfalls could have been over six feet in diameter, a horrendous task for a man with a hand crosscut saw. The rate of trail building and the view of broken country ahead of them suggested another route.

During their assault on the Elwha route, the soldiers worked hard, in hand with the settlers, to clear a trail. The settlers were free with their labor, housing their stock and offering advice. One settler suggested the Elwha route be abandoned and Ennis Creek be used as entry into the interior. Ennis Creek flows into the Port Angeles Harbor, the source south of the town. I have fished this small stream as a youth, a small rugged stream that leads nowhere.

In six weeks' time, the O'Neil expedition reached Hurricane Ridge and somewhat beyond. Their adventure in trail building matched their Elwha experience — it was awesome. They got to view the alpine meadows, the prolific amount of summer game, and the interior of the Olympic Mountains. They thought no other white man had ever been there — until they ran across an abandoned hunter's cabin towards the end of their journey.

The drive on a modern highway to Hurricane Ridge takes about fifteen minutes today. It took O'Neil almost six weeks.. The expedition was curtailed prematurely when O'Neil received army orders to report to another post. Nevertheless, O'Neil's report was perhaps the first written document of a view of the interior of the Olympic Mountains, a view that encouraged others to expand the knowledge of the peninsula's forbidden interior.

Lt. O'Neil got his second chance to penetrate the Olympics in 1890. His first expedition was motivated by a sense of curiosity and adventure. He now heard the settlers' speculation that there was mineral wealth in the Olympics, giving him a practical reason to explore the area. Stationed back at Vancouver Barracks, he was invited to join the newly established Oregon Alpine Club, and elected secretary. The club planned a scientific expedition to explore the Olympics, with the club furnishing the scientist, and the Army providing the logistics. O'Neil sold the army on the project.

The major effort was commanded by O'Neil, who was to construct a mule trail into the interior, aided by eleven Army personnel, three scientist, and a dozen pack mules. The expedition was the dubbed the Olympic Exploring Expedition (OEE). History recognizes the project as "the second O'Neil Expedition". Just 27 years old, O'Neil and the army personnel with him were bored with garrison life and welcomed the adventure. They had the whole summer to accomplish his goals. For some reason, he abandoned the Elwha route and decided to approach the mountains from Hood Canal, planning to barge the supplies to Hoodsport and pack the supplies to Lake Cushman, about six miles northeast of Hoodsport.

The North Fork of the Skokomish River flowed into and out of the lake. They planned to follow the river generally northwest to its source and to the ridge between the North Fork of the Skokomish River and East Fork of the Quinault River, which flowed west to the ocean where the expedition would exit to civilization. The expedition landed, but because of bad advice, they landed instead at Lilliwaup and had to pack their supplies on a poor trail to Lake Cushman.

Their first camp was on a ranch adjacent to the lake. Beyond the ranch was a trail going upriver that led to a miner's camp. Trail building started there. The plan was to leave the lowlands and reach the high country with its alpine meadows and sparse vegetation. There they would send out scouting parties to explore the mountainous Olympics.

In early September, the expedition had established its last camp on the Quinault side of the divide between the Quinault River and the North Fork of the Skokomish River. They thoroughly explored the area, particularly the rivers in the southern part of the Olympics. At the same time, the Hoquiam Board of Trade was constructing a trail from Hoquiam up the Quinault. As planned, the expedition was broken into groups to explore various sections of the southern Olympics.

The most significant adventure was reported by one party that reached and climbed Mt. Olympus, the central and highest peak in the Olympics. They placed a copper box at what they thought was the summit, but the box has never been found to confirm their climb. The adventurers returned to civilization west down the Queets drainage, where friendly Indians led the impoverished men to civilization. The Indians and settlers were helpful to the expedition on all occasions, and several settlers joined in the adventure.

The bulk of the exploring parties met in Hoquiam and then returned to the Vancouver Barracks and home. Hoquiam gave them an appreciation banquet to send them on their way. Later, the Oregon Alpine Club honored the explorers with a banquet in Portland. On November 16, 1890, O'Neil submitted his official report to the army. He wrote in detail of the topography, streams, and the resources. He noted the timber would be a great product for the region for many years, while the precipitous portion of the Olympics was a candidate for a national park. Conveniently, only the park recommendation has been recognized by modern writers, while O'Neil's comments on the timber resources have been ignored.

Coincidently, Judge James Wickersham and his Banner Expedition started up the North Fork of the Skokomish River, passed the O'Neil expedition and were in the interior of the Olympics before O'Neil. It was a race to the top.

The year before, Wickersham and four friends had hiked to Lake Cushman on an exploration for adventure in a nearly uninhabited and untouched forest. Wickersham and another man left their two friends at Hoodsport late in the afternoon and hiked about four miles to a settler's ranch at dusk. The settler gracefully lodged them for the night. As was the tradition of the west, the travelers were given the best the couple had to offer: a good supper, clean beds, congenial breakfast, and lively conversation. The host's wife, half Indian, half white, kept the household neat and tidy.

Wickersham's four-man party met on the trail and proceeded to the head of Lake Cushman where they camped to hunt and fish in the quiet woods and river. Wickersham and his boyhood friend decided to go farther up the North Fork of the Skokomish River. They wanted to know about the mountains they could observe to the west of their camp on the lake.

The two men left their base camp at daylight on June 8 with enough basic food for two days — hardtack and canned beef. Each man carried his gun, ammunition, hunting knife, and compass, but no blankets or sleeping accommodations. They would sleep around a campfire. The two men walked a short ways and soon left all signs of civilization. They assumed they were treading on ground unseen by white men. The elk trails were followed whenever possible until they reached a point where they could see about 15 miles up the river. It was decided to return to civilization then, as they didn't have the resources to accomplish anything meaningful with further travel. Wickersham and his friend reached their base camp the following day to be greeted by anxious fellow explorers.

Wickersham wanted to further explore the Skokomish leading to the mountains to the west. He organized the Banner Expedition, composed mostly of family. The Banner Expedition's name was derived from the *Buckley Banner* newspaper. Wickersham's boyhood friend and member of the party was the editor of the paper. The Banner party started with a dozen people, but only six would go beyond Lake Cushman, three men and three women. The women were Wickersham's wife and his two sisters.

The Banner Party met Lt. O'Neil at Hoodsport towards the end of July. The meeting was cordial. The lieutenant offered to carry the party's packs on his mules as far as the army had constructed their trail. He even furnished a mule to help the women get as far as Lake Cushman. In turn, the *Buckley Banner* published a story belittling O'Neil's efforts.

The Banner Party of six quickly trudged to the end of the army's mule trail where they left the army and their trail construction and followed elk trails to the divide between four rivers: the Skokomish, Duckabush, Dosewallips, and the East Fork of Quinault in the heart of the Olympics. They camped for several days in the high meadows enjoying the breathtaking views. The O'Neil party arrived at this location a couple of weeks later.

The Banner Party had hoped to cross the mountains to the Elwha River and exit the mountains north to Port Angeles, a feat in that era that would have been truly spectacular with three women along. However, they looked at the Quinault gorge and the rugged country beyond and decided it was too much for their limited resources. So, they turned down the Dosewallips River to Hood Canal and headed for home. They had been in the mountains three weeks. The last week they ate cakes made of flour and water. The Banner Party was the first to reach the divide between the four rivers, to explore the headwaters of the Duckabush, and descend the Dosewallips — at least the first people to write about their feat.

Wickersham was also the first to recommend that the Olympic Mountains should be encompassed into a national park. Shortly after arriving home, he wrote to three publishing companies (without being published) about his exploration and recommendations. Finally he wrote to the Director of the United States Geological Survey on July 21, 1891, recommending a park 30 miles long from north to south and 40 miles from east to west — 768,000 acres. He believed it would center on the headwaters of the rivers flowing out of the park, a location which would not cripple private enterprises, including the settlers' interest. The park would serve two purposes: "a great pleasure ground" and protection for forests and wildlife.

Judge Wickersham was touted a visionary by progressives and even perhaps the father of the Olympic National Park. Of course, his dash and fervor in taking three women into a wilderness where "no man had trod" would fit the image of the modern progressive thinkers.

Ironically, five years earlier, Wickersham had been a member of the Committee of Fifteen in Tacoma who chased the Chinese from the city. He was indicted along with many others. The jury exonerated the judge and his associates. He went on to become a federal judge along with other honorable responsibilities. He was an open-minded visionary to want to preserve the rights of the settlers and private enterprise when making his recommendations for a park. Wickersham's vision should be honored by today's society.

There was one other significant expedition into the Olympics in 1890, an expedition set up for publicity. A Seattle newspaper, *The Seattle Press*, became interested in a story after the governor told a *Press* reporter the previous year that there was a need to explore the unexplored Olympics. After the report appeared in the newspaper, several readers expressed interest in the adventure.

A woodsman and sometimes adventurer named James H. Christie, who lived in the north, was short of funds and wrote to the *Press* in early November 1889 to propose entering the Olympics immediately. After an interview with the owner of the *Press*, the paper outfitted Christie to start the journey in early December.

Christie and four men described as having an "abundance of grit and manly vim", arrived in Port Angeles in early December. The *Press* justified the expedition on the basis of scientific information collection, knowledge of topography, minerals, timber, and the feasibility of settlement. In reality, the paper wanted numerous stories from the first people to cross the Olympics. Some people would call this motivation *greed*.

The plan was to start at the Elwha River near Port Angeles and travel to the Quinault River, then to Lake Quinault and civilization. They were the first white men to traverse the Olympic Mountain Range. The five men made their first camp on the lower Elwha River on December 19. They had a ton of supplies furnished by the *Seattle Press* at their camp by December 23. For Christmas dinner, the men dined on bacon and beans. It was snowing hard. On the advice of the local "experts", they started to build a boat of green lumber to carry their supplies up the river. They finished the boat in four days, loaded it, and immediately watched it sink. The men pulled the boat out of the water, built fires under it and caulked the cracks, reloaded it, and they started up river.

The men used a tow rope to move the boat upstream, an operation that kept them up to their waist in water often to get leverage on the tow rope. With more than three feet of snow on the ground and freezing temperatures, their clothes froze when they got out of the water. When a logjam across the river at the mouth of Indian Creek created an obstacle, the settlers and the nearby Indians helped portage the boat around it. The five men continued to move the boat slowly upstream for about two weeks, before abandoning it as impractical. In this time they had moved four miles closer towards Lake Quinault.

The snow reached a depth of five feet and the explorers were confined to the cabin of a sympathetic settler. Two months had passed and the expedition had not traveled past the last settler's cabin. However, their American Heritage of that era and pride in themselves, plus their contract, dictated that nothing but success was acceptable. So, they decided to move across the mountain on foot. Each man backpacked 50 pounds through the snow, their snowshoes sinking into to eight inches of snow. They packed 800 pounds for a mile and a half each day. They had a ton of supplies to move across the landscape in successive stages of packing.

They also had to scout ahead to locate the path for a trail and rough out the trail to accommodate the two mules when conditions permitted. Of course, making camp, cooking, hunting, and fishing along the way were necessities. Their personal needs were taken care of after the necessary chores were completed. They followed this routine until they neared the Quinault River, when they had no mules and were eating only flour-soup — a mixture of flour, salt, and boiling water.

Finally, at what became Low Divide Pass between the upper Elwha and the North Fork of the Quinault River, they killed a couple of bears to keep themselves from starving. From there they continued downstream to a trapper's cabin on the Quinault River. The trapper furnished canoe transportation down to and across Lake Quinault. They arrived in Aberdeen in the middle of the night and found it difficult to find rooms, but, in the morning they enjoyed a hero's welcome. Upon their return to Seattle, their adventures were published in the *Seattle Press* — on July 16, 1890.

The three explorations in 1890 — O'Neil, Wickersham, and Christie were full of drama, emotion, hardships, and valuable information. It took two quiet, unassuming men working almost alone to put together the needed comprehensive data to define the proposed national park and adjacent lands. These men were Theodore F. Rixon, an engineer who had been a railroad engineer and independent timber cruiser, and his partner Arthur Dodwell, a government land surveyor.

President Grover Cleveland created the Olympic Forest Reserve in 1897. Two million acres were taken away from the local citizens to be controlled by an arrogant central government in faraway Washington DC. The federal government needed to know what they had stolen. It is unkind to accuse our government of stealing; nevertheless, a few academics/preservationists circumvented due process of law to create the Forest Reserves. A small group surreptitiously temporarily took most of the Olympic Peninsula from the local people. They stole the land.

The United States Geological Survey's geographer was given the responsibility to obtain the information. He hired Rixon and Dodwell to make the survey at $300 a month for the two men. The geographer probably made the best financial deal in the government's history. The men worked from 1898 through 1900 to get to a final comprehensive report. The report covered 3,483 square miles, and with a separate report for each section, that adds up to 3,483 reports. The reports listed: "the timbered, burned, cut, and non-timbered areas; the depth of humus and forest litter; the total stand of timber; the stand of the principal species recognized by the lumber trade; the average height, diameter, and clean length; and the percentage of dead and diseased trees."

The two men had several assistants, and the party climbed many of the peaks for both the survey and their own pleasure. Trails were few and far between, forcing the party to travel cross-country much of the time. The logistics of supply were quietly taken care of, so be assured there were no more meals comprised of flour, salt and boiled water. These men were professional woodsman and engineers who lived their lives in the forest for years. With this experience, they tackled thousands of square miles of survey as routine work.

In 1905 the Forest Reserves became the Forest Service under the leadership of Gifford Pinchot, Chief Forester. The Forest Service and the vast Forest Reserves were now in a department committed to producing agriculture products and more. The Secretary of the Interior, whose organization was oriented to holding land, lost a large part of his empire. There was contention and ill will over this movement of lands for decades. The Park Service was part of the Department of Interior and the Forest Service was in the Department of Agriculture.

On the Olympic Peninsula, more than two million acres became the Olympic National Forest, dedicated to growing trees, which made the residents on the peninsula relieved and more optimistic about their future. The vast government ownership was to be productive. The mill workers, loggers, farmers, merchants, traders, and entrepreneurs (timber barons) had a future. Their property would gain value as the government developed their land to serve the community and the nation. Nevertheless, the peninsula residents were apprehensive of a fickle federal government; they had experienced the eastern politics creating the Federal Reserve that took their land, and Victor Smith who created a Port Angeles Federal Reserve in the 1860s.

The Olympics were explored and thoroughly evaluated by the Rixon/Dodwell survey. The survey stated there was little opportunity for the settlers' ranches or mining, just a vast timber resource. However, the elite mountain climber/recreationist had a play area. The Mountaineers planned a mountain climbing outing in 1907 to take advantage of the Olympics made accessible by the 1890s expeditions and others. The Mountaineers, formed in 1906 with the aid of the Sierra Club and Mazamas Club of Portland, Oregon, grew to include members in several states and Canada. The club was interested in the conservation of natural resources and the preservation of the landscape by protective legislation or otherwise. Of course, they would climb mountains and enjoy the wilderness experiences. The members were primarily educators, with many of them part of university faculties.

The Mountaineers sent scouts into the Olympics in May 1907, their primary goal to climb Mount Olympus and be the first to do so. The scouts, accompanied by a local woodsman, went up the Elwha River to the base of Mount Olympus. They located a camp for their outing, but found the trails were inadequate for the pack animals that would supply their camp. Without resources to build or upgrade the trails to their camp, they appealed to the city leaders in Port Angeles for help. The town residents turned out in force to improve the trail system. In that era, the spirit of the community was there for projects to improve their land. They naively believed the Mountaineers would help them convert the wilderness into forest communities for the local people.

The Mountaineers' outing was to be the first to ascend Olympus. However, shortly before, the Explorers Club of New York had climbed one of the Olympus peaks. This event took some of the spice out of their endeavor, but the Mountaineers still attacked the adventure with glee.

The first group left Seattle by steamer on July 24. The 64 Mountaineers were faculty members of three universities, instructors, and scientists, members of the legal and medical professions, a minister, and a few ordinary folks. The trek up the Elwha to their camp took four days.

The men and women explored the high country, climbing lesser peaks around Mount Olympus. On August 9, 46 Mountaineers left the camp to climb Olympus. They began up the slope of the mountain only to have a gale wind and snow force them back to camp. Then they returned home.

The storm precluded the party from obtaining its major objective, to reach the summit of Mount Olympus. However, the social aspects of the outing were a complete success. After dinner, evening campfires were informative and fun with hilarious story telling. The meals were prepared and served by indulgent cooks who made elaborate meals that were finished off with delicious desserts. Multi-course meals were served to up to 75 climbers. Fresh beefsteak was available, as livestock was herded up the Elwha trail to be butchered on the site. The homesteaders and business people on the peninsula must have been awed by the elites' life style.

O'Neil/Wickersham honorably recommended a national park in the Olympic Mountains' interior. Further, they believed the park would not interfere with the industry and settlers in the area. They certainly earned the right to make their recommendations. The progressives/preservationists appropriated the earlier Forest Reserve covert process, leading eventually to a larger Olympic National Park.

In 1909 President Teddy Roosevelt named Mount Olympus a National Monument by proclamation. The monument was 620,000 acres, over half of it forested, and all of it closed to hunters, loggers, and miners. The President's dictatorial proclamation was hurried to prevent a calamity, but in reality to further the preservationists' agenda.

The calamity struck the imagined endangered elk. Elk were being killed by professional hunters in large numbers for their teeth, sold as fobs to the Benevolent and Protective Order of Elks. Generally, the rest of the animal was wasted. An Elk National Park was proposed in Congress, and failed. The state in 1905 outlawed elk hunting, but some poaching continued. In 1906 and 1908, game refuge bills were proposed and failed. The preservationists overreacted or used the perceived elk emergency to further their agenda. Federal legislation was not the solution. The poaching had to be controlled in the lowlands outside of the monument boundaries, and the state eventually solved the problem. Today's elk herds attest to the fact the elk were only temporally stressed. Still, the preservationists used any potential calamity to take land for their government playgrounds.

Hungry elk over-ran the second forest near Forks WA in the early 2000s

Furtively, a Seattle Congressman met with Roosevelt two days before he was to leave office. It was a meeting of "nature lover to nature lover". The Congressman communicated the problem and, without any further information, the monument was created. The President acted like an imperial potentate without concern for the local people affected by his decision. After leaving office, Roosevelt went to Africa on safari to kill animals for trophies, much like the trophy elk hunters on the Olympic Peninsula.

The monument was a fact. The local people struggled to reduce the size of the monument through the honorable political process throughout the administration of President William H. Taft (Roosevelt's successor), without success. Then came World War I, and the Secretary of Interior for President Woodrow Wilson came to the rescue. He was anti-preservationist. The country needed manganese for the war effort and the metal was thought to exist in the Olympics. In 1915, President Wilson reduced the monument to 328,000 acres, of which 259,000 acres were above the timber line. Although there was manganese mining in the area, economic mining failed to become a reality. To the distress of the preservationists, the local citizenry could normalize their lives.

The maturation of the Olympic Peninsula seemed to be progressing to serve the local people. Not to be!

The Emergency Conservation Committee (ECC) was formed in 1930, composed of three elites whose purpose was to maintain the bulk of the Olympic Peninsula in its undisturbed condition. The progressive/preservationists were desperate to preserve the last wilderness in the country and move the white interlopers from their encroachment. The committee would use the will of the people of America to drive away the "destructive timber barons" and their associated *nonpersons* on the Peninsula. The nonpersons, like the pioneer "Iron Man of the Hoh" objected to their agenda, and were ignored by the committee as unimportant.

The three who formed the ECC were Willard Van Name, Rosalie Edge, and Erving Brant. Van Name was a wealthy so-called environmentalist in the 1920s, who wrote preservationist articles that defined the will of the people. In other words, it was *the will of the people as defined by Van Name*. The ECC literature was structured to "educate" the public to the preservationists' agenda. He also had the wealth to fund publications and salaries for lobbyists.

Rosalie Edge had a prominent position in the New York social register, giving her access to anyone of importance in politics or society. She was a prolific writer and a tireless worker for the cause. The saving of the rain forest at the end of her career was a high point in her life, although she never saw it.

Erving Brant was a citizen activist who skillfully involved himself in the government. He attended top level meetings with the President, the cabinet secretaries, Congress, and the governor of Washington State. Brant became a consultant to Secretary of the Interior Harold Ickes and President F.D. Roosevelt on Olympic National Park matters. He crafted speeches for Ickes and developed the strategy to make the big park a reality. The locals on the Olympics Peninsula referred to Secretary Ickes as *Icky*.

Two other citizen activists completed the team for ECC. Irving Clark, a wealthy Seattle lawyer and a secretary of the Mountaineers, was the ECC liaison to the Northwest, with political and preservationist contacts able to undermine Washington State's Congressional delegation unity. William Schulz was another citizen activist from the Northwest who filled the local newspapers with letters to the editor. Ickes hired him as his personal representative.

The Great Depression of the 1930s brought a progressive preservationist government to Washington DC, a government that embraced the ECC and its agenda. With Brant directing policy on park matters, the people's fight for their heritage against the arrogance of a central big government was lost. The folks in the region could only try to minimize the damage to their economy and the loss of jobs. They simply wanted to use their land to enjoy the American dream that was being created. The pioneers settled generally on the Peninsula's rivers. The local people appreciated the lakes, rivers, and the scenery like no outsider could. The federal government should have been an expediter to further their visions.

The greed of the progressive preservationists' government could best be described by the euphoria of the Mountaineers as they attempted to climb Mount Olympus in 1907. Trails to access the Olympics were developed by explorers and peninsula citizens. The Mountaineers had what was equivalent to catered meals, beef driven miles over the Elwha trails to furnish them with fresh beef and other "fancy" amenities. Meanwhile, the peninsula citizens labored in the mills, logging camps, and isolated farms to create forest communities and wealth. The wealth was beginning to create a good life for the peninsula people, and even a few folks, with exceptional talent and skills, became "rich" by local standards.

The ECC formulated a strategy to create the Olympic Peninsula wilderness built through the structure of an Olympic National Park.

First, it had to define the enemy: the large timber and mill owners who conveniently were labeled as timber barons and the U.S. Forest Service. These were the people who wanted to create wealth by harvesting and growing trees. The remaining stakeholders residing on the peninsula were nonpersons, ignored because the public could and would sympathize with their loss of land and jobs.

Ironically, the Forest Service and the timber barons could have been natural enemies. There was always uneasiness in their relationship. How could there be otherwise? Pinochet lobbied to nationalize the private forests for most of his life, and many of the Forest Service personnel sympathized with him. The Forest Service was always suspicious of the private sector's motivation. They were slow to regenerate the forest and they were suspicious of the economic dealings between the two parties.

The Forest Service and private sector were forced to deal with each other on a host of issues, with timber sales as the major point of concern. Competitive bidding was complicated by timber appraisals, the timing, size, and the location of the sales. Most timber was sold on the basis of volume determined by log scales (measurements). The Forest Service/private sector created a cooperative bureau with a board of director's representative of all timber interests to scale logs. A transportation network (roads) had to be shared equitably in the intermingled ownerships. Land and timber trades were made to the advantage of both parties.

The timber interests generally had to cooperate equitably to survive. And, there was competition between the Forest Service and the private interests as there should be. More importantly, there was fierce competition between the timber owners and mill owners. This competition led to suspicion between the parties, but it was the competition that created and maintained honesty. This honesty could only be created by real competition that government could not achieve by means of regulations.

The ECC and its allies attacked this honesty viciously to further the wilderness agenda. The group identified the triad of the Forest Service, timber industry, and the College of Forestry at the University of Washington as being "tree butchers with axes on their shoulders". There was no economic need, only commercial greed. The forest was chopped down, land stripped, devastated, and utterly destroyed, to be left idle, compounded by federal timber give away legislation. The ECC name-calling was based on an emotional appeal supplemented with biased photos and graphs. The triad victims were expected to treat the ECC with respect and honor, which they did publicly without reciprocal treatment.

The ECC took up Pinchot's argument that the country was running out of timber. However, contrary to Pinchot's sustained yield strategy, the solution was to preserve the timber for an eternity. Apparently the country didn't need lumber. Further, private timber was obtained by fraud, a fraud that was generally not prosecuted because it rarely existed. That fact was conveniently ignored. The ECC did not honor the American concept that a person is not guilty until convicted in a court of law. It believed the ends justified the means, thus ignoring any sense of fairness.

President Roosevelt decided to tour the Olympic Peninsula in 1937 to settle the national park issue. He took a naval ship from Seattle to Port Angeles where he was met with dignity in front of the courthouse with bands and children. A banner on the court house implored the President to give the county a national park. It didn't state how big. Irving Brant, of the ECC, briefed and handled the President on the tour, while the Forest Service was in charge of the arrangements. With Brant's coaching, the President stated that eight out of ten Forest Service people were hand in glove with the lumber interests. This statement was made in the face of Pinchot's work to create the most incorruptible organization in the federal government; the Peninsula's folks disagreed with the President. The local folks dealt with the Forest Service on a regular basis and never questioned its honesty and independence. Timber baron Michael Earles refuted the President's statement of collusion by paying a $30 fine for cutting Forest Service trees at the Sol Duc Hot Springs.

The triad of tree growers had their problems. The Port Angeles citizens were interested in pulp wood because the town's economy depended on three pulp mills. They wanted the hemlock on the coast to be available for their mills. Grays Harbor had big sawmills that depended on the big Douglas fir. Here was a conflict of interest. The Forest Service was dedicated to a long-term sustained yield of wood to support local economies and work with the local people. The Park Service also wanted to blend into the local society, and the College of Forestry wanted its students employed in the forests.

Early on, the triad made a critical mistake. They tried to sell their big tree economic situation. They ignored the future improvements in technology in the mills, logging, and tree growing. Hindsight is unfair. Coming into the 1980s, the technology in the mills and logging were nearing obsolescence. By the 1990s, a small tree economy utilizing all conifer species was the norm. Generally, sawmills made lumber out of four-inch diameter logs and the pulp mills largely used waste from the lumber mills and logging. For decades trees have been planted immediately after logging, and modern forestry practices have prevailed on a drastically reduced land base.

The Forest Service had a good story with its sustained yield program, but it was an academic exercise in the late 1930s, and the ECC told everyone it was propaganda. The Forest Service seldom demonstrated sustained yield in the forest. They had a wonderful opportunity to do so when President Roosevelt toured the Olympic Peninsula. Even though the ECC had its person guiding the President, the Forest Service could have arranged the agenda better. Apparently they showed him the scenery of mature timber, lakes, streams, and a recently logged and burned area. They should have taken him to several different aged-young forests leading to a forest of the future that included ages of trees from seedling to 100 years old. They had the Sol Duc burn of young planted trees to demonstrate, if nothing else. Certainly, the logged and burned area he did see should have been where the "devastation" was put in context with sustained yield. It wasn't!

The President's tour in September 1937 around the Peninsula was a disaster for the Forest Service and the long-term economy on the Peninsula. The President's decision on the proposal to convert a large portion of the Peninsula into a wilderness was influenced mostly by a stumped and burned area created, in his opinion, by a "son of a bitch", apparently his impression of the Peninsula's inhabitants. Roosevelt inadvertently viewed a clear-cut north of Lake Quinault that was harvested and broadcast burned. It appeared to be a disaster to the citified President. He blamed the clear-cut on an individual, the progressive's so-called timber baron. However, the clear-cut was a forest community endeavor. The local custom dictated by experience was to employ the community's seasoned woodsmen to create sustainable wealth for the local people and the country. Private forest engineers carefully marked the boundaries of the clear-cut (setting), located a rail line into the setting, and sited the yarder to move the logs to the rail line. A railroad construction crew built the railroad into the setting. A group of skilled fallers and buckers were then transported by rail to carefully fall the trees, and buck them into logs. A rigging crew followed to set a yarder in place and rig a spar tree with guy lines to strengthen the tree. Then cables were carried out into the setting to move the logs to the railroad. The rigging crew worked the equipment to bring the logs to rail cars, which transported them to a sawmill or pulp mill where several hundred men turned the logs into products for use by the world.

Finally the last step: the setting was broadcast burned. It was an extra cost deemed necessary by the community, a cost today that would be called an environmental cost. In the 1930s and later, only prime logs had value, that is, large straight-grained logs without significant defect or knots. So, the biomass of wood (slash) on the setting was enormous and soon became tinder dry. Experienced woodsmen knew that without a controlled burn the probability of a wildfire was high, and the controlled fire immediately after logging facilitated the natural seeding of the setting to create a new forest. Undoubtedly, the new healthy forest created by 1930s logging and burn has been utilized again by the community. The third forest was to be ready for a regeneration harvest in about 2012, and will sustain the economy of the community for another generation.

The Forest Service was charged with designing the tour, but Brant superciliously controlled the agenda. Brant and Interior Secretary Ickes had spent months poisoning Roosevelt's mind against the Forest

Service. Brant wrote a memo for Roosevelt, outlining the strategy to implement the park, of course, conforming to the ECC vision.

The strategy was furthered by the tour's overnight stop at Lake Crescent, where the President was briefed by the Forest Service on its vision of the Peninsula. They wanted to provide for diverse recreation (multiple-use) and grow tress on a long-term sustainable basis to serve the local community, contrary to the ECC vision. The President contemptuously grilled the Forest Service and dictated his wants as defined by the ECC. Apparently, the final solution to create the park was made long before the tour started. Later the Forest Service man responsible for the tour was removed from his position by the President. A professional person's career and dedication to his organization's values were ruined by a special interest group.

The Lake Crescent discussion formulating the park and the future for the Peninsula was almost exclusively an inter-government discussion. Local people were involved only for publicity. The Lake Crescent discussions circumvented the public as well as to their vision of democracy. Carsten Lien, a former president of the Mountaineers in Seattle, describes the Lake Crescent discussions in his book, *Olympic Battleground, The Politics of Timber Preservation*: "Power politics removed a Regional Forester and displaced many pioneers from their ranches established decades ago in the wilderness."

The progressives' power politics also brought a modern word into our American language, *ineptocracy*. *The New World Dictionary* defines *ineptocracy* as a "system of government where the least capable to lead are elected by the least capable of producing, and where the member of society least likely to sustain themselves or succeed are rewarded with goods and services paid for by the confiscated wealth of a diminishing number of producers." On the Olympic Peninsula the producers were reduced, not because the big old trees were preserved, but because the soil for growing trees was taken from the producers. The mineral wealth was also taken. As an example, the seeping oil at the mouth of the Hoh River is suggestive of oil wealth.

After the President's tour and much political posturing, a large wilderness park seemed inevitable. Perhaps the erstwhile forest ranger, Chris Morgenroth, was responsible in moderating the park legislation. He and three others were dispatched to Congressional hearings in 1937 in Washington DC by the Port Angeles Chamber of Commerce. Thomas Aldwell presided; Morgenroth, with his intimate knowledge of the Olympics and the local inhabitants, was instantly respected by the eastern political community, who attempted to persuade him that the will of the people demanded a large wilderness park. He thought otherwise!

In February 1938, Morgenroth was sent again to Washington DC, this time to confer with agency officials and Washington State Congressman Mon Wallgren, sponsor of the park bill. He wrote to his family: "I don't think they can override us entirely." He also wrote a personal letter to the President expressing his views. As a result, he was invited to a private conference that included Congressman Wallgren and several agency folks.

Big government didn't override Morgenroth and the peninsula people who thwarted the ECC hope for a large wilderness park. It was agreed the park would be 680,000 acres and not designated as wilderness, a major concessions by the government. The park officials also agreed to build roads, especially the long proposed road between the Olympic and the Sol Duc Hot Springs. It was never constructed.

Morgenroth and most local people wanted to manage the scenery while developing the park so all citizens could view the beauty, i.e., the Hot Spring's road. A wilderness policy generally prevailed over the years. On June 29, 1938, President Roosevelt signed the Olympic National Park bill creating the 680,000-acre park. However, there was a provision that would allow the President to increase the park size to 892,000 acres by proclamation, a provision Morgenroth called a betrayal.

And, it didn't take long to increase the park size again. President Roosevelt believed his bureaucrats had overlooked an ocean strip, the Queets corridor, and the upper Bogachiel he wanted. His bureaucrats could not face a controversy that might overpower them in a debate to obtain additional park legislation, so again Brant was given the task to find a way. The park legislation specified a park enlargement would require consultation with the Forest Service, Park Service, and Washington State's governor. The federal agencies of course did not question their boss; after all, one Forest Service person had already lost his job. The governor strongly objected. Money to obtain the land had to be made available by the Congress and the governor, and people on the Peninsula could delay or stop the park expansion by taking their concerns to Congress. Brant had to find a way to get the money without going to Congress.

Brant found a way. The Public Works Administration (PWA) had almost unlimited money. The PWA was formed in 1933 to reduce unemployment by constructing highways, dams, and public buildings. It was a breach of public trust to use it for another purpose; however, Brant felt the ends justified the means. The PWA allocated $1,750,000 to acquire 187,411 acres of land and adjunct assets. The PWA acquired a corridor two miles wide down the length of the Queets River from the park to the Pacific Ocean. The ocean strip started near the mouth of the Queets River north past Lake Ozette. Also, tracts of land were acquired in the Hoh and Bogachiel River valleys.

The anger over Roosevelt's proclamation was almost violent on the Peninsula. The legendry pioneer John Huelsdonk best expressed the anger by carrying a sign to Olympia that read: "This isn't Russia — Secretary Ickes has no right to take our homes away from us." He saw the governor and told him it was unfair to change the rules to enlarge government control of his landed heritage. He and his friends had given their lives to wilderness ranches only to lose them to the government under the right of eminent domain. The Iron Man asked the governor to call out the National Guard to keep the federal government from taking the land. He was also a visionary when he contended the forest didn't belong to all the people, but the forest should belong to those who knew how to live in it and utilize the soil. The Iron Man's activism perhaps saved his ranch. It was not condemned and is still available to the family. But, more than 500 individuals did lose their property.

One progressive author writes that the wilderness ranchers on the Queets were thriving when the PWA began taking their property through the eminent domain processes in 1940. There was no empathy for these nonpersons; on the contrary, the author applauded the action for the people, people who will never see the wasted ranches. The families of the ranchers periodically visit the location of the ranches they once owned to reaffirm their American Heritage, but time and the Park Service have destroyed them.

The Iron Man's family had their property condemned, a small business near the beach on Highway 101. The PWA took the property and eventually transferred it to the park. They went to the federal district court in Seattle and lost the first round in the justice system. Their lawyer recommended they appeal to the Ninth Circuit Court in San Francisco. They didn't have the funds to travel to San Francisco, let alone pay the lawyers. The resources of the federal government directed by special interest groups had made a mockery of American justice. In turn, this injustice created pioneer family dislike — or even hatred — for our government and their agencies. On the Peninsula, the dislike was directed at the Park Service.

During one of my numerous visits to John Huelsdonk's granddaughter to trade stories about the history of west Clallam County, she asked my advice about a Park Service naturalist who wanted to interview her about the quaint ways of the area's pioneers. She wanted to refuse the request because she didn't want to contribute to the park in any way. I advised her to tell the naturalist her feelings about the park. Ironically, the condemned property on Highway 101 would be valued in 2011 at the same purchase price of the entire park addition in 1940.

The PWA purchased the addition to the park while the park administered the newly purchased property. However, the addition was not classified as a national park until 1953. The PWA/Park Service's unethical collusion in displacing private property owners by condemnation and purchase of the park addition was not commonly known outside of the Peninsula.

Historians and writers barely, if ever, refer to the collusion. On the contrary, progressive author Carsten Lien wrote of the cleverness of the government and progressives. The families of the people who were forced off their land never forgot the improbity of the federal government. In 1953, in his last few days in office, President Truman signed a proclamation adding the Ocean Strip and the Queets Corridor to the park. The proclamation again created fervor over the injustice of big government. Of course, it was too late. The "people" won and the non-persons on the Peninsula were ignored.

Most writers and historians suggest the controversy was over utilization versus preservation of the forests. The progressives go further and claim it is preservation or destruction of the forest and scenery forever. Still further, the forests will not be renewed and the scenery destroyed by greedy developers, which will make the Peninsula a waste land.

Contrary to the 1930s preservationists' propaganda, the 2011 forests outside the park have been renewed, the wildlife is flourishing, and the scenery is spectacular. The two lakes the city fathers treasured in the 1890s remain a valued asset. Lake Sutherland is outside the park and Lake Crescent is inside the park. The Sol Duc River is inside *and* outside the park. The land outside the park has created wealth for the Peninsula and the country for decades in the form of forest and farm products, jobs, tax revenue, and tourist trade.

The fight is much more significant. It is a classic choice between ineptocracy and our American Heritage. The Olympic National Park experience is extended across America. Are we going to continue to destroy the productive people in this country?

The rate of expansion of federal ownership on the Olympic Peninsula, combined with the expansion of rigid preservation on the Peninsula, suggests that productive endeavors, e.g., the utilization of natural resources, will soon extinguish the productivity created by the pioneers. The federal government owns about 50% of the land in the western states, and the government's ownership is expanding at an alarming rate. The land is rapidly being taken away from productivity. The pioneers' utilization of the land made America the most productive nation the world has known. Without utilization of the land, America becomes a third-world country.

Carsten Lien in his book, *Olympic Battleground*, defines the fight for dominance in directing the use of the park: "The struggle began in 1954 and was led by seasonal naturalists. Their major responsibility was to interface with the tourists to explain the park's flora and fauna.

The seasonal naturalists were generally college students enrolled in some form of the earth sciences that emphasized preservation. There was logging being done in the park at that time to salvage dead, dying, and 'danger trees'. In addition, trees were cut to facilitate roads, trails, and construction projects. The park legislation in 1938 excluded the park from wilderness status purposely to allow this type of activity. Nevertheless, some tourists questioned this activity and the naturalists failed to explain the work. Besides, the naturalists were shocked at this flaunting of the preservationist program."

The seasonal naturalists in 1954 were housed in the Morgenroth log cabin on Lake Crescent by the Park Service. As with all academic young men, they held evening sessions (bull sessions) expedited by cheap wine. The sessions quickly were confined to their horror of logging ancient trees, both dead and living.

The lead seasonal naturalist was Grant Sharpe who led the sessions and the smoldering revolt against the park's logging. Grant and I attended the University of Washington's College of Forestry together. I was a tree grower, while Grant was a preservationist/ recreationist.

In 1956 Sharpe left the Park Service to be replaced by Paul Shepard, an ecology graduate of Yale University. Shepard was the conservation chairman of the National Council of State Garden Clubs and had ties to the preservation groups throughout the land, including close ties to environmental groups in the Pacific Northwest. Shepard was outraged with the logging and continued the lively evening sessions condemning the practice. Then in mid-summer the naturalists were required to photograph all the back-country where trees were damaged by the winter avalanches. The phenomena was always blamed on logging activity. But, avalanches occurred in the wilderness without any logging activity. Hypocritically, these people would have blamed the avalanches on logging, rejecting the idea that nature was involved.

The simple chore of photographing avalanches panicked the naïve naturalists. They assumed the avalanche areas were going to be systematically logged and the logs floated down the rivers, destroying fish spawning beds. And because they took photographs, they would be responsible for destroying mostly *dead* trees and killing salmon in the rivers. The novice naturalist knew nothing about the practicality or the economics of logging. The back country logging was not possible without uneconomic roads, roads that would take years to construct. Also, log drives had been abandoned decades earlier. Their knowledge concerning salmon was rudimentary at best.

Nevertheless, the evening sessions immediately turned into fabricating a plan to stop the whimsical backcountry logging along with all logging. That is: let all dead trees rot in their forest.

The Park Service salvaged dead trees in log jams in rivers and natural catastrophes, as well as diseased (bug trees) and danger trees. Healthy trees were removed on construction projects. The salvage logging was wisely authorized in 1938 when the park was enabled by legislation that specified non-wilderness status. However, healthy trees were logged in addition to and beyond park policy. This activity was undoubtedly not condoned by the park administration, although the environmental community believed it was authorized.

The logging was done by small independent contractors (gypos) who were utilized by the timber industry, Park Service, and the Forest Service. The gypos had a production incentive (more truck loads per day) to cut illegal trees close to their operation. The taking of illegal trees was sometimes initiated by the contractor and sometimes his crew. The logs were not stolen, as they were included in the log scale (accountability) of all the contractor logs taken from the timber sale.

The timber industry had little problem with gypo loggers they employed. If a gypo cut illegal trees or other indiscretions, they were not employed by the industry. The Forest Service closely watched the logging operations and had ferocious penalties for cutting illegal trees. It was apparent in the 1950s that the Park Service had inexperienced supervisors to control the gypos. Unfortunately the park superintendent and the citizens on the Peninsula were punished by this flaw in supervision. Nevertheless, the naturalist would have prevailed. This indiscretion made the crusade for preservation easier. Honorable people would have recognized the flaw in the Park Service's procedures and worked to correct them instead of furthering their agenda to stop all logging in the park.

The naturalists' work ceased at the end of the summer and the naturalists scattered. Before they left, Shepard was delegated the responsibility of carrying on the effort to stop logging in the park. He formed a working group named the Joint Committee on Salvage Logging Olympic National Park (SLONP). The committee formed in Seattle included the Sierra Club, Mountaineers, Seattle Audubon Society, Olympic Park Associates, and the Federation of Western Outdoors. A naturalist's friend was administrative assistant to a local Congressman, who demanded an accounting of every logging contract in the park.

The Joint Committee visited logging sites in the park and confirmed the naturalists' report. Any logging was devastation, and they believed healthy trees in large quantities were being removed from the Park. Shepard had also pieced together a coalition of eastern and national groups. Letters and telegrams inundated the Park Service within a few weeks of the birth of the Joint Committee.

Shepard wrote a letter to the boss of the park superintendent defining the devastating logging in the Olympic National Park. The letter stated in part that a ring of logged land practically surrounds Lake Crescent.

My first car trip around Lake Crescent was in the mid-1930s as a boy and continued periodically through 2011. I never observed "intensive" park logging during this time. In fact, the lake frontage is more primitive today than in the 1930s. Shepard wrote there was logging far up the Elwha River, presumably above Lake Mills. My friends have hiked the Elwha trails for years and have not noted logging above Lake Mills. He claims there was intensive logging at the Olympic Hot Springs. I hiked the abandoned road and could not find stumps along the road or at the razed hot springs resort. However in addition to the salvage logging, there were perhaps two acres of green trees logged above Lake Mills to enable tourists to view the lake. On other occasions, a few green trees were cut for viewing purposes. Local woodsmen can document almost every tree cut in the park and testify that the few trees cut were to enhance the park for the tourists' benefit. And, the local woodsmen know the Park Service followed the non-wilderness intent of the park legislation passed in 1938.

Shepard's letter was undoubtedly circulated widely and used as the manual in defining a catastrophe to the preservation groups and the public. In addition there were pictures taken by the Joint Committee and others that portrayed devastation. A classic was a huge stump at the LaPoel Campground on Lake Crescent. The description of the picture states such stumps were common, suggesting the campground was logged clean. The last time I was in the camp ground the ancient trees blocked out the sun. The assumption is that the photographed stump represents a vigorously growing tree, which is pure speculation. I have studied and examined stumps and trees in the forests as well as logs in the mills all my adult life. I speculate the top of the tree or perhaps a third of it was dead; it is even likely the tree was dead. Further, it is certain the tree or snag was dropping large limbs to the ground periodically. Knowledgeable woodsmen call these limbs widow-makers, which we know kill people. Shepard, a Yale academic, is not qualified to comment on Douglas fir stumps.

Another picture shows a truck near the west end of Lake Crescent loaded with a Douglas fir log over seven feet in diameter, no other description. However, preservationists and the general public would assume a live ancient tree was destroyed. There is no confirmation of the log's origin; therefore this picture is flagrant propaganda. I would speculate this log was a tree that lay on the forest floor for a decade or more because there is a ring of dark stain around the perimeter of the log. It appears this log was a product of salvage logging that was permitted in the Olympic National Park at that time.

Among many pictures, the last one evaluated for truth is that of the scrap wood boomed (contained in the water) at the upper dam. The picture portrays scrap wood that I personally observed over four decades. The wood has looked the same over this time. My peers hiked the Elwha River trail during that time and know of the tremendous natural log jams moving down the river to ultimately reach Lake Mills and the dam. The dam owners periodically clean up this material and graciously offer the salvage to the Park Service and scrap the rest. Shepard states without qualification, this scrap wood came from logging the backcountry, that is, the Elwha River above Lake Mills. Yet, he has not documented one logging stump on the shores of Lake Mills or up the river to its source. Nevertheless, the author used naturalists/preservationist tactics of emotion instead of ethical research to destroy an honorable public servant and subvert a community to his agenda!

About two months after the naturalists formed their strategy and left their Lake Crescent log cabin, the park leadership was politically forced to meet with the leadership of the preservationists in Seattle. The superintendent of the Olympic National Park was not included. Park leadership agreed they would stop logging in the park. The people were ignored, especially the peninsula people. There were no public hearings, legislative action, nor economic or scientific studies. The democratic process was corrupted. More importantly, the government no longer manages our government forestlands. A few preservationists have de facto control of federal forest land; that is, the Mountaineers and their associates.

Fred Overly, Superintendent of the Olympic National Park, was replaced. In the middle 1930s he received a logging engineering degree from the University of Washington's College of Forestry. His degree made him a target for the preservationists and his own naturalists on the park staff. They believed he was obsessed with logging and didn't have the best interest of the park. The man had a difficult chore to balance the wishes of the local people with the preservationists' goals. The peninsula folks, Morgenroth in particular, had negotiated park legislation that excluded the wilderness designation. This compromise would allow salvage logging to utilize dead or near dead trees and danger trees. The local community pressured the park people to turn decaying wood into useful products like lumber and pulp. There is an honorable American adage: waste not, want not.

Overly believed he could satisfy his neighbors by honoring the negotiated non-wilderness designation and the preservationist's wishes. With hat in hand, he communicated with the founders of ECC, Brant and Edge, to get their permission to implement the salvage logging. He sold the logging to Brant on the basis that the logging revenue would go to purchase private property inside the park in the vicinity of Lake Crescent. His purchase of land would prevent the imagined destruction of the forests around the lake. In other words, trade dead trees for live trees and property to increase the size of the park. The proposal was an honorable one that would benefit the park, so Brant and Edge gave their permission. The power of two people to dictate operating procedures on public land is un-American and illustrates the movement towards corruption in government in the name of the people.

Ironically, the corruption was furthered by Shepard and his temporary park naturalists. They stopped all logging by forcing secret meetings with park service leaders. Overly was reassigned to the east coast. In other words, the temporary park naturalists fired their boss.

In 1958 the Port Angeles Chamber of Commerce gave a going away banquet for Overly. The banquet was crowned with dignitaries led by a U.S. Senator who praised him for creating a fine relationship with the people of the state. Certainly he brought a friendly relationship to the peninsula people by creating an inclusive big government. However, Shepard, an academic from Yale, destroyed the inclusive government on the peninsula in favor of a government controlled by the pseudo-academics from faraway Yale and like environs.

Surprisingly to the naturalists, the Park Service thought Shepard was disloyal. Shepard and "his" naturalists didn't communicate their concerns to the park leaders or even try to understand the park policy. Their park superintendent was a logging engineer, therefore the enemy to be ridiculed behind his back. They had a few ecology courses from Yale professors and elsewhere, where they were introduced to conflict negotiations. So, they created conflict outside their park organization. They never heard of team building. They used, at best, half-truths to create the impression the park was soon to be "a waste land". In the 1990s, former temporary naturalist Lien wrote that there was only an illusion of virgin forest in the park accessible to the limited park roads. In fact, the limited park roads largely run through virgin country. Lien and his associates have successfully kept the greater virgin park from the majority of Americans by fighting new road construction and abandoning roads, such as the road to the razed Olympic Hot Springs.

To his surprise, Paul Shepard was officially banned from employment in the national parks. The decision was troubling to him as he enjoyed his brief park work as a naturalist. He and his naturalist co-conspirators were dumbfounded that he was of no use to the park operations. With the exception of academia, there are no organizations that will employ non-team players.

Shepard, with his naturalists in the 1950s, presented a case study of the preservationist's conflict management strategy, a strategy that is contemptuous of compromise and foreign to American democratic principles. The preservationists like ECC have always been secretive about their view of the world.

Lein's 1990s book took the preservationists secretive strategy out of the closet. Apparently, the truth concerning their un-American power politics and lobbyists is an asset. His book was published by Mountaineers Books and is widely praised in review for his honesty, scholarship, and review of the preservationist victory over Park Superintendent Overly. It undoubtedly defines the preservationist's vision.

Lien presents several scenarios that predict the Olympic National Park's future in 2025. He believes it is impossible to maintain the American standard of living because of a lack of natural resources. As time passes, the lower standard of living will become the accepted norm. However, the national parks will be viewed with reverence. He also predicts a shortage of gasoline will drastically reduce the attendance in the national parks. He fails to tell his readers how a poor urban population can get to the outdoors, let alone to see Mount Olympus. However, he wants a high level of research to take place in the parks. Since the preservationists dictate a static park, the research will only document nature's actions that cannot be altered. There is no purpose for research that cannot be acted on.

One scenario calls for the parks to be merged with all other "wilderness" qualified government property to form a U.S. Wilderness Service. The Wilderness Service would greatly increase research and make discoveries that would assist tremendously in restocking presumed denuded forest land. Lien hasn't observed the real world. There isn't a vast area of denuded land except where his associates have created it in places like the Mt. St. Helens Monument. He might also observe that preservationist wouldn't allow the Forest Service to regenerate much of the government forest destroyed by the volcano. The tree-growing foresters planted tens of thousands of acres of volcano-destroyed forest on private lands. They used common sense to overcome the new regeneration challenge created by ash to have the area growing a forest again in a few short years. The tree-growing foresters don't want Lien's research money; they want the government to get out of their way so they can grow trees. Generously, the Forest Service was allowed to grow trees and log in a sustained yield, multiple-use way, but the Forest Service of today is mostly de facto wilderness dedicated to spotted owls and other endangered critters.

Following the Forest Service's de facto wilderness, private property can easily be taken by the government, directed by the preservationists and preserved, as the people in the Queets Corridor and Ocean Strip discovered. Half of the property in the western states is owned by the federal government and could be subjected to the scrutiny of Brant, Shepard and their associates for classification as wilderness and made so by presidential proclamation. In fact much of the western federal land is now in preservation state — no logging, mining, or oil drilling. Perhaps Lien's prediction of a lower standard of living is correct because the land has been taken away from productive people.

Lien's most likely scenario in 2025 would see the park logged, an 80% chance. With the rate of expansion of resource preservation, an intelligent person would disagree. Lien is intelligent, so it might be a propaganda ploy. He suggests the timber liquidation would be created by an emergency need for timber. This is archaic thinking. We don't need spruce as we did in World War I. The timber industry has moved to a small tree economy, and the big timber is used only in a small specialty market. What the country needs is productive soil to sustain forests to furnish the needs of its citizens.

However, Lien projects that a forest is not sustainable. He makes untrue statements through ignorance or wishful thinking. He states that Gifford Pinchot said "timber is a crop." The quote was from timber industry sources. Pinchot did think the forest was sustainable by studying on the ground in Europe with European foresters. The European forests have been sustained for centuries. But more importantly, Lien suggests it is clear that third growth forests would be sparse and the fourth growth forests would fail. If he had powers of observation, he would have seen the vibrant growth on the existing third forests in the Northwest, albeit the forests are only a few years old. Tree growing foresters know they can sustain a young forest and know there is no sustainability of an ancient forest. The preservationists love sustainable language, but carefully conceal the fact that trees die and big Douglas firs cannot be replaced for centuries.

Lien writes of the temporary naturalist venting outrage over logging in the park during the summers of 1954-55. The local woodsmen wondered if the naturalists were of this world; certainly they were young Turks. Grant Sharpe was the leader of the group in 1954-55, and he was not unfamiliar to me. We were both at the College of Forestry at the University of Washington.

The college studies were concentrated in two areas, forest management and engineering, with a few Grant Sharpes in the studies. Sharpe's specialty was labeled by the students as recreation, while the rest of us were tree growers.

The tree growers were young men (Turks too) dedicated to learning how to make the forest productive in an economic and environmentally responsible way. We were all in abject poverty without financial aid, except for the few veterans.

The forestry profession was notorious for low pay and rough living conditions. For an easy life style and comfortable living conditions, we could have become engineers. Many of us, after several years in the forests, came back for an additional degree in engineering. In our formative years, most of us were involved in outdoor work related to the harvest and growing of trees. We wanted to produce something that was renewable. Production and efficiency were a top priority, and we knew growing trees would provide more diverse recreation and wildlife than a statically preserved park forest. Most of us grew up in the forest. Sharpe's education is directed toward catering to tourists and esoteric studies that would not contribute to our goal of productivity. We ignored each other.

There were many debates on where we could be the most productive to achieve our vision — the private sector or the government. Most government work was available in the Forest Service. Many of us thought the Forest Service was too stodgy and regimented, while the private sector was in transition to the forestry operations we were preparing ourselves for. Unfortunately, we went to work where work was available. I went to work in the private sector, and it was work.

My first forestry assignment in the late 1950s was elementary. I examined about 10,000 acres of recent clear-cuts to determine the results of aerial seeding of Douglas fir. Where the seeding failed, I mapped those areas, and they were planted immediately. I examined brush fields in the 1902 Yacolt burn to plan its reforestation.

The area contained a mass of fire-killed old trees, now white snags about 50 years dead. The area had been burned and reburned, and the snags became torches each time another fire occurred. The fired snags threw fire for thousands of feet. The area had to be fire proofed by falling the snags. Primitive roads were built for access by fire trucks with tanks up to 4,000 gallons and caterpillar tractors to build fire trails. The work was done, and wild fire was eliminated. The brush (mostly vine maple) was bulldozed out, piled and burned, and the area was planted to two- or three-year-old Douglas fir seedlings. The planted trees are now being harvested and going to sawmills and into the lumber market. The new forest has contributed to new wealth and jobs in the community as well as access for recreational use.

In my early career, there was an enlightening experience concerning the deterioration of over-mature silver fir (Abies amabilis). In the late 1950s, several thousand acres of silver fir were infested with an aphid, the Balsam Woolly Aphid. The high elevation area was forested almost exclusively with over-mature silver fir at an elevation near 3,000 feet. I was part of a survey party who measured the extent and severity of deterioration. The damage was readily observed by the needle discoloration: no needles, grey needles, yellowish needles, or healthy green needles. Almost all trees had damaged needles, and their demise was near.

The cause of the disaster was clear: the trees were near the end of their life cycle of about 250 years, weak and susceptible to pestilence. The solution was obvious. In a few years, over-mature trees would convert to product for consumers, and the area immediately regenerated to healthy young trees. The aphid no longer had a weak host. The healthy second generation of forest in 2011 was ready to harvest, and be renewed with a vigorous third generation forest.

I went on to be a part of many of these operations and a whole host of activities that put me in an office for a long time, but still made me a part of the action of growing trees. I achieved my dream of being productive, creating forests, jobs, wood products, and wealth in an environmentally recreational responsible way. It is too bad Grant Sharpe missed the action.

In early 2000, Grant and I attended alumni meetings at the college and had a congenial relationship. He was a navy guy who served in World War II off Okinawa. I was a marine at a later date. Of course, most of our conversation revolved around who won the war in the Pacific, the navy or the marines. Lien praises conflict management; Sharpe and I resolved any conflict with friendly conversation. Conflict and enemies are regressive to our distant barbarian past.

Ironically, Grant Sharpe's vision prevailed over the tree grower's vision of forestry. Our college has been incorporated into a comprehensive environmental group. Tree growing education has been mostly replaced by Sharpe's discipline. Paul Shepard's musing prevails. The funding and grants that fuel the university's studies are enabled by politicians allied with the preservationists. The research and education are concentrated on designing forest management based on theoretical techniques dictated by politically correct musings. Graduate students study lichen growth in the upper reaches of 250-foot trees growing on the Olympic Peninsula, disease in palm trees in West Africa, and other irrelevant studies unrelated to maintaining our Washington State trees. Most of the 1950s college class of tree growers no longer attend alumni events at the University of Washington.

Lien has (arguably) documented that the preservationists have taken de facto control of the Park Service and the University of Washington forestry studies. Nevertheless, he contends the Olympic National Park is in jeopardy because of private profiteers. Instead of being on the defensive, the preservationists again attack the Olympic Peninsula tree growers and the wealth they bring to the community. In the late 1980s, the preservationists/progressives demanded the removal of the Elwha dams, the dams that Aldwell and the citizens had worked vigorously to built to bring industry and wealth to the peninsula in the early 1900s.

Crown Zellerback had operated the dams for years, the dams that brought a Crown Zellerback and its pulp mill to Port Angeles. The mill employed my father for years. It also gave me temporary work to fund my college education.

The lower dam was far downstream from the park while the upper dam was inside the park. In 1929, President Coolidge, by proclamation, eliminated the dam site and reservoir from the Mount Olympus Monument. The community had depended on the government's commitment to a historical structure and the structure's boost to the local economy through the years. The preservationists thought otherwise. For more than ten years, the dams were operated with annual licenses, and the conditions of the licenses were made more onerous and costly. Again the preservationists' strategy was to superciliously demand the government to make licensing difficult or impossible, therefore confiscating private property. It worked!

Finally the licensing conditions required the dams' owner to transport fish over the dams thus making their economics questionable. The owner then asked the Park Service to share the cost to make a community asset viable. The Park Service initially agreed, with park leaders believing the sharing would be a fine example of "a good teamwork relationship between private enterprise and government." The preservationists demanded the park study the teamwork arrangement, a study the Park Service said would create much discussion and controversy in the local community. The study wasn't made. There were easier ways to bring about the dams' destruction.

In 1990 the Park Service joined the multi-government bureaucracies to bring down the dams. The park superintendent was well aware of his predecessor, Fred Overly, being fired by the preservationists. Elwha

River Ecosystem and Fisheries Restoration Act of 1992 (The Elwha Act) authorized the Secretary of the Interior to acquire the dams.

Fish and Wildlife Service studies contended the revenue from the restored Elwha salmon run would far exceed the revenue generated by the dams. Here again, it was another government agency dominated by the preservationists and fish interests. The dams' revenue was real wealth while the fish value was based on intangibles. More importantly, the dams were an essential backup to power for the North Olympic Peninsula should the BPA electrical power be terminated. We are warned continually our power grid is a prime target for terrorists and others. It is pure speculation on the wild salmon success in the river and the value and cost of wild salmon versus hatchery fish. The Indians would harvest much of the salmon, a harvest that would return no wealth to the community. The sports fishery contribution would be minimal at best, as there are many alternatives in the Peninsula's attractions. And, the commercial fisheries are better served with hatchery fish. My speculations are as valid as a biased Fish and Wildlife Service. Perhaps an honest man should be consulted. The Iron Man of the Hoh and his woodsmen have earned the right to decide the economic future of the Elwha and the rest of the Peninsula, not Yale educated Paul Shepard and his associates.

A common theme used in the preservationists' battle for a wilderness Olympic National Park was: The preservationists and their educated naturalists want recognition as scientists not as impractical purists, as most professional people view them. Conflict management is policy and teambuilding is rejected; all the productive people are identified as the enemy; nature should not be adapted to human needs; preservationists are the unilateral authority on land management decisions; preservationists' goals are always attributed to the will of the American people.

Finally, the lobbying preservationists were able to nationalize the Elwha River from the park to its mouth on the Strait of Juan de Fuca. They arbitrarily took the river away from the local community to spend more than $300 million federal dollars to destroy two dams. To get their way, they would have spent more if needed.

The progressive/preservationists foresee a drastic reduction of the American standard of living, which would take away our vehicles so they can confine us to urban ghettos. This vision has been carefully held a secret, a vision that could not be supported by the people. All American productive people are labeled as greedy profiteers: ranchers, loggers, miners, millworkers, and entrepreneurs on the Olympic Peninsula, the same folks who fund the progressive/preservationists' agenda and are excluded from the decision making process.

Arguably, the preservationists have de facto control of almost half of the western states to exclude all productive enterprises "for the people". Historically, all tyrants justify themselves with the people's will!

Forest Death by Fire

The Washington and Oregon forests are made up largely by Douglas fir west of the Cascade Mountains. There is a small strip of hemlock-dominant forests along the Pacific Coast of Washington, although Douglas fir grows well there too. At higher elevations (above 3,000 feet) in the Cascade and Olympic mountains, Douglas fir is largely replaced by other species, especially silver fir (Abies amabilis).

Fir forests have subordinate species, including hemlock, western red cedar, alder and others. However, by stand biomass, tree size, wood strength, growth rate, and commercial utility, Douglas fir dominates. Before the 1850s, this forest prevailed, a mosaic of age classes, that is, homogeneous areas of the same general age. The areas commonly encompassed 10,000 acres or much more. The forest ages varied from 300 to 800 years old. Fir trees at this age were labeled old growth and yellow fir. Tree height generally varied from 180 to 300 feet. The diameter at the base ranged from four to six feet or more. The size of the tree was dependent upon the quality of the soil, rainfall, and elevation. The old growth trees usually have flattened dead tops, which precluded top growth, and the diameter growth is minuscule, making them stagnant and dying. However, old trees were the only ones of value until about the 1950s. Cedar was one exception, used for making shakes, shingles, and fencing; the spruce used for airplane frames in World War I was another.

There were younger Douglas fir forests, but these were insignificant. The trees were commonly called second growth or red fir. The bark was thin, the wood reddish and brash by the early day standards.

In the early days, these trees were much sought after for poles, pilings, and ship spars. As with all young things, they are resistant to disease and have vigorous top and diameter growth; they are the future forests.

The Douglas fir forests were created by catastrophes, almost always by fire. Fir is a so-called *intolerant* species. It cannot survive for long overshadowed by other vegetation. The mature tree casts seeds for regeneration irregularly. Then, the few viable seeds must find mineral soil that has available nutrients, moisture, and heat to germinate and grow. The organic material (duff) covering the forest floor usually dries out in summer and the germinated seedling withers for lack of moisture.

A dramatic example of the creation of a Douglas fir forest was a catastrophic ancient fire that occurred on the coast of Washington over 500 years ago. This fire started at Willapa Bay and destroyed nearly everything in its path as it burned parallel to the Pacific Coast north to Lake Ozette and beyond. About three quarters of the north/south coast of Washington burned, and the fire extended east from the ocean almost to the base of the Olympic Mountains. It cannot be determined whether the fire happened in one sweep or was a series of fires. It matters not; the fire destroyed a huge forest and almost everything in its path. A legend perpetuated by the Quinault tribe states a great fire forced the tribe into the sea about 500 years ago. The tribe's village was and is at the mouth of the Quinault River located between Forks and Aberdeen.

Investigators found a 500-year-old cedar tree in the old burn, growing around a fallen cedar that was downed in the ancient fire. It appeared that an ancient cedar forest had been generally replaced by a Douglas fir forest. Further, this also suggests that the extensive Douglas fir forests in western Washington and Oregon were created by similar disasters over the centuries. And, without the catastrophes of fire, wind, clear-cut logging, and regeneration, nature's Douglas fir forests are doomed to extinction.

Fire and smoke were endemic in the forest before the American settlers came to the region in the late 1840s. The Hudson Bay Company's people were the first to write of the endemic fires. In 1844, forest fires approached Fort Vancouver, but the facilities were saved from destruction. The origin of the fire was unknown and the size was described only as *extensive*. Joseph Thomas Heath, a Hudson Bay farmer located near Steilacoom, reported an "awful fire raging throughout the forests". The fire was at some distance but visibility was only a few hundred yards. He described the fire as 30 miles in length and 4 to 10 miles wide. These fires suggest that they were common in the Douglas fir forests in past centuries.

The fire and smoke continued as the Americans settled the area. A Coast and Geodetic Surveyor, John Francis Pratt, commented in August 1887: "Much of the time at this season of the year, it is impossible on the Sound to see more than one-fourth mile off. Older steamer captains are obliged to navigate by compass from point to point as much as if they were at sea." There were many other writers of the smoke on the Sound. Some smoke forced canoes and small schooners to anchor or go ashore until the smoke abated. However, there were no forest fires in Washington of consequence recorded until the Yacolt Burn in 1902.

But during the 1800s, forest fires were killing people in another part of the country. Wisconsin/Michigan/Minnesota was a thriving region of developing forest communities. Railroads crisscrossed the countryside; logging camps as well as sawmills proliferated the region; and settlers carved out farms from the forest. This region furnished much of the lumber that built America. However, settlers cut trees and burned them indiscriminately to clear land; loggers were careless with fire; and locomotives discharged sparks into the forests. Fire in the woods was not thought to be important.

Peshtigo, Wisconsin was a town of about 2,000 people in 1871, built around a sawmill and a factory that turned out wood products, like broom handles and clothes pins. Eight hundred people were employed in the industry. In September, a fire from the forest leveled the town and killed 1,152 people as it burned 1,280,000 acres of forest land. Subsequently, Wisconsin had eight fires up to 1936 that ranged from 500,000 to 1,000,000 acres apiece. These statistics don't include the "small" fires.

Michigan had similar forest fire tragedies that year, two million acres burned, according to the authorities. They undoubtedly minimized the horror and the size of the fires which were more like two and a half million acres. In one day, seven villages were destroyed and six were damaged. The people largely escaped from the villages, but the settlers suffered an unknown number of deaths. The stories told of the recorded tragedies were awful; the parents on one forest farm accidentally escaped the fire, but heard their two young girls die a screaming death in their house. Similar family experiences were common.

Michigan's forest burned again 10 years later. This time the deaths were recorded: 169 killed and a million acres burned. Contrary to previous fires, Sergeant William O. Bailey of the United States Weather Bureau toured the blazing inferno and documented his observations. Bailey noted the fire had withered leaves of trees two miles from its path, and whole fields of corn and potatoes in the fields were roasted. The fire generated wind that blew down buildings, lifted people off the ground and rolled big boulders along the ground. When the sergeant was asked the causes of the fire, he cited uncontrolled weather factors, such as high wind, and extreme temperatures. He was precise in stating the controllable facts: First were the many acres of dead timber (snags) created by the 1871 fire, combined with the logging slash; and second, the settlers' careless land clearing to create pastures. The settlers' fires were many and scattered throughout the forest. They were created without thought to critical fire weather conditions or any other prudent precautions.

The Hinckley Fire in Minnesota was the most notorious forest fire in America. It killed 418 people in 1894. Thousands of acres burned. Forest fires roared down on Hinckley on the first day of September. Some people were lucky enough to flee to a water-filled gravel pit and others to a waiting train. The train was finally overflowing with desperate people, its heated paint running down the side of the cars. As the trainmen watched men, women, and animals go down screaming in the town's streets, the train pulled out of a burning station. The train passed through a village without being asked to stop by the villagers. Soon afterwards, that village of 45 people perished without survivors. The train reached a flaming bridge to find the watchmen dead, well charred. The train crossed the bridge with flames lapping at the passengers. Once across and safely out of danger, they watched the bridge collapse. Horror stories such as this would fill a book.

After the fire subsided, the dead were laid in piles along the railroad grade. People flooded into the area from neighboring towns to help the survivors and take care of the dead. Survivors blamed the tragedy on the people's casualness with forest fires, that is, the inattention to the settlers' clearing fires and other small fires in the forests, combined with logging slash. There was no help from the state legislature or the federal government. However, after the holocaust, the burned-out lumbermen raised $5,000 a year to prevent fire in the forests to save the trees and people.

The Hinckley Fire was perhaps the first great fire to define the seriousness of forest fire. However, it was not the first or last of great fires. Fire scars on trees in a Minnesota County documented fires: in 1819, 1842, 1864, 1874, and 1885. Obviously there were severe fires before the area was settled. In spite of the fire warnings, other fire deaths continued.

The Hinckley tragedy was repeated in Minnesota in 1910: two lumber towns burned and about 2,000 people escaped in flaming trains while many missed the trains. Forty–two people died and 300,000 acres were burned.

Americans seemed to be helpless or careless, for in 1918, Cloquet, Minnesota, a town of 10,000 burned as a forest fire encompassing about a million and a quarter acres roared through. The town was proud of its five sawmills, a pulp and paper plant, and its people who made it one of the most important forest communities in America. The saloons survived the fire, as did three of the sawmills and the pulp mill. The fires not only swept through Cloquet, but other regions in the area. Again, the railroad evacuated the town, with 8,500 people quietly boarding trains to leave town.

When the fire was over, the mill workers and loggers returned to a burned-out town to begin their life anew, wondering if their livelihood that was dependent on the mills would still be possible. The mill and timber owners worked with the citizens to build a new town and industry. The forest around the town was destroyed. Where would the wood come from to run the mills? They found a way without the aid of indifferent state and federal governments. They salvaged the dead trees for several years before the fungus and bugs made the trees useless for the mills. Then they had to find other sources for "logs". Perhaps the greatest tragedy was the loss of the young trees that came after their earlier timber harvest. The young trees were destroyed by successive forest fires, a disaster that made it difficult at best to sustain an "important forest community" like Cloquet. Interestingly, the Cloquet tragedy still didn't resonate with Americans. Between 1914 and 1942 almost eight million acres burned or reburned in the Minnesota forests, suggesting forests were discounted. Sadly, during this period about 1,000 people were incinerated. And, in 1940, the Minnesota forester estimated four million acres needed to be planted.

During the period that Minnesota, Michigan, and Wisconsin were burning, the federal government became concerned for the nation's forests. The American Forestry Association requested the Secretary of the Interior to make a detailed report on the "nation's forest assets". The Secretary asked the National Academy of Sciences to investigate. It appointed a Commission of academics to do a study. In 1896, the Commission made a brief study by visiting Yellowstone and other pristine wilderness areas in the far west. Gifford Pinchot and John Muir were perhaps the de facto leaders of the commission, the two people that would lead the progressive political movement in the country.

The forests in Minnesota and vicinity had been burning for years and people were dying. The Commission ignored these forest tragedies to look at the western scenery. They had sought no data or solutions to the forest problems. They recommended the government create Forest Reserves, which they did in 1897 that totaled 21 million acres. The Reserves were made without any thought for protection of the huge land area from fire or anything else. The academics had their agenda before they began the investigation and set a pattern of behavior that is followed to this day; in addition, the Commission's de facto leaders profited by their efforts. Pinchot was rewarded by being appointed the Forest Service's first Chief Forester, and Muir was able to organize and lead the progressive Sierra Club for decades.

Sanctimoniously, the progressives led by Pinchot and Muir cited the greedy timber and mill owners for getting out of the Minnesota forests to devastate the far western forests in like manner. The citizens and mill owners of Cloquet demonstrated they wanted to utilize the Minnesota forests forever. The two men preached that a timber and lumber famine was imminent because of destructive logging.

The forests were not depleted by logging; the forests of the Minnesota region were converted into temporary wastelands by continual forest fires. The region's fire tragedies were ignored by the progressives while they accused the Minnesota lumbermen of destroying their forest. People died in Minnesota because of the progressives' agenda and their failure to provide ways to reduce the threat of more fires.

The Forest Reserves largely became National Forests under the leadership of Chief Forester Pinchot. In 1910, Idaho's fires consumed three million acres, mostly on Forest Service land. Eighty-five people died; 75 of them were fire fighters. There were more than 3,000 separate fires controlled by fire crews, and then gale winds combined the fires into a holocaust. There were 3,000 organized fire fighters battling the blazes. It was the first well organized firefighting effort in the country; nevertheless, again the citizens had to be evacuated by railroad from the raging fire.

The Idaho fire, combined with other forest fires in the country, finally got the attention of the country. The newspaper coverage was dramatic and continuous for months. The country was shocked out of its lethargy. A fire strategy was developed to go forward, and the federal government started to understand the fire problem.

William Greeley was a Forest Service District Ranger with responsibilities for containing the Idaho fire. Greeley took his fire experiences and the need for a cooperative effort by all parties — federal and local governments, the people and the timber owners — with him to become Chief Forester in 1920. Pinchot had involuntarily retired in 1910.

Further, the aftermath horrors of the fire were tracked and communicated. First, the bark beetles immediately infested the burned area and spread to the adjacent green trees to destroy millions of board feet of white pine. Salvage of the burned timber was a cooperative effort of the Forest Service and the lumber companies. The rapid decay and bugs destroyed the usefulness of the trees quickly, so only about 10% of the trees were utilized. Also, the inaccessibility of the area contributed to the waste of the burned and bug-killed trees. However, it taught the foresters the best defense against the bark beetle infestation is to remove dead trees quickly. More importantly, the burned areas, covered with dead trees (snags) and felled trees, contributed to many reburns of the Idaho 1910 fire.

The Minnesota and Idaho fire history is important to understand because of its influence on the Douglas fir region. The Washington timberland owners were generally aware of the fire danger to life and resources, while many of the residents just wanted the timber gone, to facilitate their farms and businesses. There had been few fires of consequence in the region as the settlers began to develop the area, starting in the 1850. Then, in 1902, the Yacolt Burn south of Mt. St. Helens, and supplementary fires shocked people into concern and primitive action. The total fires in western Washington and Oregon at that time was 110, with about 38 people killed and others missing.

The Yacolt Burn was in excess of 200,000 acres. The forest ranger at the Mount Rainier Forest Reserve on the east side of the burn sighted the fire and watched it burn. He had no resources to do anything else. Citizens in front of the fire fled for their lives, and some weren't fast enough. The fire traveled 36 miles in 36 hours. No group was available to organize an effort to control the blaze. The fall rains eventually extinguished it. In the meantime, one settler near the village of Yacolt watched the hills behind Tum-Tum Mountain light up with fire. He had observed how snags created by a fire in 1868 lit up like matches ahead of the main body of the fire.

In 1955, fire expert C.S. Cowan writes: "There are 100,000 acres covered with snags and no trees in the old Yacolt Burn. The extreme fire weather, combined with the snags, has led to repeated fire across the brush-covered 100,000 acres. The fire would leap from snag to snag above the heads of fire suppression crews, neutralizing any effort to control the blazes. The snags are coming down and the acreage will soon be growing a vigorous Douglas fir forest that stands a much better chance of reaching maturity."

The Yacolt Burn terrified Washington State's large timberland owners and the citizens of the state. It was evident to the owners that something would have to be done to prevent fire holocausts.

The federal government was dominated by the progressives that created the Mount Rainier Reserves and others. The ranger on the Reserve had been told to eliminate his small crew of firefighters, making the ranger the only government observer of the fire. The state government was uninterested in protecting the forests from fires, and the settlers were unorganized. The forest landowners and their loggers were responsible for fires, but so were the settlers with escaped clearing fires, recreationists, railroads, and nature's lightning. Later, cigarettes became a major problem along highways and in the woods.

In 1908 many of the major forest landowners came together in western Washington to form the Washington Forest Fire Association. A Chief Fire Warden was employed to lead the organization, and instructed to employ as many fire wardens as he thought were necessary to protect the state's forests. Their chief function was to patrol the forests to detect fires and take appropriate action. A program was also started to educate the public in fire prevention.

There were an estimated 12 million acres of private forest land in western Washington. Association members paid an assessment of two cents per acre on their lands of 2.8 million acres to fund fire protection efforts. The Association was strictly voluntary, and many landowners did not participate, particularly the small landowners. Initially, the Association's puny force and the landowners' loggers were the only forest protection resources in the state.

By necessity, the competitive (and often unfriendly) landowners were forced together to protect the forest resources in the state. They knew the solution and responsibility of protection must be delegated to the state political structure, a structure most of them detested. Hence, the Association began to educate the state of the needs to protect and enhance the state's forest resources. The progressives would label this effort as selfish lobbying, but unlike in Minnesota, it saved Washington's forests.

The Association compelled the state to put in place a fire warden's group in 1909. The fire season the following year was frisky. The state fire warden ran out of money to protect the forest. He could not obtain funds from either his employers or state politicians, so he came to the Association for funds. Some individual Association members subscribed $10,000 each to enable the fire warden to continue in his efforts to save the forest.

Inexplicably, in 1911 the Legislature didn't believe the forest resource was worth the cost of protection and wouldn't adequately fund the state fire warden. The state owned about two million acres of timber with its principal source of revenue from the private forests. The Legislature's decision was made contrary to the Association's plea to assess all forest lands a few cents to protect the assets from fire. Most of the forest landowners were willing to pay for fire protection. Unfortunately, it took the death of five fire fighters to move the Legislature to fund the state's fire fighters.

The Association didn't wait for the state in 1913. They instituted a logging camp inspection by their fire wardens. There were 1,450 donkey engines and a multitude of locomotives that were wood-burning and spewing sparks into the forests. The wardens called attention to the fire danger and asked for spark arresters for the machines. Most landowners complied, and there were only 31 minor fires caused by donkey engines and 16 by locomotives. The Association was begging the state Legislature for support to make spark arrestor's mandatory for all machines, plus some regulation of settlers' burning. The progressive federal government wasn't interested in the landowners' needs or even understood the reality of forest protection except to exclude people from the forests.

The Association and the state fire organizations advanced in their battle to protect the forests with little federal support. In 1920, protection revenues from the Association's 2.7 million acres was .0375 cents per acre. Fire crews had been increased to nine. The state placed 30 fire wardens in the field while the Association had 125. A potential air patrol of the forest failed because of a lack of support by Congress, but the concept was visionary. A public relations system was in place that featured movies at theaters showcasing slides about forest fires. The press carried fire prevention messages, and prevention signs were posted in the forests and towns. The message was: "Prevent forest fires, it pays." Eighty logging camps employed their own fire wardens who maintained fire equipment and audited fire prevention operational procedures.

In 1923 the cost of forest protection in the state was shared: federal 4%; state, 7%; and private landowners, 89%. The critics suggest that all the costs should be funded by the landowners to protect their property, but most of the fires were caused by the public who are the responsibility of the government. The government theoretically should compensate the landowner for their fire losses when the public started a fire. In 1924 the Clarke-McNary Act was passed in Congress to encourage cooperation in forest fire protection. It would share some costs in the states' fire prevention and suppression programs.

Sophisticated instruments and techniques were finally brought into the forest to fight fire in 1922. A study of fire behavior at Berkeley,

California determined that fire spread completely out of control when the humidity reached 30% or lower. Fire weather was now measurable. It took time, but soon most logging operations had an instrument to measure humidity and shut down the operation when the humidity reached this critical point. The authorities and landowners had instruments to measure humidity in their offices and radios to communicate with the loggers to audit their conformance to shut-down standards. Loggers jeopardized their employment if they logged below 30% humidity. Weather forecasting was incorporated into all operations in the forest, and areas were closed to logging and public use when weather conditions became critical. The humidity critical index was combined with other indexes as the information became available.

The Association and the state soon constructed fire lookouts for coverage of the state and private forests. The lookouts were connected to fire crew dispatchers in the early days with telephone lines and later with radio for early detection and attack on wildfires. In modern times, the lookouts were replaced with air reconnaissance. The Association and large landowners began to access their forest lands with roads and developed water "holes" along the roads. Roads gave quick access for water pump trucks (some holding 4,000 gallons) and bulldozers to get to a fire before it became large. Several operations I observed in the 1960s on private operations could have about twenty 4,000-gallon water trucks, 10 or more D-8 bulldozers, water-dropping helicopters, and about 200 hardened loggers to combat a wildfire in about an hour. Of course, the state fire people would be notified so they could bring their resources to the fire.

Progress was being made to reduce fires and protect the forest in spite of a hostile progressive government in the mid-1930s. The Federal Administration flooded the press with stories of forest destruction and lack of reforestation directed at the private landowners. As the negative rhetoric flooded the media, both Congress and State reduced funding for fire prevention and control. In 1935 there were 1,341 forest fires in western Washington: 25 logging fires, 6 lightning, 469 recreationists, 245 by land clearers, 316 by incendiaries, and 209 by miscellaneous causes. In 1936, 50 per cent of fires were caused by incendiaries. They burned more than 15,000 acres.

At this time the Association cooperated with the government to write fire regulations to reduce fires. The industry wanted regulations to enforce good practices uniformly across the state to rein in the few mavericks; generally the industry voluntarily put the regulations into practice. The courts negated the Lumber Code, which codified the fire regulations. The Association then unsuccessfully asked the government for legislation to enforce good fire prevention practices.

The progressive government in this era had its own agenda that preferred to attack the private landowner and sacrifice the forest.

The future of the Douglas fir forests in western Washington lies with its second growth. In 1935, the Association requested the State Forester to give a value to the second growth destroyed by fire, to provide the real value lost in a fire year. Only old growth had a value. The state refused to value the second growth. This attitude reflected in the public's perception that suggested a second growth fire shouldn't be a concern, so let it burn. The Association members knew that second growth was the future for an industry that was the chief generator of state revenue. Between 1927 and 1935 almost a quarter of a million acres of second growth had burned. The state classified these lands as brush lands of no consequence.

In 1941, second growth was given a value of $6 per acre. This was based on the cost of planting an acre of Douglas fir seedlings. This price suggests a prudent person would not plant trees on bare forestland when they could buy 60-year-old second growth for the same price. Nevertheless, some landowners did plant trees. Four million acres of "fully stocked" second growth existed in western Washington in 1943. The second growth statistic refutes the mid-1930s progressives' propaganda that landowners in Washington were not regenerating their land after timber harvest. It also confirms the private sector's visionaries who had faith the forest would naturally regenerate itself if the cycle of burns and re-burns was broken, that is, keep wild fire out of the forest.

The loggers in the big railroad camps were generally convinced the slash had to be burned to keep fire out of the woods. The 1921 Forks blowdown created a wildfire hazard that motivated the landowners to burn 70,000 acres of slash created by logging old growth that year. The loggers had years of experience with their spark throwing machines that resulted in wildfires that burned their equipment, camps, and railroad trestles. Practical experience dictated that the fuels generated by logging slash should be eliminated by controlled fire to preclude wildfires in the slash that would rush into the green timber. Inadvertently, the loggers were mimicking nature's fires to establish Douglas fir forests.

The state agreed with the loggers and codified a law that made slash a fire hazard that must be reduced by burning unless a greater hazard would be created by the burning. The hazard would also be mitigated with the passage of time. In the meantime, the logger or landowner was liable for the cost of any fires started therein, including the suppression cost. Today's better utilization of the timber resource and other concerns has made slash burning for fire safety virtually unnecessary.

In 1951, the Legislature passed a law requiring snag-falling in and near the operations as "snags have always been the bane of forest fire fighters". Snags were also a safety concern as they were slowly breaking apart, creating an overhead hazard. Since the 1990s, snags have been left in the woods for wildlife, a policy that might increase the population of woodpeckers slightly, but contribute to more fires and human injuries.

In the late 1940s the state took over all the responsibilities of forest fire protection, and the services of the Association were no longer needed. District buildings and equipment were set up throughout the state. In 1947, I was a sophomore in high school and was hired as a summer fire fighter. Ten high school boys formed the crew led by a college-student foreman. We were equipped with a tank truck with 500 gallons of water, a crew truck, a D-4 bulldozer on a truck, and hand tools. We had on-the-job training, and some of the urban boys had never handled an ax or shovel. I spent three summers in the crew. We put out a few small roadside fires. When the fire weather was not critical, which was most of the time, we cut brush encroaching on forest access roads or cut wood with hand crosscut saws to supply wood to heat the headquarters' building. A serious fire would have required an influx of men and equipment from the local loggers.

The Association didn't believe the state had the resources to protect high hazard private forestland, so they funded several fire districts of their own. But, the Association generally turned its attention to other activities.

Taxes on timber and land were an issue almost as important to a landowner as was fire. In 1923 it was noted that taxes on timber had increased 323% in ten years and cut-over (logged) lands' taxes ranged from nine to thirty-four cents an acre. Land reverted to the county because of delinquent taxes on cut-over land. Timber is a long-term investment. In the modern world, the land and trees would have been held and taxed for about 50 years: high taxes could force landowners to cut-out and get out of their property. Fortunately, the Association convinced the Legislature to defer most the taxes on land and timber until the timber was harvested, but it took years to get totally equitable forestland and timber taxes implemented.

The Association also identified an outbreak of hemlock looper, a defoliator, in Pacific County located in southwest Washington. The state had land in the area and was asked to cooperate, but refused. The pest had the potential to become an epidemic across a much broader landscape. It was 1931, and the technology to combat the pest was sketchy. In the middle of the Great Depression, the Association planned the operation, and designed a delivery system to make 120 flights over the infected area by spraying a chemical to control the pest. The airplane that made the flight was the sister ship of the "Spirit of St. Louis" and the chemical was calcium arsenate. The cost was $3 per acre, a lot of money for the landowners in a slumping lumber market. The area sprayed saved the old trees from damage or death. Subsequently, the area was harvested (logged) and a new young vigorous forest replaced the old forest that was often subjected to forest insect and disease. For the next 80 years the new forest was free of hemlock looper or other destructive infestations, making the use of chemicals archaic. The use of this chemical today would result in the progressives going to war. As in most of the progressives' angst, there was no damage done to the environment by spraying calcium arsenate on the forest.

The Association continued to protect the forests of the state and identify problems. In 1955 a hard freeze damaged the forest. There was a mild November and the trees were still growing with a moist cambium layer when the temperatures dropped to eight degrees below zero at Ryderwood. The cold continued for several weeks. The freeze killed several years of top growth of young trees that were about 20 feet tall, over a large area in southwest Washington. The loss of growth was serious, causing apprehension over future defect in the damaged trees.

I worked to map the damage and took part in the speculation of the damage. Of course, the exercise was futile as nothing could be done about it. However, thirty years later, I walked through many of the 1955 damaged trees. There was a crook in the trees roughly twenty feet from the ground at the point the freeze killed the trees' top growth years ago. There was no defect in the trees, but the crook would downgrade the value of the first thirty feet in the tree. My observation was interesting but useless.

The Washington Forest Fire Protection Association celebrated its 50th anniversary in 1957. During the first year of its operation there were 1,102 forest fires of unknown acreage. On its 50th anniversary, there were only 554 fires encompassing only 368 acres in the state of Washington. This record is made in the face of a huge increase in population, road mileage, and more logging operations. The Association's timberland owners accomplished a miracle in the face of a sometimes hostile government, an effort that started and was led by Washington

State's timber barons. The private sector in Washington State is growing and harvesting trees in healthy and vigorous forests while sustaining the forest communities.

The Minnesota/Michigan/Wisconsin timber industry, along with their tree growing capacity, was largely destroyed with repeated and continuous fires over this period. The progressives were wrong; Washington State did not cut and get out because of its citizens dedication to sustain their forests. The progressives will continue in their attempts to reduce tree growing along with jobs in Washington State, but Washington's forests will continue to be saved by the productive people in the forest communities.

CREATING A FOREST

The Americans started to impact western Washington's Douglas fir forests in the 1850s when they arrived by wagons, horses, and ships from the east or California. These Americans were reinforced by an influx of others from all over the world, but mostly Europe.

The forest was the chief attraction. It was the principal cash crop that could be immediately converted to gold in the California market and further afield. The timber resource seemed inexhaustible and an obstacle for those who cherished the dream of a farm — the settlers. The visionary settlers like John Huelsdonk on the Hoh River soon understood the potential of river valleys and prairies for farmland and the hills for tree growing, a combination that would support thriving forest communities.

Numerous sawmill villages and towns began to flourish integrated with an industry that largely funded local and state governments, while furnishing permanent and temporary employment to the citizens of the territory. The territory would soon become the state of Washington.

The Pope and Talbot Company was among the first to construct a sawmill and village at Port Gamble in the early 1850s. The village housed the millworkers. The firm was more or less duplicated in western Washington along numerous bays and rivers in the region. The early mills were furnished logs without thought of ownership of land on what was largely public domain — a situation that was generally unsatisfactory to the mill owners, government and citizens. But it was a necessity because the people of the region arrived before the government could become completely functional. Logging was done by independent loggers, settlers, and companies. Most mill owners yearned for ownership of land and timber to assure a supply of logs to facilitate sound capital investments in developing mills, coupled to an operating forest that would continuously supply them raw materials.

Pope and Talbot and many others over the decades finally achieved their goal of having their timber resource to complement their mills. There has been much written negatively about the transfer of the public domain to the private sector by people who don't want to understand the complex problem. The government and politicians couldn't keep up with the aggressive American people who built the country. As it should be, government bureaucracy followed the entrepreneurial people and expedited their efforts.

As the timber industry matured, many thoughtful land and mill owners began to think about the necessity of sustaining the forests. The first and foremost problem was to control and reduce wildfires. In the early 1900s, burning and re-burning the forest made the practicability of forest sustainability untenable. I looked at the history of one section (640 acres) southeast of Aberdeen and found it burned five times in twenty years. The landowners attacked this problem without much help from their government as a start to forest sustainability.

It was thought mill technology was not available to deal with small trees. One mill manager observed a 50-year-old Douglas fir forest and remarked that the industry would be out of business if forced to use the small trees. The industry was generally oriented to milling big logs — some more than six feet in diameter — considering it impractical to grow trees for three hundred years or more. It does make sense to grow Douglas fir trees for forty to eighty years. Far-sighted people knew technology could and would adapt to a younger forest.

Timber was plentiful and cheap up through the 1950s; therefore low-cost wood products were generally in oversupply. There was little economic incentive to enhance the forests. For example, the state of Washington put no value on second growth fir until the 1940s. Optimists were confident that as the old growth timber supply dwindled, second growth would increase in value to sustain the forests, communities, and the timber industry.

More importantly, the art of creating forests was almost non-existent. The observant timber owners, settlers, and woodsmen believed second growth was the future for the state. They had observed how the old burns and logging had been naturally regenerated with Douglas fir seedlings, only to see the infant trees go up in smoke. Like many Americans of this era, there were people optimistic about their ability to conquer all problems and were working to do so.

In the meantime, academics were establishing forest science and studies mostly in European universities. Graduate foresters from these universities, were awarded levels of degrees to PhD. The studies concentrated on the European forests that had been cultured for centuries, usually on gentlemen's estates. Also, the European countries' economies and structures were not as dependent on wood as in America, while the mass production of wood literally built and fueled the New World. European forestry studies emigrated to the east coast of the United States and formed the basis for American forestry studies. In addition, European forestry academics emigrated too. In the late 1800s, Gifford Pinchot started his forestry education, as did many other Americans. He went to Europe to study, then brought their science to America. Pinchot was honored and named the "Father of American Forestry".

Fortunately, university forest studies were adopted by western universities, such as the University of Washington and Oregon State. The forestry professors and students were usually westerners who were raised in or near the forests and adapted the European knowledge to the reality of the western American forests. They focused on the wildfires that continually destroyed the forests and the concept of forest sustainability.

Sustainability, as adopted in today's world, was first theorized and initiated in the forests of America. The government and most landowners were demanding the forest be sustained to furnish timber resources to the local communities and the country. A sustainable forest was one that guaranteed a continuous harvest and growth of trees to stabilize the businesses and employment in the local communities. Starting in the 1930s, the public also demanded sustainable "yield" from the nation's forests. There were even many efforts to regulate a continuous timber harvest from local forests without success. The progressives forced the federal government to abandon the sustaining concept in the 1990s in favor of preservation.

The author beside one of the trees he was responsible for planting in 1972, east of Eugene, OR.

In the early 1900s the western universities graduated foresters that usually were employed by the government, but were slowly brought into the landowners' organizations, most of whom were interested in the forests sustainability. The government foresters operated within an organizational structure that changed little over the years. The industrial foresters (employed by the private sector) increased dramatically after World War II when a multitude of factors came together. These factors activated forest culture practices, such as controlled burning and regeneration. The government foresters' story is a separate history. The foresters' role combined with the landowners is the major factor that furnished wood products to build the nation for more than a century.

The forest cultural systems started in the early 1900s and were confined to controlling fire and public education. Much of the early primitive research and experimentation by the private sector, universities, and the government, enjoyed cooperation and agreement among all parties in learning how to deal with Douglas fir sustainability.

Planting Douglas fir seedlings seemed a simple procedure for the German-trained foresters; collect seed, germinate the seed in a nursery, and out-plant the seedlings in the forest after maybe two years in the nursery. Seed was collected from mature trees willy-nilly, and ten years later the trees were pathetic. Years later, it was learned that seed must be collected by elevation and geographic area and returned to that location for optimum growth. Then, these plantings thrived, failed, or did not conform to expectations because of many other factors.

First, the number of trees to plant on an acre to create the optimum mature trees was a mystery. Many organizations planted almost 1,000 trees to attain 100 trees on that acre two years later, and there seemed no reason for the 800 trees that perished. It took years to develop proper tree planting procedures to maximize survival and good spacing of trees. The puzzle was solved mostly by the foresters who planted the trees and tracked their growth progress, not the academics.

It was discovered the tree roots had to be planted in mineral soil with the roots straight into the soil, and there must be a minimum of competition and certainly little or no over-shading of the seedlings. The planting season was critical. At first, October to April seemed reasonable, but then December to March was found to be satisfactory with February/March being the optimum months.

Almost completely ignored initially was the effect of wildlife on seedling survival and growth. Late in the game, foresters determined the best protection was immediate regeneration after wildfire or logging, before the critters invaded the prime habitat created by logging. The havoc created by deer and elk was critical. The elk trampled and pulled seedlings out of the ground. A few landowners fenced elk out of their clear-cuts and hoped eventually a liberal hunting season would reduce the problem. Elk converged on the clear-cuts. The deer browsed the seedlings. I once observed a Douglas fir tree of four feet for five years that appeared to be a bonsai. In spite of a deer repellent developed in the 1970s and hunting seasons, tree damage by wildlife continues to be a problem.

Other wildlife that went unseen were varmints, generally rabbits, voles, and mountain beavers. Rabbits colonized the brush areas, and unless the brush or rabbits were eliminated, seedlings survived only about six months. I observed a planted area three months after planting and found no trees. The voles (mouse-like creatures) inhabited the meadows. Part of the Mt. St. Helens blast area was seeded to grass immediately after the event and planted with fir seedlings. The voles girdled the seedlings shortly thereafter; they were virtually eliminated and new plantings were successful. Mountain beavers (mole-like) in some forest areas precluded the establishment of a forest. The beaver population can be reduced by high cost trapping or poisoning, at least long enough for the trees to grow large enough to survive. Of course the beavers do not thrive in a mature forest. It has been speculated that some openings in the old fir forests were created by mountain beavers that continually destroyed seedlings over many years.

There were other problems besides wildlife in birthing a forest. One concerned planting trees on abandoned cultivated fields. Several forest "experts", including a PhD, gathered around a field to speculate why the seedlings were perishing. A retired curmudgeon farmer joined the experts, wondering at their stupidity. He informed the group that, year after year, plowing created a sheer plane at the depth of the furrow that was impenetrable to the seedling's roots. The solution was to rip the plane with a D-8 tractor and plant the trees in the rip so the roots could extend into the soil. This technique was used in a few forested areas with difficult soils.

In the early 1930s, the Douglas fir forest structure was defined, a break-through that allowed forest owners to predict the makeup of the forest by age classes and predict the value of a forest at various periods of time. In 1928, Senator Charles McNary of Oregon was one of the sponsors of the McSweeny-McNary Act that authorized fourteen Forest

Service Experimental Stations. The senator was elected by the forest communities that wanted to further the understanding of their forests. The stations researched the forest and provided bulletins, among many other communications.

Forest Service Bulletin #201 was compiled of individual forests of specific age class and measured the trees by numbers and size. For instance, a 50-year-old forest of Douglas fir was separated by five site qualities (growth potential) to state the volume of wood grown in 50 years along with a multitude of tree statistics. The Bulletins furnished the data to calculate the sustainability of a forest at a multitude of timber harvest ages, which would produce a variety of volumes of wood in cubic, scribner, or other measures of wood that could be related to economics to make forest production policies which could be related to other variables, such as wildlife. All the factors could be incorporated manually or by computer to simulate different forest management strategies.

The Bulletin also guided the foresters in setting goals in regenerating the forest and other forest culture activities. For instance, Douglas fir trees were commonly planted at 800 trees per acre whereas natural regeneration might result in 1,000 trees per acre or more. The Bulletin documented that a 20-year-old Douglas fir forest might contain 400 trees per acre on about 10x10-foot tree spacing. The trees numbers were reduced by competition, as the growing capacity on an acre would only support 400 trees per acre of that age.

The Bulletin's data was compiled from even-age forests throughout western Washington and Oregon, forests created by natural regeneration after a catastrophe of fire or logging. The data represents nature's Douglas fir forests that were successfully regenerated, just like the forests that were created by the ancient fires. These forests also represent the greatest production of wood fiber and sequestered carbon, relative to alternatives that humans might engineer, such as a selective harvest that creates an uneven age stand structure contrary to nature's Douglas fir forests.

Over the years, several groups or people have tried without success to corrupt nature's Douglas fir forest by planting exotic tree species. Even native species planted outside their normal areas struggle to survive. A few species that failed outside their area have been Sitka spruce, Port Orford cedar, and coast Sequoia. One living example of a tree that struggles out of its range is the high elevation noble fir that has been planted as an ornamental in the Tacoma area, a beautiful young tree that grows rapidly. It usually starts to die at age thirty, when the tree normally lives for hundreds of years. Many eastern progressive people continually ask for diversity and believe the Douglas fir should be diluted with other tree species. This is contrary to the nature of Douglas fir because this competitive fir usually eliminates the other species. Also, there are at least a hundred species of vegetation in a "pure" Douglas fir forest, albeit mostly understory vegetation.

The details of forest knowledge are tiresome to the average reader and ignored by many academics. As late as the 1990s, a Yale-educated progressive wrote that a massive government program should be funded to discover how to regenerate a forest. Obviously, the Yale progressive was ignorant of what had taken place in the Douglas fir region for over a century. The layman needs only to step off the road and walk through the region's young trees to understand the wondrous new forests. The forests created by private landowners after the 1980 Mt. St. Helens eruption would be a good place to observe forestry in today's world.

The evolution of creating sustainable forests on private lands began slowly in western Washington. The key to achieving sustainability was accomplished mainly with two factors: the landowners and dirt foresters.

The early landowners had to control the wildfires in the forest before they could invest in the forest. The alternative was to "cut and get out". Many landowners had sawmills associated with timber holdings and wished for a reliable timber supply to continue their business. In addition, they wanted to perpetuate their companies for decades as legacies for their families. The landowners who were in the business for the short term were eventually incorporated into other long-term landholders.

Pope and Talbot began milling and logging in the 1850s and was still growing trees on its properties in 2012. Weyerhaeuser who became a force in timber in the early 1900s is still growing trees. Simpson, in Shelton, has been growing timber for decades. Merrill and Ring who began logging at Pysht on the Strait of Juan de Fuca in the early 1900s is still growing trees there. An example of a short-term operation is Bloedel/ Donovan, who purchased Clallam County forestland from a timber operator in 1924 and, in turn, was purchased by Rayonier Incorporated in 1945. Rayonier is still growing trees on the north Olympic Peninsula and beyond. Almost all of the property in western Washington follows the Bloedel/Donovan and Rayonier pattern of ownership and continuing sustainability of the forest. In addition to the large landowners, the small landowners, homesteaders, and settlers sold their properties to other forest owners and, in many cases, held forest properties in their families or revisited their vacated "home places" to continue their family legacies.

Until the early 1980s, most of the large timberlands was owned and managed by the timber industry, an industry that was a vertical organization — forestland was combined with logging and manufacturing facilities. The industry's heritage dated from the 1850s with efforts for more than a century that developed a land stewardship responsibility leading to a sustainable and responsible stewardship of forest land in close cooperation with the forest communities.

In 1983, the institutional investors discovered timberland was a profitable investment. The investors included insurance companies, pension funds, mutual funds, and hedge funds. The cumulative return on investments between 1986 and 1992 was over 25%. Between 1983 and 2009 the investors' timberland totaled 43 million acres valued at $40 billion nationwide. The federal income tax (REITs) policy favored the investors over the vertical timber industry and made the classic industry almost uncompetitive for raising trees. Weyerhaeuser Company was the only significant vertical intergraded forest products company "still standing" in 2009.

The federal government inadvertently almost destroyed the classic timber industry that was closely tied to local forest communities. The maligned timber barons kept the nation's forests from being nationalized while developing the lumber that built America. The institutional investors, mostly in the east, concentrate on profits not the communities. They lack the political history or acumen to keep the progressives from regulating them out of the timber business, or, hopefully, they are fast learners. On the other hand, the investors have vividly demonstrated the value of the forest. In actuality, the federal government has the potential to sell about 43 million acres of forest land to investors for $40 billion and receive in addition generous taxes from these investors annually.

In the early days of local private forest land in Washington State, the owners were interested in the sustainability of their investments in manufacturing facilities and forest land. However, the science of growing trees in the region was in its infancy — and foresters' educated in Europe were of little help.

The landowners worked closely with the western universities to develop the basic skills needed to grow trees. The universities were staffed mostly with local educators who taught students raised in western forests. The studies were crafted by local people to fit the regional needs, in partnership with the schools, students, landowners, state government, and the U.S. Forest Service. The universities graduated highly motivated foresters dedicate to improve the countries forests; especially to protect the forests from fire, and reforest the brush fields created by repeated fires. Foresters filled many positions at all levels in the industry and government organizations.

Perhaps the most significant forestry graduates were the so-called dirt foresters who had dedicated their lives to being in the woods culturing trees, often turning down advancements to remain with their trees. The dirt foresters had a variety of titles over the years in a variety of organizations. They had one common denominator: they got their hands dirty. I was never a dirt forester, but I was associated with them for more than 40 years.

The major effort of the early dirt foresters was protecting the forest from fire. They were in a human environment that was dominated by logging operations and the public that used the forests. Their only regeneration tool came from nature, that is, seed deposited by the wind from mature trees. They worked with the loggers to prevent operational fires and to contribute to burning slash shortly after logging to prevent future wildfires. The foresters also communicated the need to burn slash to prepare the ground for the seed flying into the burned area from adjacent trees. At first location of logging and slash burning was willy-nilly until observations suggested that seed blocks or delayed logging could be planned to facilitate more efficient use of wild seed. Then slash burning became a tool to expedite the germination of seed and survival of the seedlings. This method of regeneration was usually successful, but was slow because the seed cast from Douglas fir is irregular.

The dirt foresters were experimenting with techniques to improve the forest while carrying out primary responsibilities by planting a few trees or by seeding. They monitored the rate of the young trees' struggle to grow while challenged with the competition by vegetation and wildlife. The effect of removing "brush" with an ax, or later with herbicides, was observed by the foresters, along with the damage done by the elk, deer, and rodents. A small experimental area (exclosure) was fenced, perhaps 30x30-feet by 15 feet high, to keep the animals from the seedlings. At times the trees inside the exclosure grew to twenty feet, while outside trees were three feet or perhaps nonexistent. The results were spectacular, but frustrating. A partial solution became apparent. Plant trees immediately after logging or wild fires before the animals moved into the area to utilize the swift re-vegetation of the area's weeds, grass, and brush. The dirt foresters waited impatiently for funds to be available to practice this craft.

In the early 1900s the landowners had waited impatiently for wild-fires to be moderated and controlled in the forest and for wood product prices to rise to a level to support an investment in growing trees. The lumber market and fire conditions dictated the sustainability of the for-est, the forest communities, and businesses. Fire control and the wood products market came together in the 1950s to rapidly make sustainable forests a reality. It started by replacing the inefficient and slow seed cast from trees with artificial seeding by helicopter that yielded an immedi-ate forest if done properly.

This gave the dirt foresters the funds to start a massive regenera-tion effort on private lands. The first step was to set up buying stations in the fall to purchase fir cones from the public (seed companies also bought cones). The cones were separated by geographic zones and ele-vations to assure the seed was returned to its natural environment. The government, seed companies, and private landowners were involved in extracting the seed from the cones for use in the forest.

At first, untreated seed was dispersed on the land with poor re-sults; the rodents ate them. When the seeds were treated with endrin (a pesticide), the seeding was successful, except when the ground was inadequately prepared. The seed-eating varmints avoided the seed af-ter being conditioned with sickening endrin. I personally traversed a grid of approximately 100-feet square over thousands of acres to con-firm that when the seed reached mineral soil and was not covered with organic material or brush, vigorous seedlings were growing — thanks to endrin. Contrary to the progressive perceptions, the dirt foresters didn't need the government or the academics from Yale to direct tree growing efforts.

However, aerial seeding required a receptive ground, a condition similar to a rough clearing for agriculture. A proper seedbed required slash burning, mechanical disposal of slash, or the harvest of timber that was not defective or interspersed with brush or low vegetation. Hand planting trees cost about ten times that of aerial seeding and was not economically viable in the 1950s. Aerial seeding, to be completely successful, had to be followed with planting the failed areas; a planting could be accomplished by digging through the organic debris, sometimes an impossible task. In addition the brush fields generally created by repeated wildfire required elimination of the brush by mechanical means and planting.

The economics and technology of the 1960s led to another level of forestry culture. The larger landowners began to plant trees almost immediately after logging, usually within a year. The preparation of the site before planting became a priority to get an even distribution of seedlings. The topography and logging residual didn't allow the planting in even rows (as in agriculture), but planting in an uneven grid pattern, which was practical. The number of trees planted per acre was an economic issue.

Poor nursery planting stock and out planting in the forest had to be improved. Sometimes 800 or 900 trees were planted per acre to obtain four hundred healthy trees in two decades. Planting a large number of trees and thinning the poor trees in about a half decade was practiced at times. However, with the addition of new nurseries and better nursery culturing, along with additional supervision of planting crews, nearly 100% survival of seedlings could often be obtained.

Because deer and other animals browsed the seedlings, animal repellents were formulated to treat the seedlings in the nursery. The repellents were temporary, so plastic screens were developed to protect the seedlings in animal-critical areas. Also, seedling size and age were managed to fit the out planting environment. The early era planting of one-year-old seedlings was abandoned for two-year-old seedlings. A one-year-old seedling was transplanted in the nursery to yield two-year-old out plantings in the forest. A super seedling was developed that was grown two years in the nursery, transplanted in the nursery to yield a three-year-old transplant. Transplanting toughened the seedling. Also, "plug" seedlings were grown in greenhouses.

The seedlings were planted, and the dirt forester carefully audited their growth. If the brush competition became a problem, a herbicide might have been used to release the fir seedling from death due to both too much shade and competition. However, with site preparation and prompt planting, brush competition was hardly a problem.

In about two decades, the Douglas fir seedlings became trees with crown closure. An aerial photograph reveals trees and not the ground features. At this time, many landowners fertilized the forest with 300 pounds of urea fertilizer that was 40% nitrogen, and again every five years thereafter until time of harvest. Some landowners might commercially thin the trees at this age. Weyerhaeuser thinned some of its plantings created after the 1980 Mt. St. Helens devastation, at this age to produce 2x4 lumber. A few owners pruned their fir trees at age 20 to produce clear lumber in the first log (I6+ feet from the ground) at harvest.

In the 1970s, the "old growth" timber on private ownerships in western Washington was mostly harvested, in order to be replaced by second and eventually third growth Douglas fir. The visionary timberland owners had anticipated and, given their primitive means, tried to manage their forests to sustain their enterprises. Western Washington property was roughly a mosaic of age classes from seedlings to mature second growth. A classical regulated forest contained roughly an equal distribution of age classes to rotation or harvest age. If the harvest age was 50 years and the property was 50 acres, an acre would be clear-cut every year. Arguably, such a forest would be more diverse than the ancient Douglas fir forests of centuries past.

The modern manufacturing technology and markets now made it possible to harvest and manufacture products from this young age, a situation that was not feasible a century ago. In fact, the processing of trees into products was no longer labor intensive. A clear-cut harvest of 40- to 80-year-old timber yields the greatest sustainable volume of wood to perpetuate the forest communities.

In the late 1800s and early 1900s, lumber was the principal product realized from the forest. The lumber sawn from the logs was utilized, while the wood from squaring the round log — sawdust, planning shavings, and bark — was wasted. In today's world it is possible to realize most of the biomass produced in the forest, including: lumber, plywood, laminated beams, fiber panels, biofuels and pulp. The pulp products are produced from the whole or part of a tree or the waste from producing lumber and plywood. Pulp products range from writing/printing paper, tissues, packaging paper, rayon for clothing, and a host of other products.

The Northwest timberland owners and the dirt forester quietly saved the Douglas fir forests from extinction. The destructive Minnesota/Idaho fires were largely avoided, as were the preservationists' ideological crusade to exclude the forests from the working people.

The owners and the dirt foresters slowly incorporated their skills to produce a healthy sustainable forest on private land that produced jobs, communities, and a healthy forest environment with a larger wildlife population than the region had ever experienced, especially in the elk and deer populations.

The progressives believed and propagandized the lack of wildlife when the dirt foresters practiced their craft of growing trees and the developers built houses and businesses. Let us examine what is happening on the north Olympic Peninsula. The deer and other critters have invaded the urban areas where they have never been. My uncle in Port Angeles had to fence the deer out of his garden where the choice deer food was to be found. During my 1930s boyhood, that deer would have been in the stewing pot for Sunday dinner.

In addition, urban areas as well as rural areas harbor large populations of raccoons, possums, skunks, coyotes, and crows, along with a host of other critters. Domestic animals are endangered, and there is little recourse for citizens to protect their cats and dogs, or even their children. In some rural areas, toddlers or babies are not allowed in yards without an adult to protect them from cougars and bears. The progressives argue the animals' habitat is destroyed, but the truth is they go where there is food, and the food is optimum in gardens, lawns, and chicken houses.

Citizens protect the wildlife from predators. An urban area of parks, golf courses, and open spaces is a perfect habitat for most wildlife, contrary to what the public has been told by the progressives. The public has been informed that elk would not tolerate roads and human structures. The elk were believed to be endangered in the early 1900s, but now occur in healthy numbers on the Forks Prairie where they are in the farmers' pastures, people's yards and on the Forks airport runway. Elk cross Highway 101 in the vicinity of Sequim in large numbers, endangering motorists and elk. Most wildlife seems to be thriving on private lands, even in and around the towns. Some knowledgeable old timers even suggest that wildlife is fleeing the federal lands for sanctuary in civilization.

The dirt foresters live among the wildlife in the forest and work with public and wildlife resource people to manage the critters. Some large landowners brought forestry science specialists into their organizations or enlisted the aid of the universities and the Forest Service Experimental Stations to perfect forest cultural opportunities. It was a cooperative effort to create a new forest. However the unrecognized fact remains, that the dirt forester, through hard hands-on work, created the forests of today on privately owned lands.

It took a century for the dirt foresters, allied with big and small landowners, woodsmen, and people of the soil to create sustainable forests in America. The federal government joined the effort in the late 1920s with their own dirt foresters to create sustainable forest on government land until recently. In the Douglas fir region it was (gasp) clear-cut and burn, to re-vitalize the forest with young trees.

The government forests, the old Forest Reserves, are now unsustainable under any definition. Most of the forests are over-aged and near death, candidates for terminal disease and fire. Disease and fire are already almost out of control in the western pine that destroyed the old trees, and re-burns destroy any regeneration of the forest. Old trees cannot be preserved. The American forests can only survive if people of the soil manage the forests — dirt foresters and associates. The progressive cabal of urban environment groups, politicians, and academics must be taken out of forest policy decisions.

Mount St. Helens volcano blast zone, 1980. The federal land is still largely treeless after three decades.

Mount St. Helens, regenerated and flourishing 30 years after a devastating volcanic eruption, thanks to private and state landowners who planted more than 50,000 acres.

FOREST COMMUNITIES RAVAGED

The U.S. was mostly created by people who fled the tyranny of Europe to a wilderness in the new world — an American wilderness blessed with natural resources, mild climate, and fertile soil that awaited a vigorous people who could create a democratic society that would be all-inclusive to its citizens, a civilization without the rigid classes and tyrants of the old world. It took a revolution against the tyrants of the old world in the 1700s, a Civil War in the 1860s, and two World Wars that terminated in 1945 to create the most inclusive democratic society and powerful nation the world had ever experienced, a model for the world to marvel at and emulate.

From 1945 through the 1980s, the forest communities were prospering along with the nation. Our American Heritage was motivating the country to do even better. However, the Green Movement came alive again in the 1960s, and soon overwhelmed America. The Green Movement's luxury was made possible by the wealth created by the forest communities, along with other communities in the nation. The Green Movement attacked all activities in the country that were contrary to the progressives' interpretation of nature. The movement coalesced into ecosystem identification and management.

An *ecosystem* is defined as "a study of nature". A unit of nature is generally used by academics in a pure sense, that is, the wildlife and vegetation devoid of people, a wilderness. Our American forefathers took great pride in "taming" the wilderness. In other words, they moved from the east coast to the west coast to create an American civilization to raise the standard of living of all Americans. History tells us people have gone into the wilderness to adjust nature to benefit human beings since the beginning of time. An uncontrolled natural wilderness could support only a primitive and nearly destitute people. The tales of taming the wilderness were included in the Christian Bible before Christ.

The preservation of our heritage and wealth depends on fully utilizing our millions of acres of newly created so-called ecosystems. Certainly, our heritage included preserving noteworthy features like Yellowstone and Mount Rainier, but not millions of acres. To do so automatically reduces our wealth, leading to a lower standard of living and unemployment. The late author Carsten Lien (*Olympic Battleground*) projected future American citizens being forced to live in city ghettos without automobiles. The projection was based on a depletion of natural resources. However, the resources are available, but now largely on government land and unavailable to use in un-American ecosystems.

The ecosystem and similar concepts have come to be largely incorporated into the universities. Up until the middle 1900s, universities were oriented to educating productive people to support commerce. In the 21st Century, barren and esoteric studies started to dominate the universities. The University of Washington, College of Forestry was incorporated into the College of the Environment and Forest Sciences. A director of the college was appointed in 2012, a director noted for his expertise in terrestrial ecosystems. He is a European who has no feeling for the American forestry heritage nor on-the-ground experience in the northwest forests. It is apparent the new director is not expected to understand the people in the forest communities as past leaders in the college did.

Further, there is no longer an undergraduate study in forestry at the University of Washington or Washington State University. The new colleges obviously assume that basic forest skills and knowledge are for technical schools and the unprofessional. This assumption repudiates more than a century of experience and success to enhance the state's forests. The father of American forestry, Gifford Pinchot, would be horrified.

Academics and emotional progressives are studying nature on hundreds of millions of acres of federal forestland. It follows that their studies and recommendations will anticipate expanding their vision to private landowners through purchase, regulation, and condemnation. The study of nature, that is, the interface of critters, the creepy crawlies, fish, and vegetation have no direct practical application, as humans should not interfere with nature in the progressives' view. It follows that the productive Americans who create the nation's wealth should have no incentive to fund those in the universities that contribute nothing to the country's economy or the generation of meaningful jobs.

In the 1900s, the forest landowners funded much of the universities' efforts to educate productive young people to create and educate a workforce that would create wealth for the nation. In the 21st Century, forest landowners were mostly replaced by progressive government funding of the universities. Arguably, most of the forest scientists, now ecosystem scientists, are biased toward the progressives' preservationist agenda.

In fact, many people in the forest communities — experienced woodsmen — believe there is an unstructured cabal that is composed of enviro (environmental) clubs or organizations, the federal government, and many of the academics. The cabal is believed to have nearly destroyed the communities who have depended largely on the forest for the natural resources that created wood product jobs and community wealth. These communities are composed of several generations of families whose forefathers were guaranteed sustained resources from the forests, before the public domain was taken from the pioneers to create federal land monopolies in the form of the U.S. Forest Service.

Parts of the western forests are in danger of ecological collapse under the progressive government's "stewardship". There is agreement by everyone that the Ponderosa and Lodgepole pine forests from the Great Plains west to the coastal forests need to be rehabilitated. The progressives, in their preservation mode, insist that drought, global warming, insects, and disease are destroying the forests. The fact is, the stressed trees are old and near the end of their life cycle, which makes the trees susceptible to disease and insects. This fact is ignored by the progressives and academics and is not considered a factor in forest health. The young trees beginning their life cycles are generally healthy. Logic would suggest the old trees should be removed and replaced by young trees. The progressives, allied with many academics, are researching and inventing vocabulary to support the preservation of dead and dying trees. There are regulations that prevent the removal of dead trees (snags) that are thought to enhance some wildlife.

The preservationists' emphasis is on thinning young trees by mechanical means or prescribed fire to improve forest health, while retaining the old, often diseased, and dying trees. The progressives' solution to forest health is funded by the federal government and, to be effective, should be applied over millions of acres. The common method for thinning is to slash the trees with a chain saw and leave the downed trees to rot. An alternative is to pile the slashing to rot, or burn the piles. If not burned immediately, the slashing creates an extreme fire hazard, a ready host for beetles, and reduction of acreage for re-growing young trees.

A prescribed fire, as generally used, is a fire that burns the small trees and brush under the bigger, older trees. To use this method in older forests is risky — some experienced woodsmen would suggest insane. The older western pine forests commonly have a third or more big trees dead or near dead; the big trees constitute the bulk of the biomass or fuel in the forest. Even my grandmother knew better than put fire near a dead tree. She used lighted candles on a fresh cut Christmas tree in her house for the first week, then ceased lighting the candles. She knew the tree would explode with fire when the needles lost their succulence. The Forest Service's "Los Alamos" wildfire of 2000 was an escaped prescribed fire. The cost of the fire was more than $1.3 billion. It burned thousands of acres of forest, 861 structures, and threatened the Los Alamos National Laboratory.

In the first decade of the 21st Century, several interior states in the west have seen record fire seasons with a few half-million acre individual wildfires. It seems the forests in the western pine region are to be consumed by wildfire under the stewardship of the progressive cabal. The carbon released is enormous, and the pollution generated by these fires is greater than many years of human activity in the area. The destruction of businesses and homes is costly. The potential for loss of human lives is great, and the loss of wildlife is real.

Perhaps the greatest tragedy is the death of the forests and risk in renewing the forests under the progressives' stewardship. The progressives' goal is to preserve the old and dying trees without regard to the regeneration of the forest. The Forest Service's Mt. St. Helens Monument is a frightening example of the future of the western pine forest. Three decades since the St. Helen's forest was destroyed by the volcano eruption, the monument is much like a moonscape with little sign of birth of a new forest. However there is no forest to be endangered by wildfire. Contrary to Mt. St. Helens, the western pine forests killed by fire usually have residual standing dead trees plus regenerated low vegetation to fuel a reburn, historically, a fire hazard that requires additional fire protection.

Ponderosa pine is the principal tree species in the interior west. The mature tree produces seed cones prolifically in only three to five years. And, in the hundred-thousand-acre fires experienced in the 21st Century, a mature tree would be unavailable to seed much of the burned forest. The progressives' agenda inhibits artificial regeneration, such as tree planting. Huge wildfires are endemic; therefore, ponderosa pine forests are endangered as the cabal researches and studies. The other significant western pine is lodgepole. Different than open grown ponderosa, lodgepole is a smaller tree (about 80 feet in height) which occurs mostly in dense even-aged forests and is a prolific seeder. Invariably after wildfire the perennial cones open to reseed the waiting mineral soil created by the fire. The resulting seedlings are often so dense the trees stagnate after reaching several feet in height. The stagnation often may persist for many years, creating an unhealthy forest of small trees.

The smaller lodgepole was underutilized for wood products while the larger Ponderosa at one time was widely used for lumber and was second only to Douglas fir in the U.S. The historic Ponderosa pine logging was generally a cyclical and selective harvest of the slow growing or dying trees. The cycle was generally frequent enough to reduce or eliminate the dead fuel in the forests; some would call this tree harvest a sanitization harvest that eliminated the weak trees susceptible to attack by beetles. It also reduced or eliminated the snags and dead downed trees that constituted the bulk of the highly flammable fuels in the forest, the highly flammable fuels as defined by a century of on-the-ground experience.

However, the progressives have defined a new policy: thin the young vigorous trees and preserve or ignore the bulk of the forest biomass that is highly flammable. The Ponderosa pine forests are burning and unhealthy because of current human policy that regresses to the severe historic fires that created the western pine. The alternative is nature-polluting wildfires or regeneration harvests and the use of the trees in wood products.

The endemic and catastrophic fires are not new to America. In the late 1800s and early 1900s forests, towns, people, and structures burned indiscriminately. In that era there were little funds available for education, prevention, and suppression of wildfires. In the 21st Century, taxpayers spent over a billion dollars on the single Los Alamos wildfire, a fire that was easily preventable by eliminating perhaps negligent and nonproductive prescribed fires. The prescribed fires were planned to burn under the old and big trees without harm to the big trees, eliminating the small understory trees and brush. In the 21st Century, forest fire protection and suppression were largely dictated by the progressive cabal that ignored input by the citizens and experienced woodsmen.

In the past decades the catastrophic fires were tamed by involving the whole population of America. With inadequate funding and archaic communication, it took decades to almost eliminate catastrophic fires until the new-age fire policies. In about 1900 the private forest landowners asked and demanded the reluctant state and federal government to work with them in protecting all forest land. The government and landowners worked together to educate the public on fire safety, formulate fire strategy, acquire firefighting equipment, implement fire laws, and train firefighting crews. Initially the landowners assessed themselves a few cents per acre to form fire districts to suppress fire on mostly private land because the government wasn't moving fast enough to protect private assets. With the bitter experience of past fires behind them, the forest landowners began to "fire proof" their forest land with the cooperation of the government and informed citizens. The American people came together to tame the catastrophic wildfires.

The first priority was to spot a wildfire at its inception, and the second priority was to overwhelm the fire immediately with men and equipment. To get equipment to a fire, primitive roads were built throughout private and public property as fast as practical. A series of interlocking fire lookouts were constructed with temporary fire crews on standby during the summer. In areas where private forestland was substantial, logging crews were equipped with numerous water tank trucks on standby, along with their logging equipment, which included a host of bulldozers that could quickly be employed to build fire lines. In addition, the big logging operations had up to 1,000 loggers equipped to get to a fire at a minute's notice.

The attempt was made to carefully fire-proof the land on the landowners' own initiative. Most of the timber was harvested using clear-cuts (regeneration harvests), and the area's slash was burned to form firebreaks. Snags were felled universally in and near the harvest units to reduce the fire potential and human safety. Water holes were established wherever possible to replenish the tank trucks.

The fire strategy evolved over a century of hard fire experience. The people who depended on their livelihood from the forest for several generations lived with fire and knew how to control it.

At the start of the 21st Century, the evolution of fire cooperation between stakeholders almost ceased. The government unilater-
ally dictated fire policy. And, the urban progressives directed the
government. The most disturbing change in policy was the practice of letting a wildfire burn naturally without human intervention. The forest communities that might have been in the path of
the fire were not consulted. The pollution generated by the fire was
ignored. However, the bureaucrats asked for the elimination of gas
lawn mowers and wood stoves. A century of wildfire experience has
been discarded, and some ask if we are regressing to the fire history
of the late 1800s and early 1900s when hundreds of people periodically died in wildfires.

As the 21st Century progresses, the American forests in the western
pine region are doomed to be in poor health and never ending catastrophic wildfires. The progressives contend drought, climate change,
extreme temperatures, and the buildup of biofuels in the forest are to
blame. Their current wisdom is that excessive fuel has been built up
in the forests because humans have successfully eliminated fire from
their ecosystems, contrary to nature's way.

Again, the progressives blame humans for the deterioration of the
western pine forests. Humans are to be blamed for releasing carbon,
polluting, tree killing, and wildlife plus property destruction brought
about in the 21st Century by an eruption of wildfires because of a century of forest mismanagement. On the contrary, it affirms the century-
old fire policy that brought the American people together to quiet the
firestorms of the early 1900s to bring a semblance of health to the nation's forests. The progressives' ignorant policies brought the western
pine forests back to nature at a great financial cost to American citizens.
Both Ponderosa and Lodgepole pine forests were created after severe
wildfires. Occasionally, ground fires in the Ponderosa forests eliminated the brush and all the young pine trees that would replace the dying ancient veteran trees. Generally a severe crown fire destroyed the
veteran trees, and eventually nature reseeded the bare land to create a

young vigorous forest. As in most conifer forests, the regenerated conifers thrived in mineral soil created by fire or clear-cut logging.

The progressives' solution to the desperation in the western pine is to hold academic conferences to reduce forest biomass within the parameters of their interpretation of nature. In addition, they will fund scientific research with the citizens' wealth to reduce the forest biomass by eliminating young trees to preserve the forest of dying old trees. Most forests in the western pine region are obviously unhealthy and the older trees near death. The juvenile trees were sparsely spaced, not vigorous, and probably would not replace the dying old trees. History suggests nature would soon send a lightning bolt into a bone-dry snag, accompanied by a brisk wind that would throw fired wood for thousands of feet. The accumulated bone-dry fuel from dead trees would fuel a fire holocaust before the federal government could get their people to the several burning snags in the forest. The evaluation of that forest potential is made by an individual who has observed forest fires in the "woods" for more than seventy years, reinforced by many peers who think alike. The government lands on millions of acres in the western pine region mirror this situation.

The government's policy on a small scale is to thin the juvenile trees to add to the biomass of dead trees. A century of fire experience has documented that an accumulation of dead wood fiber in the forest creates an extreme fire hazard. The biomass might be removed by logging; however there is little market for the wood, so a landfill might be necessary. The use of prescribed (ground) fire in an extreme fire hazard forest would create a fire so intense the complete forest would burn. They could pile the downed wood and leave the piles or burn them. In both instances, this method is not practical over millions of acres, and hazardous because of the fire potential and insect infestations.

The practical solution is to learn from about a 200,000-acre private pine forest near Klamath Falls, Oregon, created by regeneration harvests that were planted immediately with ponderosa pine seedlings. The healthy and growing forest has experienced no wildfires. Plus, in the early 2000s the forest is being thinned and the wood products are processed in the local communities. Regeneration harvests will begin in the 2030s to furnish more jobs in the local communities. The young forest is surrounded by fire-prone and dying government forest that endangers a private commercial forest and the local communities. The young forest demonstrates the only solution to forest health and wild-fire taming in the western pine. That is, start an extensive program of regeneration harvests throughout the government western pine forests. The technology is there to do that right now and has been demonstrat-ed without cost to the government. Almost all of the forest biomass could be converted into product — the larger trees turned into lumber and plywood while the smaller wood is chipped for pulp, fiberboard, and biofuels. The land would be planted immediately and a healthy forest born. This technique has been proven in the private sector time and again.

However, the problem is the manufacturing facilities to process the wood. The progressive government policies have driven most of the manufacturing facilities out of the region. But, entrepreneurs could and would build manufacturing facilities if they had sustained wood re-sources to fill their mills. The past government timber sale programs or a facsimile will never support new facilities; the government has been proven untrustworthy when promising resource supply to the forest communities they distressed. The solution is to revert to our American heritage and privatize the federal forestland.

We are told time and again that privatization of government land is politically impossible. The alternative is "burn, baby, burn". Perhaps when the Los Alamos fire catastrophes continue and more homes start burning, the western pine region people will prevail over the urban progressives.

The forest land ownership in the west is dominated by the federal government, especially in the western pine. This region was featured in the story because of the fire holocausts that highlight the progressives' forest policies that nearly ruined meaningful employment in many forest communities. The effect on the coastal forests of the west is less damaging because a higher proportion of private forest is producing wood to be processed in the communities.

Many academics rationalize a difference between the private and public forests. The private landowners are generally academically ignored while the public forests are studied to develop forest practices to conform to the progressives or preservationists vision of "their" forests. Many landowners and most people in the forest communities whose livelihoods depend on sustained timber availability believe the academics are disingenuous. Further, they believe the government was deceitful when they withdrew the public resources that were processed in the communities. The government had pledged a sustained supply of timber over a century ago as they attempted to federalize forestland. Regeneration harvests are basic to an adequate supply of wood to sustain and build local communities. The building of local communities through the productive use of the nation's land was the goal of our American founders. A goal plus individual freedom created the country. The progressives, allied with many academics, are quickly eroding our American legacies.

The fragile western pine forests have been devastated by the progressives' agenda, while the western coastal forests have largely remained healthy. Regeneration harvests practiced for over a century have created a younger more thrifty forest region in part. Currently the progressives have virtually stopped regeneration harvests on federal land and attempted to reduce tree growing on private land. The progressive movement to control the nation's forests began mostly in the coastal western forests.

The first thrust in the coastal forests by the progressives was to communicate their perception that clear-cut logging permanently destroyed the forest. Further, the nation's timber supply was in jeopardy because the forests would no longer be available to build the nation. In spite of the economics of the time, they insisted the clear-cuts be planted by the landowners. Clear-cuts or regeneration harvests destroyed old growth trees, which were almost universally renewed by natural seeding after wild-fire or clear-cut logging. The natural seeding produced a new vigorous young forest on the west coast. Both the private and public landowners adopted this silvicultural practice. In the 1960s, the natural seeding was mostly replaced by hand planting to enhance forest sustainability that provided more wood for processing in the communities. The practice strengthened the community's economics and would sustain employment. In the 21st Century, regeneration harvest was mostly eliminated on the public lands and attacked on the private land without caring about the economy or the jobs of the local communities.

The early progressives' second attack on the coastal forests came to the Olympic Peninsula's communities in 1909 when President Teddy Roosevelt created the Olympic National Monument by executive order. In the more than half-million acres in the center of the Olympic Peninsula, poachers were killing elk that the state authorities were managing to curtail. There was little documentation of elk endangerment except through emotion and perhaps greed for control of land. Elk became an emotional symbol to control land use, exclusive of economic human needs.

The PhD academics began to craft guidelines to advise progressive bureaucrats on land use regulations to enhance the elks' so-called habitat. Of course, the control of tree harvest became a central theme. The academics wrote arbitrary elk management guidelines to adapt the forests to the perceived needs of elk. The guidelines evolved over time as did their influence on forest practices.

The academics made elk guidelines that encoded distances from open ground (regeneration harvests) to cover (mature trees), roads detrimental to elk or deer, traffic on roads near-fatal to elk, and a host of more guidelines. Then the progressives took the guidelines to the regulators to make laws to change forest practices. Mt. St. Helens erupted in 1980 and destroyed all life within miles of the mountain. The resulting blast zone had no cover, yet the elk thrived as in no other area in the state of Washington.

The log trucks roared through the elk herds at Mt. St. Helens as they grazed alongside the roads. Humans (thought to trouble elk) walked within several hundred feet of the grazing elk. Also, in the 21st Century, the northwest had elk grazing within the city limits of numerous forest communities. Still, the progressives continued to regulate forest practices to save the elk.

After the early 1900s of perfecting false concerns over timber supply, regeneration harvests, and elk, the academics brought numerous proposed guidelines to diminish the value of the forest to the local communities. Among one of the first proposed "modern evils" was silt, fine or coarse, that entered the streams of the northwest. It was stated conclusively that silt generated by logging or any human activity would disrupt the streams, and certainly the fish spawning gravel would be clogged with silt precluding the fish from spawning. Fish could also die because of damaged gills. The horror of a fish-dead stream was projected. It was proposed that zero silt should be allowed in the streams, and some rigid regulations were applied without recognizing the cost of millions of dollars.

The benefits of silt prevention were obscure or nonexistent. The people who live and work in the forest have observed streams for centuries and have never seen permanently silted fish spawning gravel or silt blocked streams, even when landslides or debris flows put tons of material into a stream. The natural bank cutting of the streams during flood stages and water run-off overland create enormous silt that the natural flow of the stream will cleanse in a very short period of time. The Puyallup River is silted every fall with glacier-generated silt that discolors Commencement Bay for more than a month. The silt flows down the stream, and the fish thrive in the Puyallup River and Commencement Bay.

The rivers are temporarily damaged by silt that eventually reaches salt water. Most "experts" contend this is detrimental. However, Commencement Bay seems free of silt problems; the fish thrive in the bay. Nevertheless, the silt fills the estuaries and extends the land into the sea at the mouth of many streams. The ancient city of Ephesus was moved down the estuary towards the sea as the estuary slowly was closed by silt. However, the land formed by this natural phenomenon became fertile agricultural land mirroring many estuaries. The progressives and academics were not concerned with the loads of silt through the Elwha River when the dams were breached. It appears the academic identification and regulation of silt were again selective processes to suit their agenda.

Perhaps fish became the ultimate in an attempt to dictate forest practices. A significant percentage of private land is dedicated to preservation stream buffer zones by regulation to protect the streams and fish, particularly the salmon in the west. The so-called buffer zones depressed the sustained yield of wood to the forest communities, and jobs were ultimately lost.

Stream temperature was identified in the 1960s as critical to fish. Simply speaking, the correct temperature for fish productivity would occur under the forest canopy. Therefore, buffer zones along streams would be mandatory to preserve the forest canopy. The forest landowner was obligated to leave their timber along streams without compensation, and the progressives made one more step towards forest preservation at the expense of the local community. There was little research, but regulations quickly followed, based on academic wisdom. Subsequently, meaningful research was conducted by the academics to confirm their wisdom.

The Alsea Watershed Study, located a few miles southeast of Newport, Oregon, was began in 1959 and completed in 1973. This was the first paired watershed studies that simultaneously measured water quality and flow along with fish productivity and fish habitat when subjected to different forest management practices. Three older forested watersheds were studied. Flynn Creek was the control, that is, no logging. Deer Creek was partially logged with no logging activity near the creek. Needle Branch (Creek) was clear-cut harvested and broadcast burned. There was no vegetation remaining on Needle Branch after a hard burn. It resembles a moonscape.

The study measured the variables several years before the forest management activity and several years afterward. The major fish species were Coho salmon and cutthroat trout. In the Needle Branch, the Coho density or biomass increased dramatically immediately after logging. The cutthroat density was reduced. The total fish biomass was substantially greater one year after treatment than ever achieved in the three watersheds during the study period. About a decade later, the study continued for a number of years in the three watersheds, and the fish biomass never reached the Needle Branch's record achievement. However, the stream temperatures were extreme in the Needle Branch the first years after treatment while the other watersheds had nature's lower temperature. Nevertheless, fish biomass seemed not to suffer from moonscape logging or perhaps even benefited from clear-cut logging. Certainty, the local community was enhanced economically with the sustained wood fiber produced from the Needle Branch.

Mt. St. Helens erupted in 1980, and a mud flow destroyed the South Fork of the Toutle River and its fish. This catastrophe cannot be duplicated by humans. Nevertheless, with the lapse of seven years, the steelhead (fish) returned in record numbers. Of course, there were numerous steelhead in the river, building up to the record return. Like the Needle Branch, the river and its tributaries had no vegetative cover for many years to soften the extreme stream temperatures.

In the destroyed North Fork of the Toutle River, three tributary creeks were monitored similarly to the streams in the Alsea Study. The three streams were savaged by the Mt. St. Helens' eruption, with all vegetation and life destroyed, along with the streams' channels. Nevertheless, total fish biomass reached very high levels five to seven years after the eruption before returning to more typical low levels in the following years. This is believed to be a result of a temporary increase in food availability resulting from a high abundance of aquatic invertebrates enabled by high stream temperatures. It appears after the adjacent stream vegetation ultimately cooled the streams, the fish biomass returned to its normal low levels.

Herrington Creek now supports seven different species of fish while Shultz Creek supports only cutthroat trout because of a natural waterfall that prevented re-colonization of other species. Hoffstadt Creek was stocked with fish from hatcheries soon after the eruption. Perhaps the hatchery fish have preempted the entry of other fish species into the stream. The biomass of fish remained at a relatively even level over the study period, suggesting temperature has no effect on fish biomass and that stream vegetation or cover to cool streams is not critical to fish productivity.

The academic PhDs who specialize in northwest streams and studied the research data agreed that the data is erratic at best and definite conclusions cannot be reached. However, many tree-growing specialists and landowners did not agree with the conclusions of the academics. Many laymen shout that high stream temperatures benefit northwest fish in most streams. Nevertheless, the academics' conclusions fit the progressives' agenda to set forest policy. The progressive agenda that created the Mt. St. Helens Monument depressed the local forest communities. The federal government did not salvage the dead trees to furnish employment to the local communities nor did they regenerate their forestland to further jobs in the communities.

The stream researchers have studied a multitude of variables that they perceive are a detriment to fish; they designed rules and regulations to control those variables at an enormous cost. Academic research conclusions are rationalized to support their perceived views. There should only be one standard and that is: optimum fish biomass. The clear-cut or regeneration harvest on the Needle Branch was ugly and denuded of vegetation, but initially produced more fish biomass than the other two study areas. Nevertheless, the progressives and academics continue to dictate forest cover over streams, perhaps to the detriment of fish.

There are many studies concerning the wellbeing of the forest environment and health. Also, there are many honorable academics with local experience researching the impacts of forest management on the environment in the west. It appears to the laypersons in the forest communities their research is oriented to moderate the demands of the progressives who demand preservation in the public forests while demanding private forest practices be moderated to meet their agendas.

Contrary to the academics that have spent much of their lives in the northwest forests, there are the theoretical academics whose backgrounds appear to be from another planet. Recently (2012) Mark Hudson, a sociologist at the University of Manitoba, authored a book, *Fire Management in the American West: Forest Politics and the Rise of Mega Fires*. The book was reviewed by a professor of environmental analysis who resides at Pomona College in Claremont, California.

The two professors are uniform in their theoretical evaluation of the cause of the recent mega fires. Their solution is simple: nature's fire must be reintroduced to our forests in the form of prescribed burning. The professors ignore fire history: most western forests owe their existence to mega fires, not prescribed burning. The author believes there is "a more powerful element of society — the timber industry in particular" that forced the Forest Service to manage public forests for timber production and fire suppression. This suppression almost eliminated mega fires from the forests. However, the Forest Service broadcast burned many regeneration harvests over the years to reduce wildfire potential and to grow trees. This fire tool has been mostly stopped because of air quality concerns, causing the regeneration harvests on public land to be all but eliminated. The professors ignore the point that the past forest practices undoubtedly reduced the mega fires. The elimination of these practices by the all-powerful progressive has taken the timber industry almost out of the public forests to the detriment of the forest communities.

Further the sociologist recommends the Forest Service should manage fire on a "landscape scale" to eliminate the "high cost to the healthy functioning of many forest ecosystems". The Forest Service bureaucrats directed by Washington DC would control all of the western ecosystems or most of the forestland in the west. The definition of a functioning ecosystem must be defined by the academics as they have the only lofty education to understand a functioning ecosystem, a system they have designed to exclude the citizens from policy decisions. Therefore, the academics would control rural America and people's lives in order to preserve the academic's vision of the proper relationship of living organisms and their proper environment. This concept is completely foreign to our founding fathers and our American heritage. America became strong when the citizens controlled their future through politicians and academics, not from the top down.

Arrogantly the progressives, allied with some academics, dictate forest policy overwhelming the people who tamed the wilderness forest to create much of the wealth of America over the centuries. An ancient sage wrote something like this: *Intellectuals are intellectuals because they have the only venue to write and publish.* Of course, they tell their readers they are the only intelligent ones. Today's intellectuals, as in ancient times, flourish because of the productivity of others. They seek information mostly from others like themselves and the progressives who support them. The citizens in the forest communities were largely ignored in any discussions that were held to formulate scientific conclusions nor were their experiences solicited.

Two academics have influenced the forests of the Olympic Peninsula, much to the consternation of the local pioneer families and woodsmen. In November 2011, two professors were interviewed in *The Forest Source* publication: Jerry Franklin is at the University of Washington and K. Norman Johnson resides at Oregon State University. Franklin states a regeneration harvest (clear-cut) is the only method to regenerate or "perpetuate" a forest. Nevertheless, he and his associates are studying a way to perpetuate forests in a way that would satisfy the wishes of the progressives.

The two professors label the progressives or environmentalist as *enviros*. A clear-cut is abhorrent to the enviros and is not tolerated on hundreds of millions of acres of federal land. As for the federal agencies, Johnson says, "The Agencies don't want to get hammered again." *Hammered*, of course, means the agencies know the progressives have a powerful lobby comprised of the progressive clubs, progressive politicians, and bureaucrats allied with most of the media. In addition, the courts have been made available to them via 1960's environmental legislation. The agencies have effectively been isolated from the forest communities they were designed to serve.

An effective regeneration harvest removes all of the older trees (clear-cut) to enable the reseeded or planted trees to adequately utilize the soil, nutrients, water and sun to survive and grow. The professors confirm that a regeneration harvest is the only way to renew a western forest. Most ancient forest sprang to life after massive wildfires. For over a century the western forests have been renewed with regeneration harvests or fire. The professors are attempting to renew dying and unhealthy forests by crafting forest practices that can be supported by the progressives — practices that history has shown cannot be crafted to renew the dying forests. A dying forest cannot be preserved or replaced until the older forest is cultivated by a fire or logging on extensive acres. Thus, eventually the preservationists' agenda will destroy the western forest through atrophy or wildfire.

Franklin and Johnson defied the precedence of the forestry schools and private landowners by embracing the new-age ecosystem contrivance. They cited a dictionary definition of an ecosystem as: "the complex of a community and its environment functioning as an ecological unit in nature. Ecology is the relationship between living organisms and their environment". The definition is beyond the understanding of anybody, and a vehicle to overpower the public with academic jargon.

The professors believe there is a deficiency in old forests and a deficiency in early successional forests, that is, treeless bare land. The delay in regenerating the land after timber harvest to create bare land, in their opinion, would capture ecological assets. The delay goes against more than a century of public's and landowners' demand to have immediate regeneration of the land after harvest or wildfire for both aesthetical desires and for the health of the nation. For instance, a new forest should be regenerated immediately to sequester carbon.

The professors and most of academia separate private forest land from government land when intellectualizing the management and use of forest land. The private land is generally managed with regeneration harvests that equate harvest with growth, that is, sustainable harvest that fuels the forest communities and the nation. Private forest management attempts to optimize forest growth and health to create wealth for the landowner and the community while enhancing all the forest resources. The academics largely confirm the idea that a forest community's stability depends on private ownership of forest land that is sustained by regeneration harvests. Meanwhile, the millions of acres of government forestland is dedicated to non-productive ecosystems that are dedicated to academic and progressives to play with.

I was a fourth generation inhabitant of a vibrant forest community, listened to the people around me, educated myself at a university, and traveled the forest communities throughout America. Before writing this story, I spent several years talking to the productive people on the north Olympic Peninsula to confirm or reject the thoughts I believed in for more than eighty years.

Perhaps the most vocal and knowledgeable individual was Missy Barlow, the granddaughter of the legendary Iron Man of the Hoh. She too was university educated, an elk hunter, fisherwoman, mother, artist, botanist, and an expert on the local pioneers and the history of her forest community. She told the story of local families being misused by the federal bureaucrats, with the taking of pioneer family land, and their arrogance. She would not talk to an Olympic National Park Naturalist because she thought she would be treated as a quaint symbol of the antiquated past and irrelevant to the future.

Missy Barlow on the Olympic Peninsula represents our American Heritage, a group who are being patronized or ignored by the intellectuals and politicians. Missy Barlow's grandfather in his later life referred to the American government as similar to communist Russia because he and his community had no representation in America's government.

The past vibrant forest communities that exuded our American heritage are now generally quiet retirement villages, developing little employment and wealth from the forest. The tourists visiting the communities spike the economy periodically, while the tourists marvel at the communities' heritage of American productivity.

This story represents those lost from the democratic freedom in the forest or rural communities and elsewhere. This lost freedom equates to losing our American heritage that sustained our greatness and the world's hope for justice and the reduction of poverty.

This story is not for intellectuals with footnotes. Nor is it a story for the progressives to pontificate. It is for our disenfranchised forest communities. It is a story based on honest feelings for those disenfranchised by the progressives and to give the disenfranchised talking points and hope. The American people have a choice in the 21st Century that English author Os Guinness expresses very eloquently in his book: *A Free People's Suicide, Sustainable Freedom and the American Future.* The American people have a clear choice between joining ecosystem worship leading to impoverishment or a vibrant America.

In summary, our far-sighted American forefathers dictated that the land should be productive. To create that productivity they transferred the public domain to the people who formed meaningful communities. The progressives have taken much of the land and resources away from productive communities to play with it. Our heritage is lost unless the communities are returned the land that framed our fundamental America value.

Made in the USA
Charleston, SC
03 December 2013